WIN-WIN?

THE PARADOX OF VALUE AND INTERESTS IN BUSINESS RELATIONSHIPS

Andrew Cox

Earlsgate Press

Published by Earlsgate Press
(ww.earlsgatepress.com)

© Andrew Cox, 2004

First published: December 2004

All rights reserved. No part of this publication may be reproduced, stored in a retrieval system or transmitted in any form or by any means, electronic, mechanical, photocopying, recorded or otherwise, without the prior permission of the publisher.

British Library Cataloguing in Publication Data

A catalogue record of this book is available from the British Library

ISBN 1-873439-22-9

Contents

Preface:	The Need for Conceptual Clarity	7
1.	The Complexity of Commercial Outcomes in Business Relationships	19
2.	Types of Inter-Organisational Business Relationships	31
3.	Understanding Win-Win Commercial Outcomes in Horizontal Business Relationships	45
4.	The Paradox of Win-Win and Mutuality in Buyer and Supplier Exchange	73
5.	Objectively Feasible Commercial and Operational Outcomes in Business Relationships	109
6.	False Consciousness in Business Relationships: The Problem of Subjective and Objective Interests	165
7.	On Interests, Power and Mutuality in Transactions: Towards a Science of Business Economics and Management	197
References:		265
Index:		281

List of Figures and Tables

Figure 1:	Commercial Outcomes from Business Relationships	25
Table 1:	The Scope for Opportunism in Different Types of External Business Relationships	34
Figure 2:	Feasible Commercial Outcomes in Full-Equity Joint Ventures	55
Figure 3:	Feasible Commercial Outcomes in Preferential-Equity Joint Ventures	59
Figure 4:	Feasible Commercial Outcomes in Lump-sum and Mark-up Strategic Alliances	63
Figure 5:	Feasible Commercial Outcomes in Royalty-based Strategic Alliances	65
Figure 6:	Feasible Commercial Outcomes in Non-Equity Cooperative Strategic Alliances	66
Figure 7:	Value for Money Options for the Buyer	82
Figure 8:	Value from Supply Options of the Supplier	91
Figure 9:	The Conflict and Tension in Buyer and Supplier Transactional Exchange	92
Figure 10:	Feasible Commercial Outcomes in Buyer and Supplier Relationships	95
Figure 11:	The Commercial and Operational Value Matrix	114
Figure 12:	Commercial and Operational Trade-Offs for Buyers and Suppliers	118
Figure 13:	Symmetry and Asymmetry in the Commercial and Operational Outcomes from Horizontal Business Relationships	123
Figure 14:	Feasible Commercial and Operational Outcomes in Full-Equity Joint Ventures	129
Figure 15:	Feasible Commercial and Operational Outcomes in Preferential-Equity Joint Ventures	131
Figure 16:	Feasible Commercial and Operational Outcomes in Lump sum and Mark-up Strategic Alliances	132
Figure 17:	Feasible Commercial and Operational Outcomes in Royalty-based Strategic Alliances	134
Figure 18:	Feasible Commercial and Operational Outcomes in Non-Equity Cooperative Strategic Alliances	136
Figure 19:	Feasible Commercial and Operational Outcomes in Buyer and Supplier Exchange	140
Figure 20:	Subjectively Perceived Commercial and Operational Trade-Offs in Business Relationships	184
Figure 21:	The Nature of Transactional Exchange	227
Figure 22:	Contested and Harmonious Exchange in Horizontal Business Relationships	252
Figure 23:	Contested Exchange in Vertical Business Relationships	253

About the Author

Andrew Cox is CIPS Professor and Director of the Centre for Business Strategy and Procurement in Birmingham Business School at the University of Birmingham in the UK. He is also chairman of Robertson Cox Consulting, a competence development and consulting company.

His research focuses on the problems of interests, value and power in business relationships, and the development of appropriate strategies to create commercial and operational business relationship alignment in supply chains and markets.

Consulting work focuses on assisting organisations with the alignment of commercial and operational means with strategic ends. Recent assignments have included work in construction, financial services, insurance, fmcg, healthcare, IT and computing, shipbuilding, oil and gas, travel and regulated utilities industries, as well as in the health and defence sectors.

He can be contacted at ac@robcox.com

Other Related Publications by the Author:

Business Success: A Way of Thinking about Strategy, Critical Supply Chain Assets and Operational Best Practice
by Andrew Cox (1997)
Earlsgate Press: ISBN 1-87439-76-8

Advanced Supply Management: The Best Practice Debate
by Andrew Cox and Peter Hines (eds) (1997)
Earlsgate Press: ISBN 1-873439-51-2

Outsourcing: A Business Guide to Risk Management Tools and Techniques
by Chris Lonsdale and Andrew Cox (1998)
Earlsgate Press: ISBN 1-873439-61-X

Strategic Procurement Management in Construction
by Andrew Cox and Mike Townsend (1998)
Thomas Telford: ISBN 0-7277-2599-8

Contracting for Business Success
by Andrew Cox and Ian Thompson (1998)
Thomas Telford: ISBN 0-7277-2600-5

Strategic Procurement Management: Concepts and Cases
by Richard Lamming and Andrew Cox (eds) (1999)
Earlsgate Press: ISBN 1-873439-81-4

Power Regimes: Mapping the DNA of Business and Supply Chain Relationships
by Andrew Cox, Joe Sanderson and Glyn Watson (2000)
Earlsgate Press: ISBN 1-873439-91-1

Supply Chains, Markets and Power: Mapping Buyer and Supplier Power Regimes
by Andrew Cox, Paul Ireland, Chris Lonsdale, Joe Sanderson and Glyn Watson (2002)
Routledge: ISBN 0-415-25727-1

Supply Chain Management: A Guide to Best Practice
by Andrew Cox, Paul Ireland, Chris Lonsdale, Joe Sanderson and Glyn Watson (2003)
Financial Times/Prentice Hall: ISBN 0-273-66270-8

Business Relationships for Competitive Advantage: Managing Alignment and Misalignment in Buyer and Supplier Transactions
by Andrew Cox, Chris Lonsdale, Joe Sanderson and Glyn Watson (2004)
Palgrave Macmillan: ISBN 1-4039-1904-6

Preface:

The Need for Conceptual Clarity

The ideas presented here are the fruits of many years working with practitioners in the public and private sectors. The primary aim has been to assist managers with the resolution of problems in their business relationships. These relationships include joint ventures and strategic alliances, as well as relationships when organisations act either as buyers from suppliers, or as sellers to customers.

What this experience has shown is that much of the advice that practitioners have received about effective relationship management is often misguided. This is because much of this advice has been focused on encouraging the development of operationally collaborative ways of working, based on the development of trust and win-win outcomes. To put it simply, practitioners have been advised to stop being adversarial and become more collaborative and trusting.

This "new way" to arrive at effective relationship management has led to some recently fashionable ideas in business management thinking like: long-term partnership sourcing and relationship marketing between buyers and suppliers; the outsourcing of non-core competencies; and, the development of co-opetition rather than competition. What all of these approaches share in common is a commitment to the development of open and trusting relationships between business partners, based on the idea that win-win is a better way of managing relationships than win-lose.

Intuitively, for those wishing to sustain business relationships, this reasoning makes sense. It seems obvious to conclude that, unless both parties in a business relationship obtain benefit (gains from trade), then there is unlikely to be any basis for sustaining a relationship over time. But, if this approach is best practice, one has to wonder why, in virtually all of the research and consulting engagements related to business relationships that the author has been involved over the last fifteen years, there has been only limited evidence of sustained success from the adoption of this approach. On the contrary, amongst some practitioners there has developed a dawning realisation that many of the benefits touted by relationship partners simply have not, and never will, arrive.

Some simple examples drawn from the buyer, supplier and joint venture/alliancing perspectives explain the problem. In a recent engagement the author and his colleagues reviewed four sourcing strategies for a manufacturing company. The company had recruited a CPO from the automotive sector to introduce the lean thinking, partnership sourcing and win-win practices that have been developed in that industry. The basic strategy of the company was to reduce the number of suppliers it worked with and to develop long-term trusting and highly collaborative approach with those that were preferred. The expectation was that this would create a win-win and allow both parties to appropriate higher levels of value from the relationship.

Interestingly enough, the findings of the review were that the buyer was in fact locked into highly dependent relationships with their suppliers, who has successfully closed the market to their competitors and, once this was achieved, were now in the process of failing to deliver on the original terms of the agreement unless the buyer allowed them to appropriate more value than had been agreed from the relationship. In one case the buying company had even gone so far as to outsource one of its core competencies to the supplier, who was now uninterested in sharing value, and was more interested in eventually becoming a direct competitor.

A second case explains the problem of a supposed win-win relationship, but from the perspective of the supplier selling to a customer. In this case the author and his colleagues were engaged by the seller to assess the reasons for a breakdown in their relationship with a major customer. The supplier in this case was a provider of electronic components for a final assembler of electronics equipment in the consumer market. The supplier believed that, by developing an open and trusting approach to relationship marketing, it could build a long-term and mutually beneficial collaborative relationship with this major customer. The problem for the supplier was that after two years the buyer decided to end the relationship even though it had been based on a presumption of five years or more, and the supplier had more than 80% of its revenue with this one customer.

On reviewing the case it was clear that the supplier had been a technically more proficient provider of a major component for the product range of the buying company. It also transpired that the buying company had clearly understood this, and had entered into the relationship in order to obtain the technical and operational competence of the supplier. Once this had been achieved the buying company no longer required the services of the supplier and was happy to let them go. The supplier had assumed that they were involved in a long-term win-win relationship, but the buyer was not.

There was little that the supplier could do when it found out that it was in fact involved in a win-lose relationship. This was because they trusted the other side in the relationship and had not thought it necessary to put in place contractual safeguards against this type of behaviour. Experience in consulting practice and academic research shows that these types of outcome are far more prevalent than many proponents of win-win relationships suppose. An example from a joint venture/strategic alliance arrangement in the automotive sector reinforces this point.

Honda developed a highly collaborative relationship with Rover as a way of avoiding the need to invest heavily in plant and infrastructure as they entered the UK marketplace. The relationship was clearly seen as a win-win by both sides. Rover was technically backward and did not understand the lean approach to final assembly and sourcing, which it hoped to learn from Honda. Honda, on the other hand, needed to find a quick and low cost mechanism to enter the UK market and overcome political opposition. Honda also expected that if Rover was ever sold by its parent company—British Aerospace—that it would have first refusal.

It was something of a surprise to Honda that British Aerospace decided, at short notice, to sell its stake in Rover to the highest and quickest bidder rather than allow its strategic partner to acquire the company first. In the end Honda's highly trusting and collaborative approach led to some of their technical and operational know-how being available to BMW, another direct competitor. This indicates that strategic allies may lose in the long-run if they trust the wrong partners.

Proponents of the win-win approach would probably conclude that the evidence from three cases is not proof that the approach is fatally flawed. This is because there are clearly many examples of long-term collaborative relationships that have worked very successfully for many years. This is certainly the case. This implies that, although win-win relationships can be successful, they can also fail. The primary reason for writing this book is, therefore, to try to explain why it is that win-win relationships sometimes succeed and sometimes fail. The argument developed here is that this variable performance is primarily based on three factors.

The first factor is that the win-win concept has never been properly defined conceptually, and many writers on the subject fail to grasp that the concept may not be feasible in all types of business relationship. In particular, there may be significant differences between what mutuality can mean in joint venture and strategic alliance relationships, and what is possible when buyers and suppliers interact. For example, it is argued here that win-win outcomes are not feasible in buyer and supplier relationships, although they are in joint ventures and strategic alliances.

The second factor is that many writers appear to believe that relationship partners need only to choose between win-win and win-lose outcomes. Unfortunately, this is a very simplistic view of the complexity that surrounds business relationships and what allows them to be sustained over time. As the discussion here will show business relationships are complex, and they may result in a range of outcomes with win-win as one extreme and lose-lose the other, but with combinations of win, partial win and lose for both parties to the relationship in between.

Indeed, as we shall see, business relationships outcomes can be *symmetrical* (both sides receive the same outcome) or they can be *asymmetrical* (one side receives more or less than the other). Despite this, there is considerable evidence that business relationships can be sustained with asymmetrical as well as symmetrical outcomes. A failure to grasp this complexity often leads to confusion over feasible outcomes between the parties to a relationship. It also leads to a simplistic interpretation of what *mutuality* (joint benefit) means in business relationships.

The third factor is that managers often suffer from a form of economic or commercial false consciousness. This means that managers enter into business relationships without fully understanding what their economically ideal objective interests are, either as buyers, suppliers or as strategic business allies. They negotiate business contracts with others based on their subjective (normative) perception of what their interests are, and this can lead them to misconceive how they should manage long-term relationships with others, especially when they do not understand the power and leverage benefits that may occur for their business relationship partners from pre- and post-contractual opportunism. As a result, there appears to be a significant paradox in many relationships, especially in those between buyers and suppliers, based on the way in which both parties define value and pursue their objective and subjective interests.

As a result, managers often use the language of win-win as a short hand for saying that they want to work closely with others (and often to grow "the size of the cake" that can be shared between them) without dealing directly with the difficult choices that have to be made about which aspects, and how much, of the value created in a relationship should be appropriated by either party. Unfortunately, experience shows that, when parties to an exchange start to see, objectively, the value that other parties are appropriating for themselves from an exchange relationship, win-win relationships may end in tears because the exchange is not regarded as "fair". In other words, "the size of the cake" may grow, but one party is still appropriating far more of the value than the other, leading the disadvantaged to claim a foul.

This concern about fairness arises because there is a world of difference between saying that win-win relationships exist because both parties are subjectively receiving at least something they value, and that both parties are objectively receiving "fair" value from the exchange. "Fair" here means that the value one party receives is perceived by them to be "fair" once the objective benefits that the other party is receiving relative to the value that they are receiving themselves is apparent.

Relationships that do not end in tears, in the experience of the author, are those in which both sides fully understand the power and leverage attributes of the parties to the exchange. They are also those in which each party has a clear understanding of their own and their exchange partner's objective interests, and how this will affect the apportionment of value between them pre- and post-contractually. This means that, sometimes, symmetrical outcomes are required to align business relationships effectively, but sometimes relationships can be aligned even when asymmetrical outcomes occur.

Those relationships that fail appear to be those in which either one, or both, parties to the transaction have only a vague subjective understanding of what a win-win means, do not understand objectively the operation of power and leverage, and do not fully understand their own economically ideal objective interests. In these circumstances two outcomes are likely. If one party understands the rules of the game better than another, then they will appropriate more value from the relationship than the other. If both parties to the relationship fail to understand the rules then they may both end up being dissatisfied with the relationship (Cox et al., 2004).

Practitioners, therefore, have complex choices to make about how to manage their business relationships. They must choose between win, partial win and lose outcomes for themselves, but they must also understand that within these options there are complex choices to be made about what type, and how much, of the value created by the relationship should be shared with the other party to the exchange. Even if a win-win approach is feasible and selected this does not, however, absolve either party from having to deal with the inherent tensions over value that occur in all business relationships due to the interplay of the power and leverage attributes of both parties over time.

But this is to run ahead of the discussion. The structure of what follows is simple enough. In the first chapter the complexity of commercial outcomes from business relationships is discussed. Initially, nine theoretically possible commercial outcomes are defined in business exchange between legally separate individuals or organisations.

This is followed, in the second chapter, by a discussion of the universe (nature and types) of business relationships within which win-win outcomes might be generated between legally separate organisations or individuals. The discussion distinguishes between *horizontal* and *vertical* business relationships. That is, between joint ventures and strategic alliances, and buyer and supplier exchange.

Having analysed these general issues the third chapter focuses on business relationships between individuals or organisations that collaborate to compete together in the market against others. These *horizontal business relationships* include a range of different types of joint venture and strategic alliance relationships, where it is argued that win-win outcomes are feasible, but that they are not always necessary to sustain them. This is because mutuality encompasses far more than win-win outcomes and relationships can be sustained with asymmetric as well as symmetrical outcomes.

The fourth chapter focuses on whether or not win-win outcomes are feasible in *vertical business relationships*. That is relationships between legally separate organisations, one of which is a buyer of goods and/or services and the other a supplier. It is argued that symmetrical outcomes (including win-win but excluding lose-lose) are not feasible in these types of relationship and that all buyer and supplier exchange is, and will remain, contested. This means that only asymmetrical outcomes are feasible, and also that buyer and supplier relationships are sustainable even though one party achieves more than the other from the exchange. Paradoxically, in buyer and supplier exchange it is also possible for relationships to be sustained when win-lose outcomes occur.

Chapter five provides a comprehensive overview of the theoretically possible commercial and operational outcomes from both horizontal and vertical business exchange. This is followed by an analysis of the complex range of outcomes that are practically (as opposed to theoretically) feasible from an economically rational (objective) point of view, in joint venture and strategic alliance relationships, as well as in buyer and supplier exchange. The chapter demonstrates that there are many very complex trade-offs to be made by exchange partners in all forms of transactional exchange, but that the choices open to buyers and suppliers are far more complex than those available to joint venture and strategic alliance partners.

The sixth chapter focuses on one of the major paradoxes at the heart of business management thinking, and shows that one of the key problems in aligning business relationships successfully is associated with the interplay of subjective and objective interests. This is because managers can subjectively believe they are receiving tremendous value, when in fact, objectively speaking, they are being taken advantage of by their relationship partners. This creates the possibility that managers may not act rationally, economically or commercially, through a form of subjective myopia or behavioural false consciousness. This explains why it is that there are cognitive power resources that reinforce structural power resources when exchange partners interact.

The final chapter discusses the implications of these findings for current academic analyses of transactional exchange and business relationship management. It is argued that, by adopting an objective rather than subjective way of thinking about relationship outcomes, it is possible to build on the existing work in transaction cost economics and political economy to rescue the concept of power in business economics and management from its current impasse. If this is achieved then it may be possible to develop a more holistic social science approach to the analysis of transactional exchange.

If this volume provides some illumination of these complex issues so that a more informed debate can occur about what is meant by the concepts of win-win and *mutuality*, as well as power, value and interests in different types of business relationships, then it will have served its purpose. Most of all it will have served its purpose if it helps readers to be aware of the inherent tensions and paradoxes in business relationships.

I would like to thank Paul Ireland for his extremely helpful comments on drafts of this volume and Chris Lonsdale, Joe Sanderson, Glyn Watson and Dan Chicksand for their collegial support and encouragement over many years. I would also, once again, like to thank Jackie Potter and Michele Donovan for their sterling efforts in bringing this book to publication as swiftly as I had hoped. Any sins of omission or commission that remain in what follows are, of course, mine alone.

Andrew Cox
Birmingham
2004

"There are two levers to set a man in motion, fear and self-interest"

Napoleon Bonaparte

(French General and Emperor, 1768-1821)

1

The Complexity of Commercial Outcomes in Business Relationships

The main title of this book ends with a question mark. This is because, while everyone uses the concept of win-win, it is not always clear in practice what people or organisations actually mean by it when they enter into business relationships. Furthermore, although the concept is used liberally in the English language, there has been little rigorous definition of the concept amongst academic writers. This volume seeks, therefore, to clarify the meaning of the concept by reference primarily to its objective relationship to value and interests, but also to power and leverage, in the context of different types of business relationships.

1.1 *Tautological Reasoning and a Lack of Conceptual Clarity*

Although most writing about win-win relationship outcomes assumes that one needs to say nothing more than that both parties seek mutual gain and eschew win-lose (zero-sum) outcomes, it can be argued that this type of definition is inherently vague and unsatisfactory. This is because it assumes that a win-win must exist if both parties are subjectively happy with the outcome of the relationship and they are receiving something they value from the exchange.

The problem with this type of reasoning is that it is tautological. This is because, while it explains what a win-win is not (it is not zero-sum or a win-lose), it does not really tell us what a positive-sum outcome is in any detail. It does not, therefore, provide any meaningful definition of the scope and breadth of the concept in practice. Furthermore, it does not explain in detail what is the full range of outcomes that can occur in business relationships—in most business relationships it is rarely just a simple choice between win-win or win-lose outcomes.

The concept in current usage is also imprecise because it does not specify clearly whether a win-win can encompass operational or commercial outcomes or must include both. For example, parties to an exchange can interact with either limited or extensive operational linkages or ways of working because business relationships can be *arm's-length* or *collaborative* (Cox, 1999a).

In an arm's-length relationship the parties work together, but with only very limited operational linkages. In such a case a buyer, after designing and specifying requirements and negotiating a contract, might only provide a supplier with simple information about volumes, timings and/or delivery locations. If the supplier meets these contractually agreed requirements and delivers the product or service satisfactorily this will be the extent of the relationship operationally. This is an exchange relationship that is "sharp in by clear agreement; sharp out by clear performance" (Macneil, 1974, p.738).

There are, however, other types of relationships that involve far more extensive operational linkages that are normally referred to as collaborative relationships. In these relationships, once an agreement has been negotiated, close operational linkages are formed based on dedicated investments by both parties in the relationship, supported by relationship specific adaptations and the development of cultural norms and bonds (Cannon and Perreault, 1999). In these types of relationship the operational way of working may encompass very close day-to-day working, and the joint development of the products and services of the buyer and supplier. These more extensive and operationally collaborative ways of working, which often involve bilateral dependency (Williamson, 1985), are clearly very different to arm's-length relationships.

One of the key questions that must be addressed when considering win-win, however, is whether or not the concept encompasses both of these types of relationship or only one. For some writers win-win is only really synonymous with collaborative relationships. This is because it is only in these relationships, where both sides are working together to create products and/or services, that the principles of mutual gain (through the creation of a larger cake to share) are appropriate.

The problem with this thinking, however, is that it simply confuses the operational way of working with the commercial benefit that arises from an exchange transaction. The purpose of business, after all, is to make money. At the most basic level, therefore, the win-win concept must be understood primarily in relation to a commercial rather than an operational outcome. This is because the primary purpose of business is to make money not to undertake any particular operational means.

In this light arm's-length relationships, in which there is very limited operational interaction beyond simple forms of exchange, may also be a win-win. This is because if parties to an exchange achieve some commercial benefit from the relationship then both have achieved something they value.

Whether the relationship is arm's-length or collaborative operationally is immaterial to a win-win outcome commercially. The difficulty with this conclusion is, of course, that if this is the case then, by definition, all relationships of whatever operational complexity are a win-win so long as both sides make some commercial return they value. This renders the concept tautological and relatively meaningless.

If this is the case what then does a win-win outcome mean in the context of business relationships? Common sense tells us it means that relationships cannot be sustained unless both parties receive something (operationally and/or commercially) that they value from the exchange, and also that they accept the "fairness" of the exchange. Most of us have experienced situations where we are losers from an exchange and others are winners, and this normally causes resentment on the part of those who experience the downside of a win-lose relationship. Logically, therefore, to sustain relationships with others a win-win must be preferable to a win-lose outcome.

This type of definition is common amongst writers on the subject:

"...win-win...should mean, in fact, a situation in which each issue requiring resolution has been settled in a way which meets the needs of both parties..." (Carlisle and Parker, 1989, p.36-37)

"A major part of negotiation consists of identifying potential gains from trade. This involves looking for win-win situations, moves that would make not only you but also your negotiating partner better off...Thinking creatively about the possibilities of mutual gain—ways of expanding the pie to be divided—is an essential part of negotiation." (McMillan, 1992, p.25)

"The core values of relationship marketing are found in its emphasis on collaboration and the creation of mutual value. It includes viewing suppliers, customers and others as partners rather than as opposite parties…[it] should be more of a win-win than win-lose, more of a plus-sum game than a zero-sum game." (Gummesson, 2002, p.15)

This volume does not take issue with this general conclusion that win-win outcomes (if they are feasible) are normally the best way to sustain relationships with others for any length of time. Rather, it seeks to clarify why the win-win concept can be extremely dangerous for the unwary.

The primary reason for caution is because those entering into business relationships often use the win-win concept indiscriminately. Practitioners often lack a proper understanding of the fact that it is very difficult to achieve and may not be the only desirable outcome that should be pursued. Thus, while one outcome from a relationship may be a symmetrical (50/50) sharing of the value created, this is not the only basis on which value can be shared and relationships sustained.

What this means is that sustainable business relationships may be possible with or without win-win outcomes. Indeed, as this volume hopes to show, while a win-win (or *ideal mutuality*) is possible for joint ventures and strategic alliances (i.e. both of the parties in the relationship achieve their ideal objective and economically rational goals), paradoxically, this type of outcome is not feasible in business transactions between buyers and sellers, where partial win-win, partial win-partial win and win-partial win outcomes are the best that can be achieved. Indeed, in some circumstances, business relationships between buyers and sellers also appear to be sustainable even when win-lose outcomes occur.

1.2 *A Deductive Way of Thinking about Mutuality and the Win-Win Concept*

To understand this apparently paradoxical line of reasoning it is first necessary to define what a win-win means and how this is related to the concept of mutuality. This can only be achieved by reference to the universe of theoretically possible outcomes that can occur in business relationships. As we shall see, managers and academic writers often fail to clarify what they mean by the concept, and thereby confuse win-win (one form of mutual gain) with mutuality (different forms of mutual gain).

It is important to recognise at the outset, however, that the discussion here is focused primarily on exchange between two organisations or individuals who are focused on commercial outcomes (i.e. what they ultimately value is profit). The problem of disentangling value and interests for transactions involving end consumers as individuals and/or public organisations when they interact with those who seek profit or other non-profit outcomes is not directly discussed in what follows. In the final chapter, however, the case for a more rigorous analysis of win-win and mutuality outcomes and the concepts of value and interests in all types of exchange transactions involving consumer-public and consumer-private, as well as in public-private and public-public, exchange is made.

In private-private exchange transactions a win-win outcome can be said to occur, therefore, when each party brings something that the other party values operationally and/or commercially to the relationship, with the intention of receiving something they value in return. The presumption is that by working together operationally in some way both parties will achieve a commercially valued outcome. It does not necessarily matter whether the two parties are collaborating or working operationally at arm's-length, what matters most is that they both receive something they value commercially from the exchange.

Logically speaking, therefore, if there are situations in which business relationships can result in commercially symmetrical outcomes (like win-win), then there must also be alternative outcomes—some of which may also be symmetrical and some of which may be asymmetrical. Figure 1 provides a simple way of thinking about the universe of possible symmetrical and asymmetrical commercial outcomes that can occur in business relationships between two parties (A and B).

Figure 1: Commercial Outcomes from Business Relationships

	NOT ACHIEVED	PARTIALLY ACHIEVED	FULLY ACHIEVED
FULLY ACHIEVED	(A) WIN/LOSE	(B) WIN/PARTIAL WIN	(C) WIN/WIN
PARTIALLY ACHIEVED	(D) PARTIAL WIN/LOSE	(E) PARTIAL WIN/PARTIAL WIN	(F) PARTIAL WIN/WIN
NOT ACHIEVED	(G) LOSE/LOSE	(H) LOSE/PARTIAL WIN	(I) LOSE/WIN

Rows: IDEAL COMMERCIAL GOALS OF PARTY A. Columns: IDEAL COMMERCIAL GOALS OF PARTY B.

© Robertson Cox Ltd, 2003. All Rights Reserved

As the Figure shows, when there are two parties to an exchange there can be circumstances in which both parties (A and B) fully achieve their goals (i.e. they receive everything of commercial value that they might hope for). On the other hand there can be outcomes where they only partially achieve their commercial goals, and also circumstances when they fail to achieve any of their intended commercial goals.

By adopting this logic, there are nine possible commercial outcome scenarios that two parties to an exchange relationship can experience. The first of these (cell A) is win-lose because A achieves everything they value commercially, but B does not achieve anything they value at all. The second outcome (cell B) is win-partial win because A fully achieves everything they value commercially, but B only partially achieves their ideal commercial value outcomes.

The third outcome (cell C) is where both parties (A and B) fully achieve all of the things they commercially value from the relationship. This is referred to as *ideal mutuality*. It is what most people would normally see as the "fairest" outcome from any relationship and what is intuitively meant when people talk about win-win relationships. It is also, arguably, the outcome that is seen intuitively as the most likely to sustain any type of relationship over time because both parties are achieving everything they desire.

There are, however, six other possible outcomes. In cell D it is possible for A to achieve some of what they want commercially, and for B not to receive anything at all that they value. This is a partial win-lose outcome. In cell E, both A and B receive something, but not all, of that which they value commercially. This is a partial win-partial win outcome. In cell F, A achieves some of what they value commercially, while B achieves everything they value. This is a partial win-win outcome. In cell G, both A and B fail to achieve anything they value commercially from the relationship. This is a lose-lose outcome. In cell H, A fails to win anything that is valued commercially by them, but B achieves some of the things that they value. This is a lose-partial win outcome. Finally, in cell I, A does not achieve anything of commercial value from the relationship, but B fully achieves their ideal commercial goals. This is a lose-win outcome.

It can be seen from this simple discussion that, while there are five possible outcomes in which one or both parties actually lose, there are four scenarios that involve some elements of mutuality (one or both parties gain something, if not always all, of that which they value commercially). The matrix also shows that there are only three *symmetrical* outcomes (win-win, partial win-partial win and lose-lose), while there are six *asymmetrical* outcomes (win-lose, win-partial-win, partial win-lose, partial win-win, lose-partial win and lose-win).

If this is the case then it is obvious that there is scope for disagreement and confusion over which relationship outcomes are the best for one or both parties to achieve when managing their interactions with others. Most important of all, however, is the fact that while a win-win outcome is theoretically possible, is this necessarily the only way to think about mutuality in business relationships?

There are at least four scenarios in which mutuality (some element of mutual commercial gain for both parties in the exchange) may be said to exist in business relationships. These are the win-win, partial win-partial win, win-partial win and partial win-win outcomes. Each one of these outcomes provides something of commercial value to both parties, which ought to provide the basis for a relationship to be sustained over time, but which of them is the best for each party? Is a win-win always preferable to a win-partial win for example?

These are the most pertinent questions that must be asked by those who seek win-win relationships, and the ones that experience shows practitioners often do not think about before they enter into them. Indeed most practitioners appear to believe that it is sufficient to say that they want to have win-win outcomes with their relationship partners. They do not appear to understand that to say that the other side must achieve something of value from the relationship tells us nothing at all about what the actual sharing of value in the relationship is to be commercially, or whether or not it is feasible for both parties to fully achieve all of their commercial goals in any relationship.

For example, even in a win-win situation (cell C in Figure 1) in which both parties fully achieve their commercial goals, there is still the possibility that one side in the relationship may be appropriating far more of the value from the relationship than the other. All that one is saying in the win-win scenario is that both parties fully achieved their goals, not that the commercial value in the relationship was shared equally.

So that, even in circumstances of *ideal mutuality*, there can still be tremendous inequity in the sharing of commercial value. This means that those who say they are interested in a win-win are still required to ask themselves questions related to how much of the value to be created is to be shared with their relationship partners. This is because, even within win-win scenarios, there is scope for more or less leverage of the commercial value that the two parties engaged receive from the exchange. Most writing on win-win and/or mutuality is silent on these issues.

But there is a further issue that is central to understanding the paradox at the heart of both mutuality as a principle and the win-win concept as an ideal outcome. This is the problem of economic false consciousness. This refers to the process by which individuals and/or organisations fail to understand their own ideal (objective) commercial interests and have a misguided (subjective) understanding of what these commercial interests are. If one or both parties to a relationship fundamentally misunderstand their objective economic interests, then it is possible that individuals engaged in business relationships may subjectively believe they are receiving a win but, objectively speaking, they may only be receiving a partial win or even a lose outcome, while the other side is achieving a much greater win than their subjectively misguided partner assumes.

This problem of opportunism by one party to an exchange occurs frequently in buyer and supplier relationships (Williamson, 1985; 1996). Opportunism of this type is normally the consequence of adverse selection (Akerlof, 1970); information asymmetry (Molho, 1997); post-contractual moral hazard (Roberts, 2004); and incomplete contracts (Hart, 1995) providing opportunities for suppliers to behave opportunistically against buyers. The related problem of hold-up (Milgrom and Roberts, 1992), where buyers take advantage of locked-in suppliers, ensures that sometimes the losers or partial winners from relationships can also be suppliers as well as buyers. As we shall see, these problems of pre- and post-contractual commercial opportunism tend to be less acute—although still possible—in horizontal business relationships (Das and Rahman, 2002).

The need to focus on problems of commercial opportunism in business relationships is critical to an understanding of why supposed win-win relationships often fail in practice. This is because at the heart of all negotiation and relationship management is the problem of the transparency of information about the commercial consequences of operational practices for both parties in a transaction (Bowles and Gintis, 1999). If one or both parties to an exchange do not fully understand the commercial consequences for themselves and/or for their relationship partners of the operational practices they are engaged in, then a situation of information asymmetry can be said to exist.

In such circumstances there is potential scope for opportunism (self-seeking interest with guile) and this may move a potential win into a partial win or lose scenario for one party in the relationship. This is fairly common in some business relationships, but is more difficult in others. It is for this reason that it is necessary to understand the types of inter-organisational business relationships—*horizontal* and *vertical*—that are possible. This is because some types of business relationships are far more likely to encourage pre- and post-contractual opportunism than others, and it is those that do where the major difficulties for achieving win-win outcomes occur.

2

Types of Inter-Organisational Business Relationships

In this volume we are only concerned with inter-organisational business relationships, and especially those between organisations that seek commercial returns as their primary reason for existence. The relationships that occur internally within organisations are not our primary focus, although many of the principles of opportunism over value appropriation discussed here can occur between individuals working within the same organisation. This view reinforces the claims of those writers that conceive of the firm internally as a "nexus of treaties" (Aoki et al., 1990), but our concern here is with external rather than internal business relationships between legally autonomous individuals and/or organisations.

2.1 *Types of External Business Relationships*

The primary reason for considering external contractual relationships is because, even though it may not always be true in practice that those contracted to work for a particular organisation are on the same side working towards the achievement of common goals, in theory they are supposed to be doing so. The reason for focusing on external relationships in business is because there is always the possibility of conflict and tension when two separate legal entities work together to achieve their individual commercial goals. This occurs because it is normal to put the pursuit of one's own commercial interests above those of others in business, and especially when an individual or organisation seeks to earn commercial returns for themselves. This often means that although inter-organisational relationship partners may be seeking win-win outcomes they are not always on the same side commercially. This fact creates potential problems and paradoxes for those interested in achieving win-win outcomes and other forms of commercial mutuality.

As Williamson has shown, the greatest obstacle to mutuality in business relationships externally arises from opportunism both pre- and post-contractually. It is essential, therefore, when considering whether win-win outcomes can be successfully implemented to understand what the scope for commercial opportunism is within particular types of business relationships externally.

This is critical because, as Herbert Simon demonstrated long ago, human beings suffer from bounded rationality. This means that although human beings try to be rational when making economic decisions they do not always make them in possession of perfect information. This means that decision-makers often do not know what it is that they do not know about a particular business relationship, even though they have to make decisions about what they should do now, and also assess how decisions today will affect them in the future (Simon, 1955).

Given this problem, it seems reasonable to agree with Williamson that the ideal situation for a decision-maker (bliss) is one in which there is perfect information and no scope for commercial opportunism, either now or in the future, by our business partners (Williamson, 1985). The problem is that this benign environment rarely occurs, and this is because there is often a problem over the transparency of information about the commercial consequences of particular operational practices. This information gap may be due to the imbeddedness of information and the difficulty of disentangling cause and effect, or it may be due to conscious withholding of information due to opportunism by one side in the relationship.

When either, or both, of these two conditions exist it is extremely difficult for anyone to make a perfectly rational decision about how to negotiate the terms of a relationship. In the absence of clear and unambiguous information for both parties about the commercial benefits that their relationship partners receive (now and in the future) from any operational collaboration it is difficult to know whether the terms of the exchange entered into are equitable and truly a win-win or not. This implies that win-win outcomes are likely to be most successful when the scope for opportunism is limited organisationally and contractually. This further implies that structurally some types of business relationships may be more or less conducive to the development of win-win outcomes commercially.

The discussion that follows analyses the basic types of inter-organisational business relationship from this perspective. As Table 1 indicates, the different types of external business relationship that companies enter into can be differentiated by the nature of the relationship; the typical sharing of value; the scope for information transparency and asymmetry; the ownership of risk and costs; and the scope for opportunism.

Table 1: The Scope for Opportunism in Different Types of External Business Relationships

THE CHARACTERISTICS OF THE EXCHANGE	HORIZONTAL RELATIONSHIPS — JOINT VENTURE	HORIZONTAL RELATIONSHIPS — STRATEGIC ALLIANCE	VERTICAL RELATIONSHIPS — COLLABORATIVE SOURCING	VERTICAL RELATIONSHIPS — MARKET TESTED SOURCING
BASIC DEFINITION OF THE RELATIONSHIP	Two legally separate parties remain independent, but create a new company that they both jointly own and manage to produce and sell products and/or services together in the market.	Two legally separate parties remain independent, but enter into an agreement to cooperate to achieve specific commercial and operational objectives by working together to produce and/or market and sell a product and/or service together in the market.	A legally separate and independent party (the buyer) enters into an agreement with a legally separate supplier, to source a supply input for their own products and/or services, using operational collaboration and long term contracts.	One legally separate and independent party (the buyer) enters into an agreement with a legally separate supplier, to source a supply input for their own products and/or services, on a short term basis using arm's length market testing contracts.
TYPICAL SHARING OF VALUE IN THE RELATIONSHIP	Can be full or preferential-equity based and share ownership can be equitable (50/50) or majority/minority. The issue of power in the relationship post-contractually is legally defined by the shareholders agreement.	There is no necessary fixed agreement on how value is shared in the relationship, this is still negotiable and could be close to zero-sum (99/1) or positive sum (50/50) depending on the relative power attributes of the two parties.	There is no necessary fixed agreement on how value is shared in the relationship, this is still negotiable and could be close to zero-sum (99/1) or positive sum (50/50) depending on the relative power attributes of the buyer and the supplier.	The buyer and supplier appropriate whatever value they can by negotiation and leverage pre- and post-contractually. This is normally a zero-sum game for both parties. The outcome is determined by the buyer and supplier relative power attributes.
SCOPE FOR INFORMATION TRANSPARENCY/ ASYMMETRY	Normally high levels of actual and potential information transparency for both parties due to share holding, but preference shareholders may be able to hide or delay information about trade-offs between some operational activities and commercial outcomes.	The degree of information transparency about operational and commercial trade-offs is a function of what is negotiated in a specific alliance agreement. High levels of information asymmetry are possible as well as transparency.	The degree of information transparency about operational and commercial trade-offs is a function of what is negotiated in a specific collaboration agreement. High levels of information asymmetry are possible as well as transparency.	Both parties experience high levels of actual and potential information asymmetry. Buyers have to trust that competition and market testing will provide efficient signals, and suppliers have to trust that buyers will use them again in the future, without guarantees for either party.
OWNERSHIP OF REWARDS, RISKS AND COSTS OF OPERATIONS	Both parties jointly share all of the risks and costs of operation, and both have transparency over the rewards that arise if the company is successful. The level and type of share ownership may vary the rewards outcome for each party.	Each party carries their own risks and costs of operation, and receives their own rewards as negotiated. Whether or not there is full transparency over the rewards received by the other party depends on what has been negotiated.	Each party carries their own risks and costs of operation, and receives their own rewards as negotiated. Whether or not there is full transparency over the rewards received by the other party depends on what has been negotiated.	Both parties carry their own risks and costs of operation, and receive their own rewards as negotiated. There is limited opportunity to understand the rewards received, or the risk and costs incurred, by the other party in the relationship.
SCOPE FOR OPPORTUNISM FOR EITHER PARTY	Opportunism within the jointly owned company is limited. There may be some scope for opportunism from preferential shareholding. Each party can be opportunistic about the benefits to their other businesses from participation in the joint venture.	A dominant party in the alliance can often be opportunistic against the more dependent party. The scope for opportunism by both parties is only limited by what has been agreed in the alliance agreement and even dependent parties may be able to hide the true rewards they receive.	Both parties can be opportunistic about the operational and commercial benefits they receive except for what has been agreed should be transparent. There is no direct mechanism to allow either party to understand the operational or commercial outcomes for the other.	The buyer can use false information about current and future demand requirements as a lever. The supplier can hide the true returns being made if market testing the buyer is sub-optimal and not efficient.

Table 1 makes a broad distinction between two types of business relationship. The first are those that occur between legally separate organisations cooperating operationally to produce and/or market a particular product and/or service in competition against others. These forms of external business exchange are known as *horizontal relationships*. The two major types of horizontal relationship discussed here are *joint ventures* and *strategic alliances*.

The second broad type is *vertical relationships*. These are sourcing relationships between a buyer and supplier within a supply chain. The relationship here is not between parties that wish to collaborate and to share the potential risks and costs, as well as potential benefits or losses, of competing together in the market. On the contrary, these are relationships in which the potential risks and costs, as well as potential benefits or losses from the product and/or service sourced, belong to the buyer once it has been legally and contractually acquired from the supplier. Conversely, the supplier normally is responsible for all of the potential risks and costs, as well as potential benefits and losses, from the product and/or service up until the legal and contractual transfer of ownership and responsibility to the buyer.

As Table 1 demonstrates, these vertical relationships can be short-term and arm's-length operationally (*market tested sourcing*) or they can be long-term and highly collaborative (*collaborative sourcing*). As Table 1 also indicates, horizontal and vertical business relationships have some very divergent as well as some similar characteristics. As we shall see, in relation to the scope for opportunism and the degree to which commercial value, information, risks and costs are either jointly shared or borne independently within particular types of relationship, there is a continuum running from joint ventures at one extreme to market tested sourcing relationships at the other.

2.2 *Understanding Horizontal Relationships*

Taking horizontal relationships first, of the four external business relationship types discussed here, it is clear that *joint ventures* provide the clearest legal guarantees and protections against information asymmetry, bounded rationality and opportunism for both parties. A joint venture is normally between two legally separate entities that remain independent. However, by creating a new organisation that is jointly owned, the joint shareholding within the company normally guarantees that each party has legal rights about access to information concerning operational and commercial trade-offs. This is the type of information that is normally of critical importance when opportunism is to be guarded against in business relationships.

Despite this, it is not necessary for joint ventures to be undertaken on a 50/50 equity basis. This means that, although both parties to the relationship may have similar levels of knowledge about the trade offs between operational practice and commercial outcomes, the actual amount of profit or loss to be achieved by either party may not be the same—it will depend on the share of equity participation and may be heavily weighted in favour of one party (the majority shareholder).

There is also a major distinction to be made between *full-equity joint ventures* (in which each share carries the same rights and responsibilities as all other shares) and *preferential-equity joint ventures* (in which Class A shares have superior rights and responsibilities over Class B shares). In full-equity joint ventures the relationship is always symmetrical in the sense that the risks and costs and rewards of operation are all borne equally by each share. This significantly reduces the scope for opportunism by one party relative to another, and tends to ensure symmetrical relationship outcomes for business partners. In preferential-equity joint venture relationships there is more scope for opportunism by one party over another and, as a result, asymmetrical relationship outcomes. This arises because Class A shareholders may be given superior rights to information, or first claim on profits, when compared with Class B shareholders.

Overall, however, the scope for opportunism within joint venture relationships is relatively low when compared to the other extreme of *market tested sourcing*. The primary reason is because both parties are working towards the same (or at least similar or coincident) end—they are normally on the same side operationally and commercially. This means that, although there may be some scope for differential risks and rewards in the preferential-equity joint ventures, neither side can benefit or lose commercially without the other side also benefiting or losing. Despite this coincidence of commercial interests in general, it has to be recognised that even within a joint venture there are normally no rights legally for either party to have access to sensitive operational and commercial information about the activities of the parent companies, or of the additional benefits that the joint venture may be bringing to their own independent businesses.

The second horizontal relationship type is the *strategic alliance*. These types of relationship normally involve two legally separate individuals or organisations entering into an agreement to cooperate to achieve a specific commercial and/or operational objective by working together in the market to sell particular products and/or services. These types of relationship can be quite varied in structure and encompass *technical training/start-up assistance agreements; patent licensing; production/assembly/ buy back agreements; franchising; know-how licensing; management/marketing service agreements;* and, *non-equity cooperative agreements for exploration, research and development/co-production* (Contractor and Lorange, 1988).

It is clear that strategic alliances may also hinder commercial opportunism through information asymmetry and bounded rationality, but the pressure for transparency on both parties may not be as effective as under joint ventures. The difficulty is that, in the absence of equity ownership and legally enforceable rights about access to critical information, there may be considerably more scope for information withholding in these types of relationships than in joint ventures. Part of the reason for this is because in many strategic alliance relationships—such as *technical training/start-up assistance, buy back agreements, patent* and *know-how licensing,* and *franchising*—there may often be a dominant party able to impose terms on the other party in the transaction.

In such circumstances the potential cost and risks and potential benefits and losses may be distributed asymmetrically. Indeed, each party carries its own risks and rewards independently of the other, which is not the case in joint venture agreements where the risks and rewards are owned by the joint venture company, and therefore by the equity owners, directly. Similarly, there is no necessary logic that says that in these types of arrangements that equitable value sharing will occur, unless of course each party to the relationship has something to bring to it that creates a negotiated agreement based on 50/50 sharing of risks and rewards.

Despite this, in all of these types of relationship—and in particular in *management/marketing service agreements* and *non-equity cooperative agreements* where both sides specifically need the expertise and resources of one another—both parties are clearly on the same side operationally and, in general terms, commercially. This tends to minimise the risks of information asymmetry by one party against another, although it does not guarantee it. In scenarios where one party has a dominant negotiating position, as well as critical resources, it is possible that opportunism may occur through a lack of transparency about the true relationship between operational activities and commercial returns. Furthermore, the risks and rewards for their own businesses outside of the strategic alliance are, as with joint ventures, known primarily by each independent party alone.

Notwithstanding these limitations on transparency and the realisation that there is still scope for some degree of opportunism—particularly by dominant parties over time—it is logical to conclude that horizontal forms of cooperation may be conducive to win-win outcomes, although they do not guarantee it. This is because both parties are working towards the same common goals commercially. As we shall see in the next chapter, however, while *ideal mutuality* (a win-win in which both parties are able to simultaneously achieve above normal returns commercially) is possible in horizontal relationships, this is not guaranteed and the exact sharing of value within them can vary quite widely (Das and Teng, 2002).

2.3 Understanding Vertical Business Relationships

The third and fourth types of relationship to be discussed here are vertical (*collaborative* and *market tested sourcing*) relationships between buyers and suppliers. In these types of relationship it is argued that a win-win (*ideal mutuality*) is not possible, whether the relationship is collaborative or market tested. This is because, although the operational goals of buyers and sellers can be coincidental, they are commercially in tension, or rather the relationship is one of *"contested exchange"* (Bowles and Gintis, 1988; 1993; 1999).

Two independent and legally separate parties normally undertake a collaborative sourcing relationship. The relationship is normally for one party to supply a particular product and/or service to the other, but using high levels of operational interaction and very close ways of working. Such relationships—sometimes confusingly called partnerships, alliances or partnership sourcing—usually necessitate long-term contractual agreements to encourage both parties to make dedicated investments, relationship specific adaptations and to develop cultural norms and organisational bonds with one another.

Despite this, because there is no legal equity ownership, there is no guarantee that this way of working will stop dominant parties (buyers or suppliers) from using operational collaboration as a way of forcing the other party to bear a disproportionate share of risks and costs, while limiting the share of value or reward that they can appropriate commercially from the relationship. These types of relationship are called *buyer dominant* or *supplier dominant* relationships, and are common in business (Cox et al., 2003).

It is, however, possible for buyers and suppliers to agree to operate in non-adversarial operational and commercial relationships—this is sometimes known as *reciprocal collaboration* (Cox et al., 2004). As we shall see, even this type of operational relationship does not completely eradicate the commercial tension in buyer and supplier exchange. This is because it is not possible for buyers and suppliers to achieve *ideal mutuality*. The reason for this is, as we shall see, because it is not possible for buyers to achieve their ideal objective (economically rational) commercial goals in a relationship with a supplier and for the supplier also to achieve theirs, or vice versa.

Due to this tension there is considerable scope for commercial opportunism in buyer and supplier relationships, even when operational linkages are close and highly collaborative. The primary reason for this is that, while in some regards the two parties are on the same side operationally, objectively speaking, it is rare for them to be on the same side commercially, whatever they may believe subjectively. This being the case, and in the absence of legal rights to transparent information about the relationship between operational and commercial trade-offs, there will be considerable scope for incomplete contracts, with adverse selection, moral hazard, information asymmetry and post-contractual lock-in and the hold-up problems to occur in buyer and supplier exchange (Williamson, 1985; Bowles and Gintis, 1999; Cox, 2004a).

Obviously, the closer companies work together in sourcing the more scope there is for both sides to understand the operational and commercial trade-offs in what is being done by the other side in the relationship. This implies that in *collaborative sourcing* relationships it is likely that there will be relatively less scope for commercial opportunism than in purely *market tested sourcing* relationships. In these latter relationships the exchange transaction occurs between two independent and legally separate organisations, whose only point of contact is the short-term contractual relationship, which tends to be operationally arm's-length. This means that the buyer provides basic specification, volume, timing and location information against which the supplier has to comply. The relationship tends, therefore to be operationally limited and commercially opportunistic (when feasible).

The opportunism arises because in situations of short-term market testing neither party is required—since they are not necessarily looking for long-term commitments—to provide high levels of critical information about the trade-off between operational activities and commercial returns. Given this, *market tested sourcing* relationships tend to become purely bargaining games based on the short-term maximisation of current power and leverage attributes in the market.

Unfortunately, for many buyers this is a one-sided game because they lack the time and resources to undertake the extensive market analyses that are necessary for them to properly understand the current power and leverage situation in complex sourcing markets. This often provides scope for suppliers to behave opportunistically against uninformed buyers (and sometimes buyers against suppliers) suffering from information asymmetry and bounded rationality.

In these circumstances win-win outcomes commercially are not feasible in *market tested sourcing* relationships. The point that will be made here, however, is that even though there is potentially more scope for these to occur in collaborative sourcing relationships—due to the bilateral operational commitments that both parties make to one another—in practice *ideal mutuality* (the ultimate form of win-win that is clearly achievable commercially in horizontal business relationships) is also not feasible in any types of vertical sourcing relationship.

This does not mean, however, that there is no scope for limited forms of mutuality (win-partial win, partial win-win or partial win-partial win) to occur. But it does mean that those who espouse win-win in sourcing relationships may be guilty of a failure to properly specify what the limits of this type of relationship are between buyers and suppliers.

In the next two chapters the scope for win-win outcomes is discussed first in horizontal and then in vertical business relationships. As we shall see, there are a number of interesting paradoxes over value and interests in the relationships between buyers and suppliers that do not appear to exist in joint ventures and strategic alliances.

3

Understanding Win-Win Commercial Outcomes in Horizontal Business Relationships

The primary questions that are addressed in this chapter are, first, whether or not it is possible for individuals or organisations involved in horizontal business relationships—*joint ventures* and *strategic alliances*—to have win-win outcomes. By win-win outcomes one means here *ideal mutuality*, or a situation in which both parties to an exchange fully achieve their objectively ideal (economically rational) commercial outcomes. The second question is whether or not horizontal business relationships can be sustained in the absence of these win-win outcomes commercially. The resolution of these questions is not an easy matter because of the problem of objective and subjective interests, which is discussed briefly in what follows.

The chapter first outlines a way of thinking about value in the context of horizontal business relationships. The problem of subjective and objective interests and how this impacts on perceptions of value in exchange relationships is also discussed. The final section concludes with an analysis of the types of relationship outcomes that are possible in horizontal forms of exchange. It is argued that *ideal mutuality* (win-win) is possible in horizontal business relationships, but that this is not always required for joint ventures and strategic alliances to be sustained.

3.1 *Value and the Problem of Subjective and Objective Interests*

What is it that joint venture and strategic alliance partners value when they enter into relationships? Obviously the answer to this can be multifaceted and may vary from party to party and within relationship types. Space does not allow here for a full discussion of all of the value permutations that might motivate all of the potential participants in these types of relationships. To make some sense of the problem, therefore, it is safest to assume that the primary goal of all participants in these types of relationships is, in the private sector at least, to make money.

When one raises the question of making money, however, this creates at least two additional definitional problems. The first is the problem associated with what amount of money has to be made for one or both of the parties in the relationship to be satisfied that this is a win-win commercially. The second problem is whether or not the win-win should be seen in the context of the specific relationship being analysed, or in the context of other relationships that one or both parties to a particular exchange might be involved in elsewhere. Each of these issues is discussed in more detail in what follows.

It is obvious that in business the goals of individuals are not always the same. While everyone is concerned with the pursuit of money, as psychologists understand, people have *"hierarchies of need"* (Maslow, 1943). This implies that some individuals may be profit maximisers while others may be profit satisficers (Cox, 1997a). This means that, although everyone in business must make sufficient money in order to sustain their business operations, not everyone is seeking to continuously maximise their returns. For some individuals and organisations, after their basic needs for shelter and lifestyle have been met, their psychological needs shift from money making to other interests.

This human predilection is well known, but its existence causes some theoretical problems for disentangling what is meant by a win-win in the context of a business relationship, or even a win for a self-employed individual engaged in business. A self-employed individual might be content to make sufficient money to keep their business alive and to give them a basic standard of living. Once this has been achieved such an individual (or organisation) might then be willing to pass value to customers or business partners without making large returns above these basic needs. The self-employed individual's subjective conception of what is needed (i.e. how much money or profit is required) to achieve a win for them may, therefore, be one thing, but it may be altogether another for an individual or organisation that has shareholders to satisfy.

An organisation may not only have to support the lifestyles of a number of individuals that work for it (some of whom may be satisficers and some of whom may be maximisers), but it is more than likely that such an organisation—especially if it is publicly listed on a stock exchange—will also have to satisfy the lifestyles and commercial aspirations of shareholders. While some shareholders may be satisficers, it is more than probable that most shareholders—especially the large faceless pension funds and investment companies that dominate equity markets—will tend to be profit maximisers. As a result, organisations must ultimately seek to maximise profit whatever the personal predilections of those who work for them. In capitalist economies it is clearly the case therefore that, whatever the personal or subjective preferences of individuals about what a win means commercially, in the context of any business exchange the system itself has its own laws and logic.

In this sense in capitalist economic exchange there are some outcomes from business relationships that are more highly valued than others. Thus, objectively speaking, from an economically rational point of view, in any business relationship some financial returns are more desirable than others. Put simply, economists differentiate between *normal returns* (the profits that arise from participating in highly contested and competitive markets) and *above normal returns* (the super-normal profits that arise from an ability to create isolating mechanisms that create competitive advantage in markets).

Objectively speaking, therefore, the interests of individuals and/or organisations engaged in economic exchange must be to earn above-normal returns (*rents*) rather than normal returns (*profits*). In simple language this normally means that it is better for a participant in a business relationship to earn *rents* (double-digit returns) than for returns to be below double-digit and tending to zero. Furthermore, it is also best from an economically rational point of view, if these double-digit returns are sustainable—this means that they are not one-off, but can be continuously achieved over time.

This ideal or objectively economically rational way of thinking may not be to the personal (or subjective) taste of everybody, as our discussion of the *"hierarchies of need"* problem earlier demonstrated. So there is considerable scope for subjective disagreement about what the concept of a win means commercially for particular parties to specific business relationships.

The approach taken in the discussion here is, however, straight forward. The concept of a win or a win-win has very little meaning in the business context if it simply means that it exists when one or both parties to the exchange believes that they have achieved what they subjectively desire. This makes the concept tautological and meaningless because it is not capable of definition outside of the subjective perceptions of individuals.

To overcome this problem, therefore, a win is defined here as the ability by any party in a business relationship to achieve above normal returns (*rents*). A partial win is defined as the ability to make returns that can be defined as normal (*profits*), which merely sustain the business at below double-digit levels, and a lose as any returns that fail to provide a profit and/or do not meet the ability to sustain the individual and/or organisation in business over time. This approach provides the concept with an objective rather than subjective definitional basis derived deductively from economically rational reasoning.

This definition will not, of course, satisfy those who demand that business relationships should have broader social and political purposes. Unfortunately, once these social and political externalities are factored into the concepts of a win or win-win their definition becomes wholly subjective and tautological—it becomes whatever an individual (and/or the omniscient observer of the relationship as analyst) defines it to be. This provides no basis for either theoretical clarification of the meaning of the concepts or their empirical validation.

Although this objective (or economically rational) definition of the commercial outcomes from a business relationship provides a way of clarifying the problem of win-win it does not overcome a further problem with the concept. This second problem is associated with the fact that individuals and organisations can be involved in different types of business relationships with separate parties but which may in some way be inter-connected. Thus, an individual or organisation might enter into a relationship with one party, in which a less than ideal transactional outcome (a partial win or a lose) is acceptable commercially, because it provides the basis for developing a relationship now or in the future with the same or another party that is even more commercially favourable (a win).

A simple example explains this inter-connection problem. During the Second World War an enterprising individual realised that the combined RAF and US Air Force needed to have many more airstrips than were available and this forced them to operate from farmers' fields. The combined Air Forces needed to have the grass-based airfields regularly mowed, so the enterprising individual offered to mow all of the fields in his part of England (and even those he did not own) for free. He made no money at all from the combined Air Forces, but he made himself a millionaire because he had spotted that there was a shortage of fodder for animals and that he could make a financial killing from supplying this need. He saw that the cost to him of mowing would be more than adequately compensated for by the high returns from customers who were short of fodder for their animals.

This simple example shows that sometimes, objectively speaking, it is possible to operate within one business relationship as the loser, (i.e. in what is commercially a win-lose outcome from an economically rational point of view), but still end up as the commercial winner, objectively speaking, in another business relationship. In this case the enterprising individual was the objective loser in the specific relationship with the combined Air Forces because it cost him more to mow the grass than he received (which was nothing). Objectively, in this transaction, it was the combined Air Forces that were the winners in what was, from an economically rational point of view, a win-lose relationship.

Objectively speaking, however, the enterprising individual was clearly a commercial winner overall. This was because he was able to make above normal returns from all of the buyer-supplier relationships he was able to enter into after mowing the airfields. He was able to sell his product (fodder) at above normal returns because his costs of production were lower relative to other providers in the market (he did not have to incur costs in the management of land so that grass would grow), and he was also a major source of supply when there was a shortage in the market (two clear isolating mechanisms relative to other suppliers in the market).

Objectively speaking, in these inter-connected relationships with buyers of fodder the transactional outcomes were likely to be a win or a partial win for all of the buyers concerned. This was because the buyers were desperate for the supply in order to operate their own businesses (raising animals) and to be able to sell their own products in the market. Furthermore, at this time, because of shortages for foodstuffs for consumers of all kinds, farmers were also able to make above normal and/or normal returns. Despite this, the relationships were not, ultimately, sustainable. This was because after the war the combined RAF and USAF did not have a need for anyone to mow the fields and food shortages gradually disappeared. This was only a temporary competitive advantage for the enterprising millionaire.

What this example shows is that one business relationship is often part of a more complex network of business relationships, and this makes the problem of understanding what we mean by a commercial win-win in business very difficult. The problem is further complicated by the fact that there are many examples of organisations providing 'loss leaders' (goods and/or service at less than the cost of production) in order to have a short-term impact on market forces. Thus, large multiple retailers will often provide a 'loss leader' in their stores in order to attract customers to buy other products from which they make high returns, or to wipe out competitors who can undercut their normal prices for particular goods and services but who cannot provide the same product and/or service range overall.

By 'loss leading' in this way organisations demonstrate that they are more than willing to countenance a win-lose commercially in some relationships (for a short time at least) in order to maximise their competitive position overall, or in order to make even more money in another relationship with the same or a different business partner. The problem is that these interconnections cause additional problems for understanding what is meant by a win-win.

In order to simplify this problem the approach adopted here is to assume that it is only possible to discuss a discrete business relationship to ascertain whether or not it is a win, partial win or lose for each party to the exchange. In other words, to make the concept meaningful and manageable the analysis must be confined—as it was in the discussion of the enterprising individual's relationship, first, with the RAF and USAF and, then, with buyers of fodder—to the discrete exchange transaction. This avoids confusion of transactional outcomes by reference to other separate, even if inter-related, business relationships.

The issue of the overall business strategy of either party is, of course, of major significance and must be taken into account by those trying to understand the strategies of individuals and organisations when they enter into business relationships. Nevertheless, in the context of defining what a win or win-win means commercially, the approach taken here is to limit it to each specific transaction or relationship that exists and to assess whether or not either party is, or is not, able to earn above normal returns, normal returns or be forced to operate at break-even or at a loss.

This is because, even in circumstances where parties to an exchange have to accept a loss or a partial win to be able to achieve a win in another relationship, they would ideally prefer not to have to do this, and would prefer instead to achieve a win in all of their relationships. In this sense using 'loss leaders' may be a sensible overall strategy but it is still sub-optimal at the specific transactional level from an ideal, or economically rational, perspective. This approach allows us to understand the inter-connectedness of business relationships, but also provides for an objective rather than subjective assessment of the types of outcomes possible in specific business relationships.

3.2 *Feasible Commercial Outcomes in Joint Venture Relationships*

Given this starting point, it is clear that it is possible in both theory and practice for parties in horizontal business relationships—joint ventures and strategic alliances—to achieve *ideal mutuality* commercially. This is a win-win in which both parties to an exchange achieve above normal returns—these are the ideal commercial goals that individuals and organisations in capitalist economic systems ought objectively to be seeking to achieve.

While win-win outcomes will certainly sustain these types of horizontal relationships, it is also clear that partial win-partial win outcomes may also be capable of sustaining these relationships over time as well, although lose-lose outcomes will not. Paradoxically, it is not possible for asymmetrical outcomes (win-lose, win-partial win etc.) to occur in full-equity joint venture relationships, although it may be possible in preferential-equity joint ventures and strategic alliances. These outcomes are discussed in more detail for each horizontal relationship type below.

As Figure 1 demonstrated there are, theoretically, nine possible commercial outcomes available to participants in business relationships. As Figure 2 demonstrates, however, only three of these outcomes are possible for full-equity (all shares carry equal weight) joint venture partners at the transactional level. This is because in full-equity joint venture relationships *ideal mutuality* (a win-win outcome in which both parties earn their objectively ideal outcome of above normal returns) is possible. This occurs when both parties enter into a full-equity arrangement to create a company to compete in the market and the jointly owned company is successful in creating sustainable isolating mechanisms (Rumelt, 1987).

With sustainable isolating mechanisms creating a competitive advantage, and always assuming that the costs of operation are more than covered by the revenue received such that above normal returns can be made from dividend payments, both of the full-equity joint venture parties—regardless of the size of their respective share holdings—would normally be able to earn double-digit returns (*rents*) on their investment of time, resources and money. This is a commercial win-win for both parties, objectively speaking, even if one party is earning more from the relationship in volume terms (they have a larger shareholding) than the other. The key is the objective commercial returns that are being earned by each party relative to their original investment.

Figure 2: Feasible Commercial Outcomes in Full-Equity Joint Ventures

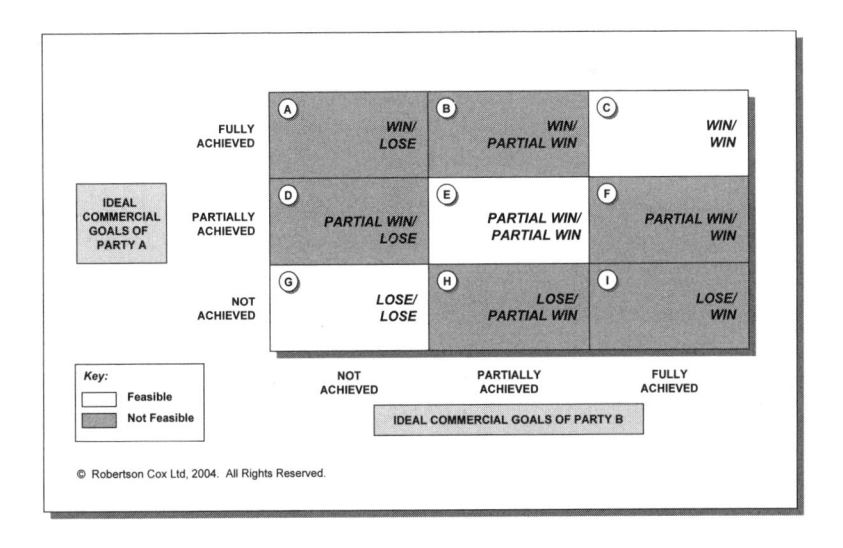

	NOT ACHIEVED	PARTIALLY ACHIEVED	FULLY ACHIEVED
FULLY ACHIEVED	(A) WIN/LOSE	(B) WIN/PARTIAL WIN	(C) WIN/WIN
PARTIALLY ACHIEVED	(D) PARTIAL WIN/LOSE	(E) PARTIAL WIN/PARTIAL WIN	(F) PARTIAL WIN/WIN
NOT ACHIEVED	(G) LOSE/LOSE	(H) LOSE/PARTIAL WIN	(I) LOSE/WIN

Rows: IDEAL COMMERCIAL GOALS OF PARTY A. Columns: IDEAL COMMERCIAL GOALS OF PARTY B. Key: Feasible (white), Not Feasible (shaded).

© Robertson Cox Ltd, 2004. All Rights Reserved.

Clearly such a relationship ought to be sustainable between the two parties. This is because, although there might be some resentment about the difference in the volume of earnings from the joint venture if the shareholding is based on majority/minority ownership, both parties still make their objectively ideal commercial returns. The only issue would be whether or not the isolating mechanisms in the relationship are sustainable or not, such that above normal returns are being earned by both parties—irrespective of their shareholding. This is a symmetrical business relationship at the level of the commercial returns achieved by each share in the company. The fact that one party may have more shares than the other is immaterial to the win-win nature of the outcome commercially speaking.

Despite this it is also possible for a full-equity joint venture to be sustained even in the absence of both parties earning above normal returns. As Figure 2 shows, a second feasible outcome from a full-equity joint venture is a partial win-partial win. In this outcome the joint venture partners are not able operationally to create isolating mechanisms to generate sustainable competitive advantages, and must compete in a marketplace where any that can be created are quickly competed away by replication and imitation. In such circumstances, profits may still be made but they will be below double-digits and tending to zero for all equity partners.

When this outcome occurs commercially then both parties to the exchange objectively experience a partial win-partial win— they obtain sufficient profits to stay in business but not enough to warrant the title of a true win-win as defined earlier. This type of relationship ought, however, to be sustainable even though it is not ideal because it involves some element of mutuality (both parties gain something of that which they value commercially). The only threat to sustainability would be if one or both parties felt it was able to invest its money more profitably elsewhere.

This outcome is once again symmetrical at the commercial level because each share in the company receives the same level of dividend return, but now at a lower level than under a win-win outcome. The overall sustainability of these types of partial win-partial win relationships depends, ultimately, on whether or not both parties believe that the levels of return are commensurate given the currently available feasible alternatives to which they could devote their time, resources and money.

If a partial win-partial win outcome is sustainable in full-equity joint venture relationships it is not clear that the same can be said for lose-lose outcomes. This is a feasible outcome from a full-equity joint venture, and it is once again a symmetrical outcome for both parties because each share receives the same level of loss as another. It would arise in circumstances where the company created by the joint venture partners was not able to create any isolating mechanisms and failed to cover its costs of operation, such that losses rather than profits were made. Obviously the full-equity joint venture partners could decide to maintain the company for a while but, other things being equal, the company would eventually have to be closed if there were no eventual prospects of making money. Obviously there might be exceptional circumstances where both parties wanted to run a company as a tax loss, but this would be an unusual occurrence if both parties sustained it indefinitely.

This discussion shows that only two commercial outcomes are likely to sustain full-equity joint ventures and that is situations of win-win and of partial win-partial win. Both of these symmetrical outcomes can be seen as forms of mutuality. Lose-lose, the third symmetrical outcome, does not appear to be a long-term viable option unless there are exceptional circumstances. As Figure 2 indicates, however, the other six possible asymmetrical theoretical outcomes from business exchange do not normally appear to be feasible in practice in full-equity joint ventures.

The primary reason for this is that full-equity joint ventures presuppose that the two parties to the relationship are involved operationally and commercially in the same enterprise. As we argued in the previous chapter in full-equity joint ventures there is normally only limited scope for opportunism for either party based on information asymmetry and bounded rationality. The reason for this is that, as joint shareholders, the full-equity partners normally have access to all of the critically important information about the trade-offs between what is done operationally and its relationship with commercial outcomes.

In this sense the full-equity joint venture parties are on the same side operationally and commercially. A commercial lose for one party is also a commercial lose for the other side; a commercial win for one party is also a commercial win for the other party. Even if there is majority/minority shareholding this fact does not change this reality—all that the majority/minority shareholding affects is how much is awarded as a profit or loss in volume terms to the parties involved. Given this, as Figure 2 indicates, it is highly unlikely in a full-equity joint venture relationship that asymmetrical relationship outcomes such as win-partial win, partial win-win, partial win-lose, lose-partial win, win-lose or lose-win can occur.

This is not the case, however, if the joint venture is created with preferential (Class A and Class B) shares because there is more scope for opportunism through the use of information asymmetry and bounded rationality pre- and post-contractually in these types of horizontal relationships. Figure 3 shows that six, rather than only three, of the theoretically possible commercial outcomes are feasible in preferential-equity joint ventures. This means that both symmetrical and asymmetrical outcomes can occur for parties to these types of business transactions.

Figure 3: Feasible Commercial Outcomes in Preferential-Equity Joint Ventures

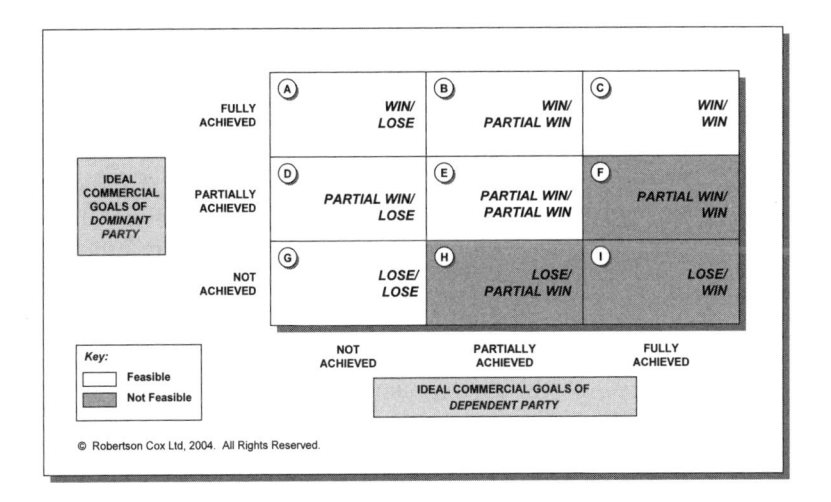

		NOT ACHIEVED	PARTIALLY ACHIEVED	FULLY ACHIEVED
IDEAL COMMERCIAL GOALS OF DOMINANT PARTY	FULLY ACHIEVED	(A) WIN/LOSE	(B) WIN/PARTIAL WIN	(C) WIN/WIN
	PARTIALLY ACHIEVED	(D) PARTIAL WIN/LOSE	(E) PARTIAL WIN/PARTIAL WIN	(F) PARTIAL WIN/WIN
	NOT ACHIEVED	(G) LOSE/LOSE	(H) LOSE/PARTIAL WIN	(I) LOSE/WIN

Key: Feasible / Not Feasible

IDEAL COMMERCIAL GOALS OF DEPENDENT PARTY

© Robertson Cox Ltd, 2004. All Rights Reserved.

In a preferential-equity joint venture relationship the three symmetrical transactional outcomes of win-win, partial win-partial win and lose-lose can occur in much the same way that they can for full-equity joint ventures. The only difference here is that Class A shareholders may have received their benefits although not their losses earlier than the Class B shareholders. Asymmetrical outcomes can, however, also occur in these types of joint venture because the Class A shareholders (shown in Figure 3 as the *dominant party*) can create superior information and commercial rights for themselves.

In these circumstances it is possible to envisage a situation in which the dominant equity partner is able to appropriate above normal returns for themselves first, and only allow the other equity owners (the *dependent party* with Class B shares) to have a return once they have fully achieved their own goals. In such circumstances it is possible to envisage (from the dominant party's point of view) asymmetrical outcomes of win-partial win (in which the Class A shareholders receive above normal returns but Class B only achieve normal returns) or win-lose (Class A shareholders receive above normal returns but Class B receive a loss) and partial win-lose (Class A shareholders receive normal returns but Class B receive a loss).

It may seem, at first, that such asymmetrical outcomes are unlikely to be sustainable given that these are joint venture relationships. Despite this, it can be argued that preferential-equity joint venture relationships can be sustained even though there are asymmetrical outcomes. It is perfectly possible to envisage a situation in which Class B shareholders would willingly accept a win-partial win outcome, especially if the partial win they receive is superior to any other alternatives that are currently available to them.

Obviously some of these asymmetrical outcomes are likely to be more or less sustainable than others. Normally only the win-partial win asymmetrical outcome is ultimately sustainable. This is because, while the dominant party may wish to sustain win-lose and partial win-lose outcomes, it is debatable whether these are feasible long-term outcomes for the dependent party—unless, of course, the joint venture was providing some tax avoidance or alternative benefits in another relationship. This implies that only those outcomes that involve some form of mutuality—win-win, partial win-partial win or win-partial win—will normally be sustainable over time.

This means that asymmetrical outcomes can sustain preferential-equity joint ventures but this does not mean that all of the nine theoretically possible outcomes specified in Figure 1 are feasible here. As Figure 3 demonstrates, three outcomes are highly unlikely to occur in preferential-equity joint ventures.

These are the outcomes of lose-partial-win, lose-win and partial win-win. The reasons for this are simple enough. It is unlikely that a dominant party (unless they were commercially naïve or altruistic) would create shareholding structures that allowed a dependent party to appropriate more of the value from the relationship than they could themselves.

3.3 *Feasible Commercial Outcomes in Strategic Alliance Relationships*

The picture is even more complex when strategic alliances are considered. In some types of strategic alliances all nine of the theoretically possible relationship outcomes appear to be feasible, but in other types this is not the case. The reason for this complexity is because strategic alliances may or may not have dominant parties, but when one party is dominant (unlike preferential-equity joint ventures) it is not always the same party that is dominant in any alliance relationship. This means that there is scope both for symmetry in outcomes and also for asymmetry.

There are many different types of strategic alliance, and this also partly explains the reason for the complexity of outcomes in these types of relationships. One way of categorising them is by the method of compensation/payment and the strategic impact on each partner's operations in the relationship (Contractor and Lorange, 1988). As we shall see, the remuneration structure impacts directly on commercial exchange and value appropriation and, as a result, it has a direct impact on the feasible outcomes from these types of relationship. Three broad strategic alliance types can be described based on alternative remuneration structures.

The first type to be considered here are *strategic alliances with lump sum and mark-up payments to dominant parties*. In this category *technical training/start-up assistance agreements* are normally found, but it can also include *patent licensing, franchising, know-how licensing* and *management/marketing service agreements* where a one-off payment or mark-up on products or service provided is made to the product and/or service originator.

These agreements normally involve short-term, one-off and limited forms of organisational interdependence because one dominant party (A) is providing the product, technology and process or know-how training or rights to another (B). After training and/or start-up B produces the product and/or service on their own in a new market, and may only make a one-off payment or continuous mark-up payments to A, so the forms of organisational involvement may be quite limited operationally on both sides. Under these types of remuneration structures A is, however, always guaranteed some commercial return from the relationship even though B may not be. In this sense A is normally, although not always, the commercially dominant party.

It is obvious, as Figure 4 reveals, that a win-win outcome commercially is perfectly feasible in these types of alliance arrangements. The originator (A) may have a unique product and/or service that it is able to provide to another party (B), who will have a significant competitive advantage in a new market as a result. If this occurs, and a lump sum or mark-up payment is paid by B to A, then both A and B may be able to make above normal returns from the alliance.

It follows, however, that if the product and/or service quickly generates competitive imitators then a partial win-partial win outcome (in which both parties only make normal returns) may be the best that is achievable. It also follows that the win-partial win outcome is feasible. This would arise if A is able to achieve above normal returns from the lump sum or mark-up payments, but B was only ever able to make normal returns. The partial win-win outcome is also feasible. This would arise if the lump sum or mark-up only allowed A to make normal returns, but B was able to appropriate above normal returns for themselves in the new market.

Figure 4: Feasible Commercial Outcomes in Lump-sum and Mark-up Strategic Alliances

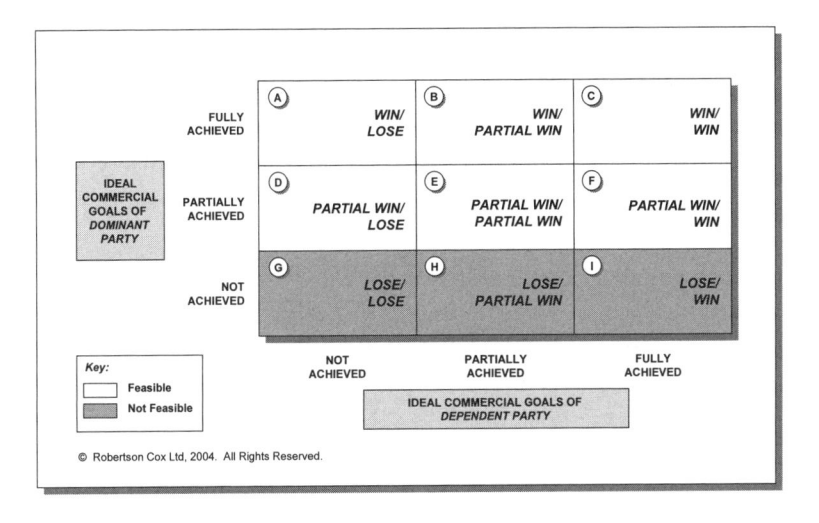

		NOT ACHIEVED	PARTIALLY ACHIEVED	FULLY ACHIEVED
IDEAL COMMERCIAL GOALS OF DOMINANT PARTY	FULLY ACHIEVED	(A) WIN/ LOSE	(B) WIN/ PARTIAL WIN	(C) WIN/ WIN
	PARTIALLY ACHIEVED	(D) PARTIAL WIN/ LOSE	(E) PARTIAL WIN/ PARTIAL WIN	(F) PARTIAL WIN/ WIN
	NOT ACHIEVED	(G) LOSE/ LOSE	(H) LOSE/ PARTIAL WIN	(I) LOSE/ WIN

IDEAL COMMERCIAL GOALS OF DEPENDENT PARTY

Key: Feasible / Not Feasible

© Robertson Cox Ltd, 2004. All Rights Reserved.

In the worst of all cases the product and/or service might not find ready acceptance in the market and this means that a win-lose or partial win-lose is possible. This is because A receives a guaranteed lump sum or mark-up but B must take the risk that the products and/or services will sell in the market and this may not occur, generating losses for B. It is, however, improbable that three options lose-lose, lose-partial win or lose-win will occur in this type of strategic alliance. This is because A will normally receive some return, at least at the level of normal returns (partial win) or possibly at above normal returns (win), from the lump sum or mark-up payment.

This in not the case, however, when *strategic alliances with royalty payments* are created. These types of alliance normally involve more extensive forms of operational interaction and include *production/assembly/buy-back agreements, patent licensing, management/marketing service agreements* and *franchising*. In each of these alliances the originator (A) normally has to provide some degree of initial and continuous operational linkage with the recipient of the agreement (B) and this may be more extensive and regular than under start-up agreements. This is because the originator (A), for branding reasons, may wish to ensure that standards are maintained and quality monitoring of B's performance will, therefore, be a key element of this type of alliance.

In these alliance relationships, if there is no lump sum or mark-up paid initially, the return is not guaranteed for A (the dominant party) unless B (the dependent party) successfully enters the new market. It is possible therefore, as Figure 5 indicates, that, while win-win, partial win-partial win, win-partial win and partial win-win can occur as outlined above, both A and B could also find themselves in the lose-lose outcome—neither party makes any commercial return from the relationship.

Paradoxically, even though lose-lose is feasible in this type of alliance relationship, it is unlikely that the lose-partial win and lose-win outcomes will occur. This is because, under a royalty agreement, if B is making a return it is inevitable that A will also make a return from the transaction. Paradoxically perhaps, it is feasible for the win-lose and partial win-lose outcomes to occur. This is because A is guaranteed a return from the transaction if B makes sales, and there may be limited cost to A in undertaking this activity. For B, however, the costs of making sales could be considerable and they might not make a return at all from the revenue they receive.

Figure 5: Feasible Commercial Outcomes in Royalty-based Strategic Alliances

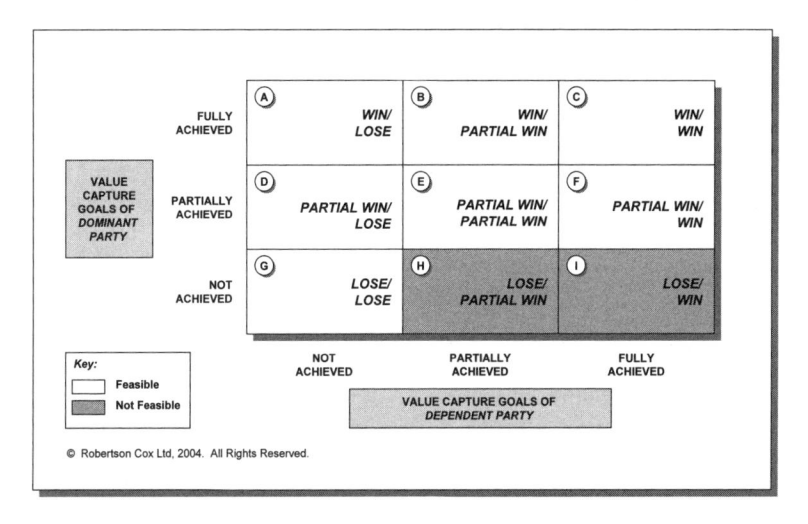

The third, and final, type is *strategic alliances with non-equity cooperative agreements*. This form of strategic alliance requires the most extensive forms of interaction and often has the most complex remuneration structures. These are relationships in which two legally independent parties normally come together to share their combined resources to undertake a particular operational and commercial enterprise that they cannot undertake on their own, but which does not require them to create a joint venture company. These alliances may be for joint exploration (as in the case of the oil and gas industry), joint research and development (as in the case of the computer industry), or joint production (as in the case of the aerospace industry).

Figure 6: Feasible Commercial Outcomes in Non-Equity Cooperative Strategic Alliances

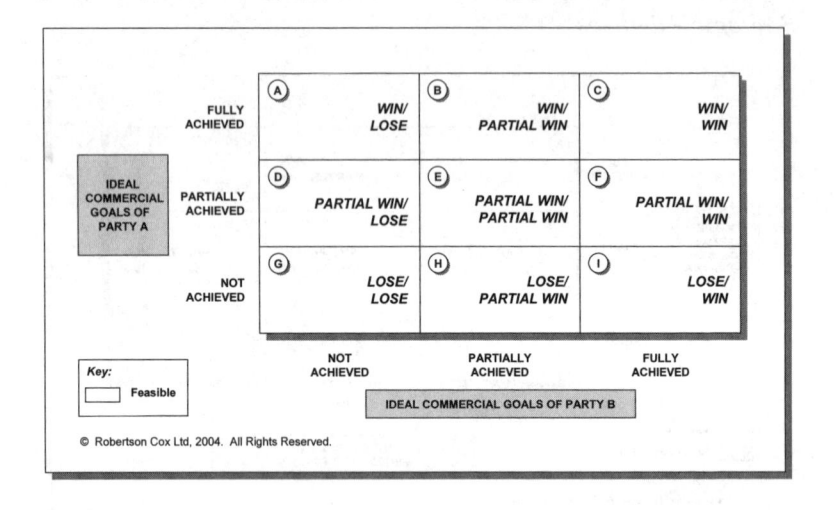

		NOT ACHIEVED	PARTIALLY ACHIEVED	FULLY ACHIEVED
IDEAL COMMERCIAL GOALS OF PARTY A	FULLY ACHIEVED	(A) WIN/LOSE	(B) WIN/PARTIAL WIN	(C) WIN/WIN
	PARTIALLY ACHIEVED	(D) PARTIAL WIN/LOSE	(E) PARTIAL WIN/PARTIAL WIN	(F) PARTIAL WIN/WIN
	NOT ACHIEVED	(G) LOSE/LOSE	(H) LOSE/PARTIAL WIN	(I) LOSE/WIN

IDEAL COMMERCIAL GOALS OF PARTY B

Key: Feasible

© Robertson Cox Ltd, 2004. All Rights Reserved.

In these relationships, agreements can be based on joint operational efforts, whose costs are shared out on the basis of an agreed formula linked to the eventual revenue earned from the venture. There may not, however, be a common formula and different types of alliance may have distinct formulae with different implications for risk and reward for the parties in the alliance (Contractor and Lorange, 1988).

Thus, in some exploration alliances two parties may agree to share the costs to be incurred and revenues to be earned (and therefore their respective returns or losses) by reference to a complex formula agreed at the outset. In these types of *reciprocal cost and revenue agreements* the commercial outcomes from exchange may be different from other types of non-equity cooperative agreements. For example, in research and development alliances the costs may be borne by each party using an agreed formula, but the benefits that are achieved may be based solely on what each individual alliance party can achieve on their own with the technology that is created.

These *agreed cost but independent revenue agreements* are clearly not the same as the reciprocal cost and revenue approach, and different outcomes can occur commercially for each party to these types of exchange. Alternatively, it is possible to have development alliances in which the revenues shared is agreed, but the costs are borne independently by each of the parties. In these *agreed revenue but independent cost agreements* the outcomes for each party can vary quite dramatically depending on the internal efficiency and effectiveness of each party in the relationship.

Thus, it is necessary to understand the feasible outcomes from these three very different risk and reward remuneration approaches. In *reciprocal revenue and cost agreements*, as Figure 6 indicates, all nine of the theoretically possible outcomes are feasible. Win-win outcomes commercially are also clearly possible. This would arise if the parties are able to find an asset that allowed both of them to earn above normal returns from the agreed share of the revenue received, even after incurring their agreed share of the costs of the exploration. If this is possible, then so is a partial win-partial win. This would arise if the returns earned by both parties failed to reach double-digit levels. The final symmetrical outcome—lose-lose—is also possible. This would occur if the costs of exploration were far greater for both parties than the revenue received.

If symmetrical outcomes arise in these types of agreement there is also scope for all of the other six asymmetrical outcomes that have been defined as theoretically possible to occur. This is because each party to the relationship may have an agreed formula dictating cost and revenue shares, but it is possible that one party may have negotiated a cost burden that is far too high relative to the revenue share being received to ensure that normal or above normal returns can be made.

In this circumstance it is feasible for all six asymmetrical outcomes—win-lose, win-partial win, partial win-lose, partial win-win, lose-partial win and lose-win to occur. Interestingly enough, since these relationships are normally one-off, in the sense that they only last as long as the exploration and discovery activity, then none of the outcomes have to persist for the relationship to be sustainable. This type of exploration alliance is inherently risky and need not be sustainable.

For research and development alliances, in which there is an *agreed cost but independent revenue agreement,* all of the nine outcomes are also feasible. This is because, while the costs are basically fixed (or at least the share that each party will incur is), the amount that each party will be able to generate is dependent on the independent production and marketing and sales capability of each party. In this circumstance, while all three symmetrical outcomes are feasible so are all of the asymmetrical outcomes as well. Once again the relationships do not have to be sustained because these also tend to be one-off, although it is likely, as it is with exploration alliances, that both parties will want to work with the other party again if they have both achieved some form of commercial win or partial win from the experience.

The same principles apply to the final non-equity cooperative agreement of *agreed revenue but independent costs*. It is also possible, because there is no dominant party in these types of relationships, to have all three symmetrical and all six asymmetrical outcomes from this type of arrangement. Once again the commercial outcome for both sides (win, partial win or lose) depends on their individual ability to manage their own costs relative to the revenue share that has been agreed.

In so far as strategic alliances are concerned, therefore, depending on the type of remuneration structure entered into certain types of relationship outcome may, or may not, be feasible in practice. In general it would appear that, when there is a dominant party (A), who is able to impose remuneration structures on the dependent party (B), then all nine theoretically possible outcomes are not feasible. As we saw, this is because dominant parties are able to protect themselves and ensure that they do not lose when the other side is in a win, partial win or lose position.

These types of outcome are most likely in strategic alliances with lump sum and mark-up payments. In royalty payment-based strategic alliances the dominant party is also able to ensure that two outcomes—lose-win and lose-partial win—do not occur; but it is not possible to stop lose-lose outcomes occurring. Finally, in non-equity cooperative agreements, where there is rarely a dominant party, it would appear that all nine of the theoretically defined possible outcomes are feasible in practice.

The other major conclusion from this discussion is that in some types of strategic alliance sustainability is clearly an issue—in particular in those relationships where royalty payments need to be earned—but this is not necessarily the case for all strategic alliances. In royalty-based relationships there is obviously a need for some form of win or partial win to allow both parties to continue their operational interaction.

Despite this, the discussion shows that sustainability, and therefore mutuality in some form or other, is not always necessary for strategic alliances to be created. This is because not all alliances are intended to be long-term, many of them are short-term, and in some of the most extensive operational forms of collaboration—non-equity collaborative alliances—the intention of both parties may be to pursue their own individual self-interest unreservedly, and without direct concern for the other side in the relationship operationally or commercially (Das, 1990).

3.4 Conclusions: Win-Win, Mutuality and the Sustainability of Horizontal Business Relationships

The discussion shows that a win-win outcome commercially is feasible in each one of the horizontal business relationships discussed here, but also that extensive forms of horizontal collaboration could persist over time without win-win outcomes. It also shows that not all forms of horizontal collaboration need to be sustained indefinitely and also that mutuality (where both parties gain) is not always necessary to create and/or operate these types of relationships.

Furthermore, it appears that only in *strategic alliances* based on *non-equity cooperative agreements* are all nine of the theoretically possible relationship outcomes feasible. In all other types of horizontal business relationships only some of the theoretically possible outcomes are feasible. In *full-equity joint ventures* only symmetrical outcomes (win-win, partial win-partial win and lose-lose) are feasible. In *preferential-equity joint ventures* the dominant party can also stop dependent parties imposing three detrimental asymmetrical outcomes on them (partial win-win, lose-win and lose-partial win).

In *strategic alliances* the remuneration (risk and reward) structure has a major impact on whether or not symmetrical and asymmetrical outcomes occur. In all types of *strategic alliance* (other than those based on lump sum or mark-up payments to one party) all three symmetrical outcomes (win-win, partial win-partial win and lose-lose) can occur. Additionally, asymmetrical outcomes occur when these favour the dominant party and force the dependent party into partial-win and lose scenarios.

This discussion confirms the view that, although win-win is possible in horizontal relationships, it is not a prerequisite for creating or sustaining these types of relationships. Interestingly enough, it would appear that mutuality in other, more limited and asymmetrical, forms is also not always necessary to sustain most of these types of relationships. Only in the case of full-equity joint ventures is mutuality clearly necessary for relationships to be sustained.

This conclusion, about the lack of a need for mutuality to support business relationships, is further reinforced when one considers the concept of win-win and the problem of mutuality in vertical (buyer and supplier) relationships. As we shall see, it is here that perhaps the greatest conceptual confusion has occurred. This is because writers have failed to specify clearly what they mean by the concepts of value and interests for buyers and suppliers, or to grasp that there is an inevitable and irreconcilable objective tension in buyer and supplier exchange that ensures that exchange is always contested, which makes the achievement of win-win outcomes in vertical business relationships impossible.

4

The Paradox of Win-Win and Mutuality in Buyer and Supplier Exchange

The previous chapter demonstrated that a win-win outcome is feasible commercially in joint ventures and strategic alliances, but that it is not essential for them to be successful. In this chapter it is argued that win-win outcomes are not feasible in buyer and supplier exchange although symmetrical and asymmetrical mutuality and zero-sum outcomes are.

This conclusion is arrived at because of the very different way in which value must be understood in vertical as compared with horizontal business relationships. As a result, win-win outcomes are not essential commercially for successful short- or long-term buyer and supplier relationships to be maintained operationally. Furthermore, it is argued that while some forms of mutuality may be necessary to sustain longer-term *collaborative sourcing* relationships, this is not always necessary for short-term *market tested sourcing*. This is because in these latter circumstances relationships do not need to be sustained beyond the term of the initial agreement.

The chapter, first, addresses the current state of thinking about win-win and mutuality in vertical business relationships and shows that it is not properly conceptualised. This provides the basis for a more rigorous and robust conceptualisation of what value means objectively for buyers and suppliers involved in vertical business relationships. As we shall see, the major difference between the specifications of value in vertical, as opposed to horizontal, business relationships relates to the position of the buyer rather than the supplier. Having resolved this conceptual problem, it is then possible to assess whether or not it is feasible for the nine theoretically defined outcomes to occur in *collaborative* and *market tested sourcing* relationships.

4.1 *Current Thinking about Win-Win and Mutuality in Buyer and Supplier Exchange*

The recent interest in supply chain management has resulted in a growing literature that discusses the operational mechanisms that can be used, either in dyadic or in more complex network relationships, to create, develop and sustain exchange transactions between buyers and suppliers. Much of this literature owes its genesis to three broad schools of writing. First, there is the *transaction cost economics approach* associated with Williamson (1985; 1996). Second, the *interactions approach* as exemplified by the IMP academic grouping (Ford et al., 2002); and, third, the *relational approach* associated with lean and agile principles of production and operations and purchasing and supply management thinking (Lamming, 1993; Macbeth and Ferguson, 1994; Fisher, 1997; Hines et al., 2000; Christopher and Towill, 2002; Lee, 2002).

Although few of these approaches focus explicitly on the value that buyers and suppliers receive from transactions by following win-win approaches, all of them do so implicitly. Most writers assume, without explicitly defining exactly what they mean, that some element of mutuality (value for both parties from the exchange) must occur for buyer and supplier transactions to be successful. This implicit view of win-win outcomes does not, however, provide any objective means to understand which elements of value must be shared to sustain buyer and supplier relationships, or the complex commercial and operational trade-offs and tensions that exist in vertical forms of exchange (whether in dyadic or network relationships). Furthermore, this thinking tends to overemphasise the operational while underplaying the commercial drivers of vertical business relationships.

Most current thinking about mutuality and win-win in vertical exchange is, therefore, partial and requires a more robust and rigorous conceptual clarification, based on an understanding of the commercial trade-offs that exist for buyers and sellers from transactional exchange. By doing so, it is possible to demonstrate why it is not feasible in practice for both buyers and suppliers to fully achieve their ideal commercial goals in any exchange transaction and why, as a result, exchange is contested and why win-win outcomes are not necessary to sustain vertical business relationships.

Most writers on vertical business relationships do not explicitly define the issue of value and what it means for buyers and sellers when they interact. Despite this, writers in the transaction cost, IMP and relational traditions argue that there must normally be some element of mutuality in an exchange for relationships to be sustainable:

"...the emphasis on value maximization requires a recognition of the interdependence of the exchange partners." (Zajac and Olsen, 1993, p.137)

"Relationship management is as much about creating, value through relationships ... Value is created through jointly planning and mutually

adapting products, processes, people and resources." (Wilkinson and Young, 2002, p.117)

"...value transparency...is the creation, nurture and delivery of value for the benefit, and thus continued existence, of both parties." (Lamming et al., 2001, p.7)

While most writers assume that a win-win is at the heart of successful vertical business relationships, there have been few systematic attempts to specify clearly what a win means, either for buyers or suppliers, in transactional exchange (Macneil, 1983). Despite the lack of common agreement on the meaning of a win there have been a number of attempts to define what value means for buyers and for suppliers. In the IMP tradition it has been argued that value is difficult to disentangle as a concept but that it can be understood for participants on at least four levels (Ford and McDowell, 1999). These are:

- *the perceived benefits that arise from the effects in a relationship* (did it achieve its intended outcome);
- *the perceived benefits that arise from effects on the relationship* (did it change the relationship as a whole detrimentally or positively);
- *the perceived benefits on a portfolio of relationships* (did it harm or reinforce other relationships);
- *the perceived benefits on a wider network* (did it harm or reinforce relationships within a wider chain or network of relationships).

This approach to understanding value (a win) is useful, but like the writers discussed earlier it also relies for its definition of value on the subjective perceptions of managers or observers, without a clear specification of what value means objectively for buyers and suppliers in specific business relationships. In particular this approach does not provide a robust and rigorous conceptualisation of the *commercial and operational trade-offs over value* that buyers and suppliers must make when they enter into *inter-organisational* exchange relationships.

This problem is compounded by the fact that many writers have a one-dimensional (buyer or supplier fixated) view of transactions. The transaction cost approach, for example, has tended to view the issue of value only from the buyer's point of view (Zajac and Olsen, 1993; Cox, 2004b; Cox et al., 2004). In contrast, much of the industrial marketing literature focuses only on outcomes in so far as they are beneficial to suppliers (Shapiro et al., 1987; Turnbull and Zolkiewski, 1995). This issue of one-dimensionality has been addressed recently, with the argument that buyers must recognise what it is that a supplier values in a relationship rather than simply thinking about their own needs as buyers and vice versa (Ramsay, 2004).

In the next section the two-dimensional nature of commercial and operational exchange for buyers and suppliers is analysed from an ideal, or economically rational (objective), point of view. This is essential because, when considering buyer and supplier exchange, it is not possible to use the same simple commercial conceptualisation of value for both parties (do they make rents, profits or losses?) that was used earlier to understand horizontal forms of exchange. As we shall see, value, for buyers and suppliers in vertical exchange, is not fully commensurable (Cox, 2004c).

The discussion demonstrates that when one adopts an economically rational view of value, and the ideal operational and commercial outcomes from exchange, for both buyers and suppliers a win-win outcome (*ideal mutuality*) is not feasible. This is because the exchange relationship is contested (Bowles and

Gintis, 1988). It follows from this that mutuality in vertical forms of business exchange is far more complex than currently assumed, and that buyer and supplier relationships can be sustained without win-win outcomes. Paradoxically, it also appears that in some types of sourcing relationships win-lose outcomes can also sustain vertical business relationships.

4.2 *The Paradox of Non-Commensurability in Buyer and Supplier Exchange*

The *power and leverage perspective* on business relationships has never been properly unified, nor has it always been focused specifically on the problem of transactional exchange. Despite this, writing in this genre is widespread and it provides a way of understanding the inherent commercial tensions that exist in business relationships between buyers and suppliers. Major authors on transactional exchange within this tradition include: Emerson (1962); Blau (1964); Cook (1977); Pfeffer and Salancik (1978); Porter (1980); Campbell and Cunningham (1983); Granovetter (1985); Bowles and Gintis (1988, 1993, 1999); Scott and Westbrook (1991); Provan and Gassenheimer (1994); Ramsay (1994, 1996a); Cox (1997b, 1999b, 2001, 2004a, 2004b); Cox, Sanderson and Watson (2000); Cox et al., (2002, 2004a) and Kim et al., (2004).

In this approach it is argued that, even though there are occasions when buyers and suppliers interact in order to increase the size of what can be shared, there is always an inherent operational and commercial tension between both parties to a transaction, whatever "the size of the cake" that can be created. This tension is based ultimately on the non-commensurability of the commercial value that buyers and suppliers seek to appropriate from their interactions (Cox, 2004c).

Furthermore it is argued that, since it is impossible for both parties in a transaction to fully achieve their ideal commercial goals, who gets what, how and when from any relationship operationally and commercially must ultimately be determined by the power resources that buyers and suppliers bring to it, and their relative competence in using these resources to appropriate (leverage) operational and commercial value for themselves. This means that, while buyers and suppliers are able to work together in both long-term as well as short-term relationships, the inevitable objective conflict and tension in their relationship cannot be eradicated—even if they are working together using extensive forms of operational collaboration.

The first problem that must be addressed when seeking to understand what buyers and supplies value, and therefore what they will see as a win from any vertical form of exchange, is why it is not possible to simply focus on whether or not both parties are able to earn above normal returns (rents) for themselves from the transaction. This is, after all, the basis by which win-win outcomes were analysed commercially in horizontal exchange relationships. The reason why an alternative view of value has to be taken is because individuals and organisations have to think differently when they act as buyers and sellers in marketplaces.

In horizontal relationships the two parties to an exchange conjoin their operational competencies in order to create a product and/or service from which they both expect to generate a return together. This is normally in a market where their combined product and/or service, once created, will have to compete against similar products and/or services. In this sense both parties are on the same side operationally and commercially, even though they may be opportunistic at the margins and over time (Das, 2004). This is because each of their returns commercially comes primarily from the success of their jointly owned and/or created product and/or service. In the absence of some form of operational and commercial success in the market for this jointly owned and/or created product or service there is no return for either party. This is not the case in vertical business relationships.

While it is clear that the success of the buying company may indirectly and directly be a pre-condition for the success of the supplying company—in the sense that without their success there might be no buyer for the supplier's products and/or services—this relationship is not necessarily coincidental. This is because suppliers normally have alternative customers to sell to, and buyers also normally have alternative sources of supply for the same products and/or services.

Even if the supplier is a monopolist this does not mean that it is always completely dependent on a single buyer for their business. This is because monopolists normally have many other customers they can sell to as well. (Obviously monopsony with monopoly can occur, making both parties dependent on one another, but it is highly unusual in business reality and is clearly an exception that proves the rule).

Given this tendency for limited degrees of dependency on one another operationally, buyers and suppliers are clearly not on the same side commercially. This is true even when buyers and suppliers enter into longer-term collaborative rather than short-term market tested sourcing relationships. Under *market tested sourcing* buyers and supplies have to ensure that they do not become dependent on one another because there is always the possibility that either party may choose to end the relationship at fairly short notice, requiring them to find alternative customers or suppliers.

Relatedly, the most important consideration for buyers and suppliers when they enter into longer-term collaborative sourcing relationships is that they do not suffer creeping dependency on the other party that hinders their ability to switch easily to alternative business partners. Buyers must always consider the problems of "lock-in" (Williamson, 1985; Cox, 2004a), while suppliers must always worry about the "hold-up" problem (Milgrom and Roberts, 1992).

Thus, while buyers and suppliers can work very closely together operationally using extensive forms of collaboration, this does not mean that by doing so either party should ignore the fundamental commercial principles of buyer and supplier exchange. The problem with much current thinking about vertical forms of collaboration is that it assumes that, just because the operational way of working changes from limited and short-term to extensive and long-term, the commercial principles of exchange ought to change as well.

It is this type of thinking that leads writers to argue, misguidedly, that all forms of operational collaboration between buyers and suppliers must involve win-win outcomes commercially for both sides. As we shall see, when we focus on what value means objectively for buyers and suppliers in transactional exchange, a win-win commercially is not in fact feasible for buyers or suppliers.

Drawing initially on the conceptualisation of value made by Adam Smith in 1776 it can be argued that, because buyers and

82   Win-Win?

suppliers are only ever on the same side in the most indirect manner, value (or a win) in vertical relationships has two principle meanings for buyers. First, it can be understood as *value in use*. This refers to the *functionality* or *operational benefits* that a given product and/or service or process may provide for the buyer. Second, it can be understood as *exchange value*. This refers to the *commercial cost* that must be borne in acquiring the product and/or service or process from a supplier. Clearly, using this formulation, it is possible to understand that value for a buyer must involve trade-offs between use value and the total cost of ownership for particular products and/or services and processes (Cox et al., 2004). The complex value for money trade-offs that buyers face is outlined in Figure 7.

Figure 7:   Value for Money Options for the Buyer

		REDUCED	STATIC	INCREASED
THE FUNCTIONALITY OF THE SUPPLY OFFERING	REDUCED	① REDUCED FUNCTIONALITY/ REDUCED COSTS	② REDUCED FUNCTIONALITY/ STATIC COSTS	③ REDUCED FUNCTIONALITY/ INCREASED COSTS
	STATIC	④ STATIC FUNCTIONALITY/ REDUCED COSTS	⑤ STATIC FUNCTIONALITY/ STATIC COSTS	⑥ STATIC FUNCTIONALITY/ INCREASED COSTS
	IMPROVED	⑦ IMPROVED FUNCTIONALITY/ REDUCED COSTS	⑧ IMPROVED FUNCTIONALITY/ STATIC COSTS	⑨ IMPROVED FUNCTIONALITY/ INCREASED COSTS

THE COSTS OF OWNERSHIP OF THE SUPPLY OFFERING

© Robertson Cox Ltd. 2001. All Rights Reserved.

As Figure 7 shows, although buyers can experience nine *value for money* trade-offs, there is one outcome that is always ideal and which they would normally prefer to receive on a continuous basis from all suppliers and in all exchange relationships. This is the improved functionality and reduced total costs of ownership outcome in cell 7.

While buyers may also be reasonably happy to receive some of the other outcomes if this one is not achievable, they will not necessarily be happy with some of these outcomes at all. Thus, buyers may welcome improved functionality/with static costs (cell 8) or static functionality/with reduced costs (cell 4) if they cannot achieve their ideal. On the other hand, they are unlikely to welcome reduced functionality/with increased costs (cell 3), reduced functionality/with static costs (cell 2) and static functionality/with increased costs (cell 6).

It is possible that improved functionality/with increased costs (cell 9) may be desirable as well—although whether it is or not depends ultimately on the impact of the increased functionality on the performance of the buying company in its own markets relative to the increased costs that must be borne. Sometimes reduced functionality/with reduced costs (cell 1) is acceptable—especially if the buyer has been over-specifying the functional requirements that are needed.

Finally, static functionality/with static costs (cell 5) may or may not be desirable depending on what is happening elsewhere in the market between buyers and suppliers. If the costs of ownership are rising for the same functionality then this could be a beneficial outcome, on the other hand it may not be if costs are coming down or functionality is improving elsewhere in the market.

What this discussion shows is that when buyers think about *value for money* in vertical business relationships they should always be concerned, first, with maximising *value for money* for themselves (in the form of increasing functionality and reducing the total costs of ownership) in order that the company they represent can maximise its own profitability. The impact on the supplier, while always important, should always be a secondary consideration. The reason for this is because the supplier's goals when they enter into sourcing relationships with a buyer are not coincidental—suppliers are also pursing their own self-interest first.

The relationship between a buyer and a supplier is, therefore, very different to most horizontal business relationships. In horizontal business relationships, and in particular in joint venture relationships, the two parties are clearly on the same side commercially and operationally. This is rarely the case for buyers and suppliers. In fact buyers and suppliers in vertical business relationships are an extreme example of the commercial tension that sometimes exists in strategic alliances, when there is a dominant player who is able to impose risk and reward outcomes on dependent parties. There is a need to work together in these circumstances for both parties to attain their operational and commercial goals, but their commercial interests are not at all coincidental in all respects.

For buyers and suppliers these problems of a lack of commensurability of commercial goals are stark. This is because they are always legally separate and independent organisations when they interact operationally and commercially. This is true whether they are involved in *collaborative sourcing* or *market tested sourcing* relationships. This means that, while strategic alliance partners tend to share operational and commercial goals, buyers and suppliers may not share either, although sometimes (especially in collaborative sourcing) they may have similar operational goals. Furthermore, in both types of sourcing relationship, each party's ability to achieve their ideal objective interests is commercially, if not always operationally, constrained by the other party.

This tension between commercial conflict and operational cooperation in business exchange is best understood if we consider what value (a win) means for a supplier. This should not be difficult because it has already been specified in general terms commercially in chapter 3. What was not made apparent in that discussion, however, was the fact that in vertical, as opposed to horizontal, business relationships there are two additional factors that must be considered.

The first factor to be considered is the complex choices that suppliers have to make about what levels of *use value* relative to *exchange value* they have to provide to satisfy their customers, so that they can maximise their revenue and returns. The second factor is that, at the transactional level, there is always an objective commercial tension between the ideal commercial goals of buyers and suppliers when they interact.

The first factor to understand is the complexity that suppliers are faced with when they enter into negotiations with buyers about the levels of operational functionality (*use value*) that must be provided, and at what cost, in order to win a contract. While the buyer ideally always desires a continuous increase in functionality and a continuous reduction in the total costs of ownership this may cause problems for suppliers. This is because suppliers are not in business to pass value in this form to buyers—whatever some writers on this subject may mistakenly believe (Womack et al., 1990; Womack and Jones, 1996).

Suppliers are in business to provide whatever minimum level of operational functionality they must in order to appropriate the maximum share of commercial value for themselves. This implies they are, ideally speaking, in business to satisfice rather than to delight their customers. This means that what a buyer wants operationally and commercially is one thing, but whether or not they will receive it depends on whether or not suppliers are forced to provide it for them. Thus, while it is perfectly possible for suppliers in some circumstances to continuously provide increased functionality with reduced costs, they are only likely to do this if it also allows suppliers to earn commercial returns that are acceptable.

This requires some explanation because the exchange trade-offs between buyers and suppliers are complex. The problem for a buyer is that their economically ideal and objectively rational outcome from exchange is that, whatever the current level of technical and operational efficiency that exits in supply markets, they should receive the maximum feasible technical and operational use value or functionality available. If this occurs buyers would be delighted because they would be achieving *x-efficiency* (the current best functionality or use value given the state of technical and operational know-how and competence).

Unfortunately, the buyer also has to consider not just whether or not they are receiving *x-efficiency* but also the total cost of ownership associated with possessing it. Thus, the ideal for the buyer will always be that they receive *x-efficiency* but at the lowest total costs of ownership that are feasible. If buyers are to receive the lowest feasible total costs of ownership then this implies that their suppliers will never be able to earn more than normal returns or less.

Thus, from a buyer's perspective the ideal trade-off in a relationship with a supplier must be to have suppliers who can provide the currently maximum feasible operational *use value* or functionality (*x-efficiency*), which they must continuously strive to improve over time (or lose the buyer's business), but they must also either earn no commercial returns (they provide the goods and/or services at cost or at a loss) or, at worst, they only ever make normal returns, which tend to zero. In such circumstances, buyers would be able to achieve maximum feasible increases in functionality (*use value*) with the lowest feasible total costs of ownership.

It is clear that sometimes—and especially in perfectly competitive markets experiencing high levels of contestation—buyers can receive this ideal goal of continuously increasing functionality (with *x-efficiency* constantly improving) and continuous reductions in the total costs of ownership (the personal computer and television market currently approximate such markets). When this occurs it is also normal for the suppliers in such markets to be receiving very low returns (profits tend to zero). In these circumstances suppliers may be satisfied with the fact that they are in business and making a living, but it is obvious that they are far from delighted, and a million miles away from achieving their ideal commercial goals of double-digit returns (*rents*).

Conversely, when there is limited competition and an absence of contestation in markets it is normal that the supplier (or a restricted number of suppliers) is able to determine cost and functionality standards for the buyer. This means that the supplier sets the standards for the level of operational functionality that will be passed to the buyer (and when), as well as setting the price and, therefore, the total costs of ownership to be borne by the buyer. The operating system software market for the personal computer approximates such a market currently.

Here a dominant supplier is able to determine what *x-efficiency* is, and introduce improvements to it in the market when it suits them rather when it might suit the buyer. The buyer is also forced to accept prices and, therefore, total costs of ownership that are determined by the supplier. In such circumstances supplier profits tend to be high and double-digits returns (*rents*) are normal.

These commercial outcomes can still occur for the supplier even though, over time, the buyer may experience some increases in functionality (*use value*) and some reductions in price and the total costs of ownership. This is because the increases in functionality and reductions in total costs of ownership provided may not be the maximum that are feasible for the supplier to provide to the buyer. The supplier could provide a higher level of operational efficiency and they could reduce their profit margins.

It is clear, therefore, that there must be a tension, if not an outright conflict, between the *use value* and *exchange value* aspirations of buyers and those of the supplier. This is because the operational requirement for the supplier is to provide a particular use value and exchange value trade-off to the buyer, but to do so in such a way as to first satisfy their commercial goals rather than those of the buyer. Thus, what is ideal for the buyer is never ideal for the supplier and vice versa.

Paradoxically, even when the supplier's operational goal in providing a particular functionality and cost of ownership trade-off is coincidental with that of the buyer, it will only be ideal for the supplier if they are also able to maximise their own commercial goals. The problem with this coincidence of interests operationally is, however, that if the supplier is able to achieve their ideal commercial goals of double-digit returns (*rents*) this can only be achieved if the buyer is willing to pay for it. By doing so, the buyer is then unable to achieve his ideal commercial goal of continuously reduced costs, with suppliers only able to earn normal returns that tend to zero.

This non-commensurability of commercial interests arises because a supplier is normally concerned with two goals—*returns* and *revenue* (Cox et al., 2004). The first is the desire, outlined earlier, to earn above normal returns (*rents*) if at all possible. In order to earn *rents* the supplier must make a decision about the level of functionality (*use value*) that must be passed to the customer and at what total cost of ownership (*exchange value*).

This means that when considering how much value to pass to the buyer a supplier must also consider the degree to which any increase in functionality and/or reduction in costs will impact upon their own profitability. They cannot be agnostic about this trade-off and assuming they are pursing their own self-interests first, which they should be doing from an economically rational (objective) point of view, it will be in their interests to only offer *value for money* trade-offs that allow them, whenever possible, to earn above normal returns and, if this is not possible, those that allow them to achieve the highest returns possible for themselves.

This means that there is always a tension for suppliers in their relationships with buyers. Transparency over the commercial consequences of particular functionality and cost of ownership trade-offs can be a dangerous game for them to play. This is because using information asymmetry about this trade-off may be one of the major mechanisms by which they can create opportunism and earn *rents* from uninformed buyers.

Furthermore, suppliers are also interested in the ability of their supply offering to win a growing market share (*revenue*) at the expense of the competition, so that effective market closure can be achieved with any customer specifically, and all customers in general. By having 100% of the revenue from a customer or, ideally, achieving market closure in a specific market, it becomes easier for suppliers to hide the true trade-offs between functionality and the total costs of ownership. This is because buyers have few alternative reference points by which to compare prices and functionality. This implies that successful companies seek to maximise their share of revenue from the customer whenever possible, and to minimise competition in markets. Both of these outcomes may not be in the best interests of buyers.

It is clear, therefore, that when suppliers interact with buyers they also experience a range of *revenue* and *returns* trade-offs. These can be referred to as *value from supply* trade-offs and, theoretically speaking, there are also nine of these, as outlined in Figure 8. As this Figure demonstrates, of these nine possible *value from supply* outcomes, suppliers will normally prefer some more than others.

Suppliers will normally see the increased revenue/increased returns outcome (cell 9) as the ideal outcome from any, and all, buyers (assuming of course they can service the buyer's requirements). After this, suppliers will normally welcome increased revenue/static returns (cell 8) and static revenue/increased returns (cell 6). They are unlikely to welcome reduced revenue/reduced returns (cell 1), or static revenue/reduced returns (cell 4) or reduced revenue/static returns (cell 2).

Figure 8: Value from Supply Options of the Supplier

		REDUCED	STATIC	INCREASED
SHARE OF BUYER'S REVENUE RECEIVED BY SUPPLIER	REDUCED	① REDUCED REVENUE/ REDUCED RETURNS	② REDUCED REVENUE/ STATIC RETURNS	③ REDUCED REVENUE/ INCREASED RETURNS
	STATIC	④ STATIC REVENUE/ REDUCED RETURNS	⑤ STATIC REVENUE/ STATIC RETURNS	⑥ STATIC REVENUE/ INCREASED RETURNS
	INCREASED	⑦ INCREASED REVENUE/ REDUCED RETURNS	⑧ INCREASED REVENUE/ STATIC RETURNS	⑨ INCREASED REVENUE/ INCREASED RETURNS

RETURNS RECEIVED FROM SERVICING BUYER'S ACCOUNT

© Robertson Cox Ltd. 2001. All Rights Reserved.

Finally they may, or may not, welcome static revenue/static returns (cell 5) unless everyone else in the market is suffering a decline and they are still making above normal returns. They may, however, find reduced revenue/increased returns (cell 3) acceptable, but only if the returns significantly outweigh any loss of revenue. Finally, they may find increased revenue/reduced returns (cell 7) acceptable, but only if there is no higher return alternative available.

What this discussion shows is that suppliers, just like buyers, must consider their own interests first when they enter into sourcing relationships, and this is true whether they are involved in short-term or long-term relationships. Thus, the primary concern for companies when they act as suppliers is not the goals of their customers, and their desire for maximum feasible operational functionality with the lowest feasible reductions in the total costs of ownership, but their own revenue share and profitability.

This does not preclude suppliers working to assist their customers with the growth of their businesses but, at whatever level of performance and growth achieved by the customer, the supplier must first consider their own revenue and profitability goals. This ensures that there is an objective and continuous tension in vertical business relationships however much the two parties in a relationship may collaborate together operationally, and no matter how long the collaboration lasts. This conflict and tension is depicted in Figure 9.

Figure 9: The Conflict and Tension in Buyer and Supplier Transactional Exchange

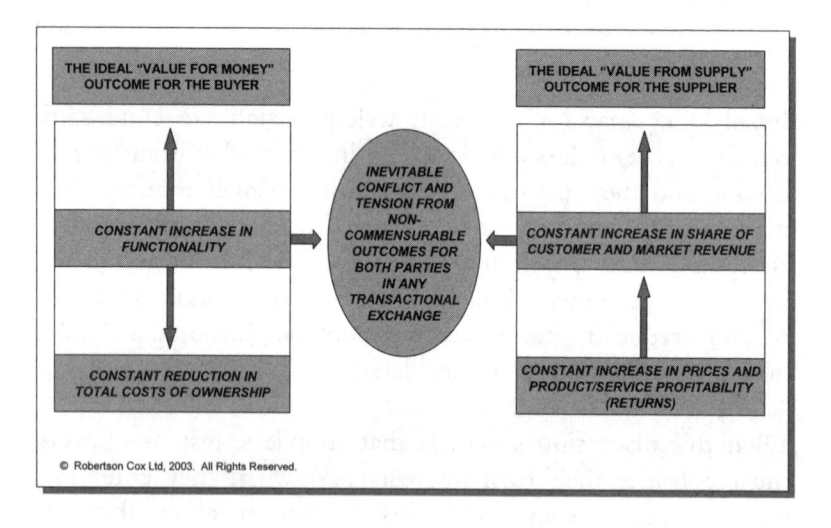

THE IDEAL "VALUE FOR MONEY" OUTCOME FOR THE BUYER		THE IDEAL "VALUE FROM SUPPLY" OUTCOME FOR THE SUPPLIER
CONSTANT INCREASE IN FUNCTIONALITY	INEVITABLE CONFLICT AND TENSION FROM NON-COMMENSURABLE OUTCOMES FOR BOTH PARTIES IN ANY TRANSACTIONAL EXCHANGE	CONSTANT INCREASE IN SHARE OF CUSTOMER AND MARKET REVENUE
CONSTANT REDUCTION IN TOTAL COSTS OF OWNERSHIP		CONSTANT INCREASE IN PRICES AND PRODUCT/SERVICE PROFITABILITY (RETURNS)

© Robertson Cox Ltd, 2003. All Rights Reserved.

As the argument has shown, the *value for money* goals of the buyer and the *value from supply* goals of the supplier are not fully commensurable commercially, and it is for this reason that win-win outcomes (in which both parties achieve their objectively ideal goals) are not achievable in vertical business relationships. This occurs because, if a buyer fully achieves the ideal goal of maximum feasible increases in functionality (*use value*) and maximum feasible reductions in total costs of ownership (*exchange value*), this can only be achieved at the expense of the ideal goal of the supplier—the ability to earn above normal returns (*rents*).

It is this search by suppliers for sustainable *rents* (the ideal outcome for any company theoretically) that makes fully commensurable mutuality (win-win) so difficult to achieve commercially in any relationship with a buyer. This is because the buyer must, ideally, always be seeking to achieve the maximum feasible operational improvements in *use value* (i.e. functionality) and at the lowest feasible total costs of ownership commercially, and this implies that suppliers should only ever make normal returns or less.

This is because, as Adam Smith pointed out long ago, in perfectly competitive markets the power of the buyer relative to the supplier is maximised by contestation. When contestation occurs suppliers can only survive in markets if they continuously pass value (in the form of increased functionality and reduced total costs of ownership) to customers. In such market circumstances of buyer power over suppliers he argued that profits would tend to zero (Smith, 1776). The history of competition in industrial markets more than adequately supports these theoretical principles. Highly contested markets normally experience buyer power with low returns for suppliers, who must compete for volume without hope of earning *rents*.

This objective conflict of interests between buyers and suppliers ensures, therefore, that a win-win commercial outcome based on *ideal mutuality* (as defined in cell C in Figure 10, where both parties fully achieve their ideal commercial goals) is not feasible in vertical business relationships. This is because, even though buyers and suppliers can work together operationally quite happily, neither side can achieve their ideal commercial goals without the other side failing to fully achieve their own commercial ideal (Cox, 2004c).

4.3 The Feasibility and Sustainability of Commercial Outcomes in Buyer and Supplier Exchange

Despite this, as Figure 10 demonstrates, even if an objectively defined win-win is not feasible in practice in vertical business relationships, all of the other eight theoretically possible outcomes are. As we shall see, however, some of these are more conducive than others for sustaining *collaborative sourcing* relationships. Thus, while all eight outcomes are feasible in both *market tested* and *collaborative sourcing* relationships, in *collaborative sourcing* some form of mutuality (short of win-win outcomes) must normally be in place to support continuous operational collaboration. Mutuality is not, however, a pre-requisite for the creation and operation of all vertical business relationships; this is because sourcing relationships can be managed by buyers and suppliers using win-lose or lose-win outcomes.

Although it is impossible to achieve *ideal mutuality* in commercial terms this does not mean that buyers and suppliers cannot achieve some form of mutuality when they engage in *collaborative* or *market tested sourcing* relationships. These relationships will not, however, be ideal for both parties because when one party achieves all that they desire commercially then the other side can, at best, only partially achieve their ideal commercial goals. Thus, objectively speaking, mutuality can have a number of meanings. Some of these can be based on *symmetrical* outcomes and some can be asymmetrical, but they all provide the basis for vertical business relationships to be sustained in the absence of ideal mutuality, or a win-win outcome.

Figure 10: Feasible Commercial Outcomes in Buyer and Supplier Relationships

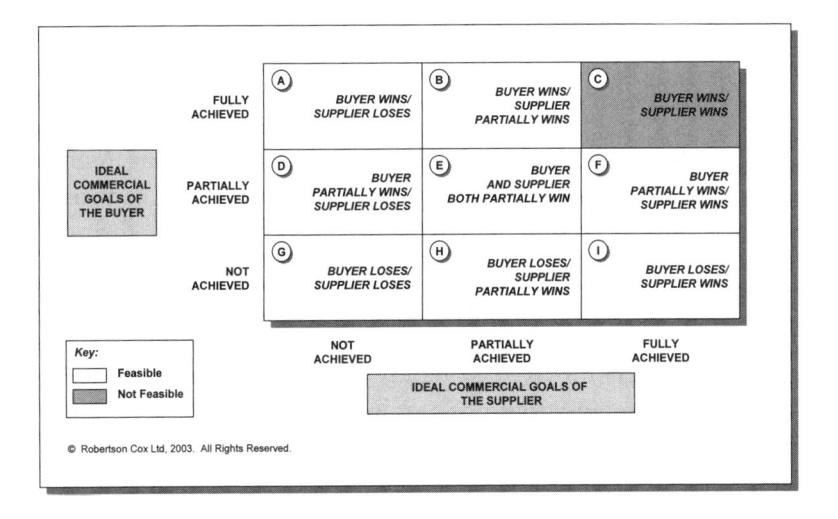

		NOT ACHIEVED	PARTIALLY ACHIEVED	FULLY ACHIEVED
IDEAL COMMERCIAL GOALS OF THE BUYER	FULLY ACHIEVED	(A) BUYER WINS/ SUPPLIER LOSES	(B) BUYER WINS/ SUPPLIER PARTIALLY WINS	(C) BUYER WINS/ SUPPLIER WINS
	PARTIALLY ACHIEVED	(D) BUYER PARTIALLY WINS/ SUPPLIER LOSES	(E) BUYER AND SUPPLIER BOTH PARTIALLY WIN	(F) BUYER PARTIALLY WINS/ SUPPLIER WINS
	NOT ACHIEVED	(G) BUYER LOSES/ SUPPLIER LOSES	(H) BUYER LOSES/ SUPPLIER PARTIALLY WINS	(I) BUYER LOSES/ SUPPLIER WINS

Key: Feasible / Not Feasible

IDEAL COMMERCIAL GOALS OF THE SUPPLIER

© Robertson Cox Ltd, 2003. All Rights Reserved.

Mutuality, therefore, can be an asymmetrical outcome in which a partial win-win or a win-partial win occurs commercially. This means that one party fully achieves all of their commercial goals while the other party does so partially, and vice versa

(Cells B and F in Figure 10). It is, however, possible for mutuality also to be based on symmetrical outcomes. This would occur if both parties only partially achieved all of the commercial value that they desired from a relationship (partial win-partial win). To say that a relationship is based on mutuality, therefore, tells us only that both parties must be achieving some element of what they value commercially from the relationship, and nothing more.

To fully understand mutuality commercially, therefore, one has to understand that it is a variable concept. Some commentators and practitioners appear to believe that mutuality should mean equity, or a 50%/50% sharing of value from exchange. It is clear, however, that mutuality can in fact mean a 99.99%/00.01% share of value for either party. Such unequal outcomes may be perfectly sustainable over time; it all depends on what are the alternative choices available to both parties to the exchange.

If 00.01% is superior to any other potential outcome (either now or in the future) for the less favourably rewarded exchange partner then it is still possible to conceptualise this form of exchange as mutuality. This is so, especially if both sides are happy with the objective commercial outcome and see what they are receiving as a win of some kind for themselves, even though one side may be less happy than the other. Mutuality in this way of thinking does not require commercial equity (indeed commercial equity is not a feasible outcome in a mutually beneficial vertical business relationship).

When considering the potential outcomes in Figure 10 it is important to understand not only whether there are outcomes that can be based on mutuality (as the outcomes in cells B, E and F clearly are), but also to understand whether they can occur in *collaborative* and/or *market tested sourcing* relationships. As we shall see, the three mutuality outcomes are essential for sustaining *collaborative sourcing* relationships, but they are not essential for managing *market tested sourcing* relationships.

In collaborative sourcing relationships, buyers and suppliers are working closely together operationally. The only issue is to what extent there is mutuality in the commercial exchange that occurs. If win-win outcomes are not feasible it is, however, perfectly possible to envisage a situation in which win-partial win (cell B) outcomes can occur. This would arise if a buyer entered into a collaborative relationship with a supplier on the understanding that the supplier could have a long-term contract, but only on the basis of open book transparency of the trade-offs between functionality and the total costs of ownership, and with the supplier passing all value in the future to the buyer, but with an agreed margin for the supplier that allowed only normal returns (tending to zero) to be earned. This would be a win-partial win from the buyer's perspective, and is what normally happens when *buyer dominant collaboration* occurs (Cox et al., 2003; 2004).

Conversely, a buyer and supplier might agree to enter into a long-term collaborative agreement and agree to have transparency and open book arrangements, but they might also agree that if any value is created in the relationship all of it should not be passed to the buyer. In such a situation the buyer would be accepting that they could not appropriate all of the commercial value and, although they might receive increased functionality, they could not reduce the total costs of ownership to a level that forced the supplier to earn low, normal returns. This would be a partial win for the buyer.

The supplier, however, would still have to continuously innovate operationally (improve on *x-efficiency*), but now would be able to earn levels of profit that were close to double-digits, but without earning *rents*. If this occurred this would be a partial win-partial win outcome (cell E). This is normally the outcome in situations of *reciprocal collaboration* based on power structures of *interdependence*, when there is no dominant player and both parties need one another operationally and commercially (Cox, 2004b; Cox et al., 2003; 2004).

However, there is a third potential outcome from collaboration that normally occurs in power structures of *supplier dominance*. In this outcome the buyer has to work collaboratively with the supplier because the supplier demands it. If the buyer will not collaborate, the supplier—being dominant in the market—can threaten to stop or delay supply and/or increase prices.

Given this, the terms of the collaboration are normally determined by the supplier and, in return for working closely with them, the supplier may be prepared to pass limited amounts of operational improvement in functionality (improved *x-efficiency* but not necessarily the maximum feasible) to the buyer. It is rare, however, for the supplier in this situation to reduce the total costs of ownership (unless they are forced to do so by competition or regulation). In this case the supplier will earn above normal returns (*rents*) and force the buyer to be a price receiver. In this situation the outcome is a partial win-win that favours the supplier (cell F).

Obviously, if relationships are to be sustained over time, and if buyers and suppliers are to make the dedicated investments, relational specific adaptations and also develop the cultural norms and bonds that are an essential part of operational collaboration, then some form of mutuality must occur. It is

The Paradox of Win-Win 99

important to recognise, however, that mutuality, as described here, does not imply a win-win commercially. On the contrary, as we have seen, mutuality can encompass power situations of *buyer dominance, interdependence* and *supplier dominance*. It is a variable concept and this is extremely important, as we shall see in the penultimate chapter, when we discuss the impact of subjective and objective interests on business relationships.

It is worth stressing also, however, that the three mutuality outcomes are not confined to collaborative sourcing relationships. On the contrary, it is perfectly possible for these three outcomes to occur in *market tested sourcing* relationships. A win-partial win that favours the buyer commercially could occur because a supplier is operating in a highly contested market, and is forced to pass value in the form of increased functionality and lower costs of ownership to the buyer. In this case, the supplier might still be able to earn a normal return that, although tending to break-even or zero, allows them to sustain themselves in business.

Similarly, in short-term *market tested sourcing* relationships it is possible for a buyer to find that in a restricted supply market suppliers will provide some increase in functionality and some reductions in total costs of ownership and profits. Once again, however, the supplier may provide more value, but not the maximum feasible improvements in *x-efficiency* available, or the maximum feasible reductions in total costs of ownership that would force the returns of the supplier towards zero. In such circumstances the buyer might receive continuous improvement in the functionality and costs of ownership trade-off, the supplier might not earn rents, but they would still make a healthy profit close to double-digits. This would be a partial win-partial win outcome (cell E).

Finally, it is possible that market testing might allow a buyer to receive an increase in functionality without any significant reduction in the total costs of ownership, or even with increased costs of ownership. This would normally occur in markets that had a limited number of suppliers (oligopoly or duopoly), where collusion between suppliers was not possible, and they were forced to compete on functionality rather than price. This often happens in consumer markets when there are dominant players, who compete on brand and functional improvements, rather than on price. In so far as the buyer receives additional value from the functionality improvements, this would constitute a partial win for the buyer whenever they came to market. The supplier would, of course, be achieving a win because they would be earning rents from the lack of effective contestation in the market. This is a partial win-win outcome (cell F).

What is clear from this discussion is that mutuality is feasible in both *collaborative* and *market tested sourcing* relationships, even if win-win is not, but that mutuality is only really necessary to sustain long-term *collaborative sourcing* relationships. This is because in *market tested sourcing* relationships the buyer is normally constantly searching the market for better *value for money* deals, and will only stay with a supplier for any length of time if they can offer the currently best *value for money* alternative in the market (i.e. the maximum feasible use value at current *x-efficiency* and the lowest feasible total costs of ownership, at cost or normal returns tending to zero).

Since sustainability is not required, neither is mutuality. This is not the case when we consider *collaborative sourcing* relationships. In these types of relationship both the buyer and supplier have to invest considerable time, resource and effort in establishing and operating the relationships. Given that these sunk costs have been incurred, with a risk of high switching costs post-contractually, it is unlikely that these relationships can be maintained in the absence of mutuality.

Despite this, as we shall see in the next chapter, mutuality does not mean that conflict and tension in business relationships has disappeared. This is because, of the three mutuality outcomes discussed here, only one (partial win-partial win) is symmetrical, the other two are asymmetrical outcomes, which one party (the partial winner) may be seeking to overturn through collaboration.

It is obvious that the remaining feasible outcomes (other than lose-lose) are difficult to sustain in *collaborative sourcing* relationships, even though one party achieves something they value and registers a win or a partial win. When this occurs asymmetrical outcomes from collaboration occur. Thus, if a buyer receives a project on time, at the lowest total costs of ownership and at the maximum feasible functional specification possible, but the supplier loses money on the transaction because they failed to price the job correctly and their revenue does not meet the costs of operations, then a win-lose has occurred commercially (cell A). If the buyer does not receive the project on time, and/or does not receive the maximum feasible functional specification and/or with additional cost, and the supplier still loses money on the transaction, then a partial win-lose outcome has occurred (cell D).

Conversely, if a buyer does not receive anything that they originally specified and there are massive time delays in delivering the project, so that it eventually cancelled as a failure, and the buyer has no redress in place against the supplier for contractual failure, then all of the costs incurred will have been lost. The buyer in this case has failed to receive the promised product and/or service and has experienced a lose outcome. It is perfectly possible in this type of scenario for the supplier, however, to have made either above normal returns, or only normal returns from the project. If the supplier has made above normal returns then a lose-win outcome has occurred (cell I). If the supplier only makes normal returns then a lose-partial win has occurred (cell H).

Obviously such asymmetrical outcomes are not likely to provide the basis for sustained collaborative relationships unless, of course, there is no other choice available to the buyer or the supplier. Buyers, for example, may have to accept that they have to collaborate with a dominant supplier, who, through the threat of loss or disruption to delivery of goods and/or services, forces them continually to innovate at their own cost without providing them with anything in return (a lock-in problem). Suppliers on the other hand may be forced to continuously provide 'loss leaders' to buyers because the supplier cannot afford to admit that they are not able to make a profit from providing the goods and/or service (a hold-up problem).

The major reason why these types of outcomes—especially those that are asymmetrical—do not last indefinitely is because one party loses and will inevitably seek alternative and more congenial partners commercially, or exit completely from the relationship, whenever it is feasible to do so. Despite this, there is still evidence in business of these types of outcomes occurring in buyer and supplier *collaborative sourcing* relationships. This is because sometimes there are no or few realistic alternatives available to one party and they must endure the asymmetrical outcome that exists.

Obviously in both *collaborative* and *market tested sourcing* relationships lose-lose outcomes are feasible but highly unstable forms of exchange. A lose-lose outcome would occur when a buyer specified a requirement and failed to receive it even though they had paid a substantial amount for it. This is clearly a lose outcome for the buyer because they have not received what they requested. It is perfectly possible, however, for the supplier to have agreed to deliver the product and/or service at a price that, even though it is exorbitantly high, does not allow them to make any return. In this circumstance the supplier would have produced the goods and/or services at a loss.

These types of relationships are not likely to be sustainable because, while the supplier might undertake such activities as a tax avoidance measure, they would soon find they could not operate this business model because they would eventually have no customers. Conversely, if they were able to provide something at a loss that the customer was satisfied with, this would not be a lose-lose but a win-lose outcome for the buyer.

Given this, just as with long-term *collaborative sourcing*, eight outcomes appear to be feasible in short-term *market tested sourcing* relationships. The reasons for the lack of feasibility of *ideal mutuality* have been explained earlier and we saw above how the three mutuality outcomes and the lose-lose outcome are all feasible for *market tested sourcing* relationships. Similarly, it is possible to conceive of asymmetrical outcomes in short-term *market tested sourcing* relationships, where one party achieves some element of gain while the other party does not.

Thus, if a buyer was able to make a supplier provide a product and/or service as a 'loss-leader' on the promise of more work or higher volumes in the future, but these promises failed to materialise, then the buyer would have achieved a win-lose outcome (cell A). This would occur because the supplier would make a loss on the transaction and receive none of the expected benefits promised by the buyer in the future. Similarly, if the buyer made equivalent promises but the supplier only provided part of the functionality or cost reductions desired by the buyer, and the buyer then failed to deliver, then a partial win-lose (cell D) would have occurred.

On the other side of the buyer-supplier divide it is possible for suppliers to achieve gains in short-term relationships even though the buyer is suffering a loss. Thus, if a buyer fails to receive the goods and/or services that have been specified, but the supplier has received a price that allows them to make above normal returns, and the buyer has no contractual recourse (in the form of penalties or other forms of restitution), then a lose-win outcome has occurred (cell I). In contrast, if the same situation repeats itself, but the price the supplier is able to charge only allows them to make normal returns, then a lose-partial win outcome has occurred (cell H). Clearly, when these types of outcome occur, and one or more party loses, then buyer and supplier relationships are unlikely to be sustained—particularly by the loser(s).

4.4 *Win-Lose and the Sustainability of Market Tested Sourcing Relationships*

Despite the common sense assumption that some vertical business relationship outcomes are not sustainable, this is not always the case, either in long-term *collaborative* or short-term *market tested sourcing* relationships. This occurs because of the problem of relationship inter-connectedness discussed earlier (see chapter 3). As a result, because parties can appropriate commercial value from inter-connected relationships, even as they make commercial losses in others, mutuality may not always be necessary for transactions to occur, either for one-off or repeat exchanges.

As Figure 10 demonstrates, there may well be circumstances in which one party fails to achieve their commercial goals and the other side fully or partially achieves theirs. These asymmetric outcomes of win-lose, lose-win, lose-partial win or partial win-lose may demonstrate, however, not a failure of business relationship management, but rather a sophisticated willingness on the part of some parties to use some business relationships as 'loss leaders' in pursuit of their broader strategic goals. This means there are often circumstances in which buyers and suppliers may, in the short-term (and even in the longer-term), be prepared to enter into relationships in which they do not achieve their ideal or even their optimal commercial goals.

While it is obvious in cell G in Figure 10 that, if both parties continually fail to achieve their goals, conflict and a termination of relationships will occur, this is not, however, self-evident for the relationships in cells A, D, H and I in Figure 10. These outcomes normally occur when buyers are prepared to pay more than they currently desire and/or receive sub-optimal use value. This normally occurs because they are locked into products and/or services and processes from which they cannot exit without unacceptable short-term difficulties. Or it may be that suppliers are providing 'loss leaders' to entice buyers to purchase other supply offerings from which they make more than enough profit for them to sustain losses from other offerings.

While these relationships may not be fully ideal or sustainable over the long-term, it is still the case that in business asymmetric outcomes (win-lose, partial win-lose, etc.) are a necessary fact of life that must sometimes be endured by one party in pursuit of other goals. Furthermore, in some circumstances (especially when the buyer or supplier does not need to sustain repeat games with the other exchange partner) win-lose options can be preferable in the short-term to any of the alternative options based on mutuality (win-partial win or partial win-partial win) that are available (Cox, 2004c).

It follows, therefore, that managers entering into exchange relationships, whether as buyers or as suppliers, must be cognisant of the additional paradox that vertical business relationships can be sustained when there are win-lose outcomes. This normally means, however, that those entering into such a paradoxical situation will have countervailing mechanisms for subsidising any commercial losses when they are on the losing end of a relationship. This means the loss is more than compensated by a win or partial win elsewhere. If they cannot then they will normally seek to exit from the relationship.

Finally, managers in business relationships have to accept that, although the best ways of managing business relationships are normally those in which there is a coincidence of interest, and both parties achieve some (although not necessarily the same) level of operational and commercial value, the search for an ideal approach to mutuality, in which both parties fully maximise their commercial goals, is illusory. In the real world of vertical business transactions, paradoxically, such an *ideal mutuality* is unachievable because objectively it is impossible for both parties to maximise the bottom-line commercially, whatever both parties may believe subjectively.

In practice, both parties to a vertical business exchange have to decide just how much operational and, in particular, commercial value they have to obtain in order to make any relationship work. This choice will be different for each party to an exchange, and it will vary under specific market and industry circumstances. It appears, however, that the primary area of tension and potential conflict is rarely likely to be about operational trade-offs. It is nearly always the commercial trade-offs that undermine inter-organisational business relationships. This is an important lesson to learn for those who devote the majority of their attention to operational rather than commercial improvements. It is also an important lesson to learn for those seeking to achieve more effective alignment in their business relationships, as the following chapter indicates.

5

Objectively Feasible Commercial and Operational Outcomes in Business Relationships

In this chapter the broad conclusions from the previous analysis are brought together. The discussion shows the full range and complexity of outcomes that are theoretically possible in business relationships by bringing together the operational and commercial aspects of exchange. This is followed by an analysis of which of these outcomes are objectively feasible for particular types of horizontal and vertical business relationships.

5.1 Theoretically Possible Commercial and Operational Outcomes in Business Relationships

The analysis so far has shown that, based on an objective view of the commercial interests of parties in transactions, there are significant differences in the feasibility of particular types of commercial outcome, depending on whether or not they occur in horizontal or vertical exchange. This objective view of interests is based on defining the ideal goals of individuals or organisations acting as economically rational actors. This implies that a win can only really be said to have occurred if the operational means used in business relationships by any actor allows them to maximise their commercial goals.

Using this approach, when an actor is involved in a business relationship, either as a joint venture/strategic alliance partner or as a supplier, a full commercial win means the ability to maximise above normal returns (*rents*), with complete market closure and the maximum share of revenue possible (i.e. 100% of the buyer's available demand). If an actor only earns *rents* but cannot fully close the market to others, or normal returns with or without market closure, this implies that only a partial win has been achieved commercially.

It could be argued that most actors would be satisfied with *rents* without full market closure, and in the real world of business practice this is often the case. However, while earning *rents* without full market closure is very close to an ideal outcome, the fact that competitors still exist in the market who may also have a share of the buyer's revenue or be able to compete in the future for a share of that revenue, means that there is always a threat that contestation will erode profitability in the future. In this sense the outcome is not ideal. Finally, if no commercial returns are made (this implies either a loss or break-even) then a lose outcome has occurred whatever the level of revenue received, or the state of market competition.

When an actor is a buyer a complete win implies that they receive operationally the maximum feasible increase in functionality that is possible given *x-efficiency*, and commercially the lowest feasible total costs of ownership possible. This means that, for a buyer to achieve their ideal commercial goals, their suppliers can only make returns that are either a 'loss leader', at break-even, or are normal (below double digits but always tending to zero). Obviously, the ideal win for the buyer in this case would be a 'loss leader' outcome if it could be sustained, followed by break-even. Since these outcomes cannot normally be sustained for very long by suppliers, the best that can be sustained in the long-term are normal returns that are as close to zero as possible.

If the supplier earns double-digit returns (*rents*) then, even if functionality has increased operationally and the total cost of ownership has been reduced, the buyer is experiencing only a partial win outcome. This is because the ideal situation for the buyer would be one in which all of the returns earned by the supplier are passed to the buyer in the form of even lower total costs of ownership than those currently being incurred. It also follows from this line of reasoning therefore that, whatever the supplier's returns, if the buyer experiences a decrease in functionality when the total costs of ownership are also increasing then a lose outcome has occurred commercially.

Given this logic, it can be argued that win-win outcomes are feasible (both in theory and in practice) in all horizontal forms of exchange. This is because it is possible for *both* parties to achieve their ideal commercial, as well as operational, goals. If interests are fully commensurable in this way then a win-win outcome (*ideal mutuality*) is, by definition, feasible.

Ideal mutuality means that it is feasible for both parties in a discrete exchange transaction to simultaneously achieve everything they ideally desire operationally and commercially.

This is not, however, the case in vertical forms of exchange. In these forms of exchange, because the objective commercial interests of buyers and suppliers are not fully commensurable, win-win outcomes based on *ideal mutuality* are not feasible. In these types of relationships the best that can be achieved is mutuality (or *nonzero-sum*) outcomes.

Mutuality here means that each party in a discrete exchange transaction can achieve all, or something, of what they ideally desire operationally and/or commercially, but both parties cannot simultaneously achieve everything they ideally desire.

This is because the economically rational desire by the supplier to achieve above normal returns and maximise their share of total revenue through market closure is in conflict with the equally economically rational desire by the buyer to achieve the lowest feasible reduction in the total cost of ownership. This means that *mutuality* outcomes incorporate all of the *nonzero-sum* asymmetric and symmetric exchange outcomes—such as win-partial win, partial win-partial win, and partial win-win—in which neither party loses, although in some circumstances one party gains more than the other.

This way of thinking also provides a basis for objective definitions for win-lose, partial win-lose (*zero-sum*) and lose-lose (*zero-zero*) outcomes.

Zero-sum outcomes mean that one party in a discrete exchange transaction can achieve all, or something of what they ideally desire operationally and/or commercially, while the other party does not receive any of their operational and commercial needs.

Lose-lose outcomes mean that both parties in a discrete exchange transaction simultaneously do not receive any of their operational and commercial needs.

When these permutations of win, partial win and lose are put together there must be a range of *symmetrical* (win-win, partial win-partial win, and lose-lose), as well as *asymmetrical* (win-lose, win-partial win, partial win-lose, partial win-win, lose-partial win, and lose-win) transactional outcomes. This also implies that, theoretically speaking at least, asymmetrical outcomes occur more often than symmetrical outcomes.

If this provides for definitional clarity, it still remains to provide a comprehensive delineation of the range of theoretically possible outcomes that can occur in different types of business relationships. This requires recognition of the fact that, although the purpose of business relationships is always defined objectively in terms of a commercial end, business relationships also involve operational means. This means that relationship outcomes always involve some fusion of commercial ends and operational means.

To assist with a more rigorous and robust understanding of these issues it is essential to understand the operational and commercial trade-offs that managers experience when they enter into business relationships. Figure 11 provides a simple matrix that shows the basic operational and commercial outcomes that the two parties to an exchange transaction can experience.

It is axiomatic that the purpose of business is not to do any particular thing operationally but, rather, to do those things operationally that allow companies to make money. Thus, the primary commercial purpose (end) for any company must be the ability to *improve profitability*. In addition, from an objective and economically rational perspective, improvement should result in the maximum feasible and sustainable *rents*, rather than normal returns. Once this can be achieved then companies ought to seek to *increase their share of market revenue* in order to increase the volume of money received at the highest possible level of returns.

Figure 11: The Commercial and Operational Value Matrix

	A — HIGH COMMERCIAL/ LOW OPERATIONAL VALUE	B — HIGH COMMERCIAL/ HIGH OPERATIONAL VALUE
HIGH (Commercial Value)	• Increased Profitability (Rents) • Increased Market Share • Differentiated Products/Services • Sustainable Isolating Mechanisms • Reductions in Total Costs of Ownership • No Improvements in Capacity Utilisation • No Improvements in Cycle Time • No Improvements in Quality • No Improvements in Customer Responsiveness • No Improvements in Supplier Responsiveness	• Increased Profitability (Rents) • Increased Market Share • Differentiated Products/Services • Sustainable Isolating Mechanisms • Reductions in Total Cost of Ownership • Improvements in Capacity Utilisation • Improvements in Cycle Time • Improvements in Quality • Improvements in Customer Responsiveness • Improvements in Supplier Responsiveness
	C — LOW COMMERCIAL/ LOW OPERATIONAL VALUE	D — LOW COMMERCIAL/ HIGH OPERATIONAL VALUE
LOW	• Static/Declining Profitability (Tending to Zero) • Static/Declining Market Share • Undifferentiated Products/Services • Unsustainable Isolating Mechanisms • Static or Increasing Total Costs of Ownership • No Improvements in Capacity Utilisation • No Improvements in Cycle Time • No Improvements in Quality • No Improvements in Customer Responsiveness • No Improvements in Supplier Responsiveness	• Static/Declining Profitability (Tending to Zero) • Static/Declining Market Share • Undifferentiated Products/Services • Unsustainable Isolating Mechanisms • Static or Increasing Total Costs of Ownership • Improvements in Capacity Utilisation • Improvements in Cycle Time • Improvements in Quality • Improvements in Customer Responsiveness • Improvements in Supplier Responsiveness
	LOW	HIGH

OPERATIONAL VALUE

© Robertson Cox Ltd, 2004. All Rights Reserved.

To achieve this commercial end, companies normally have to ensure that operationally they create *differentiated products and/or services* that allow them to offer unique and difficult to replicate supply offerings to customers, and also seek to create other forms of *isolating mechanisms* to ensure market closure even when products and/or services cannot be fully differentiated (Rumelt, 1987). Finally, in order to reduce the overall costs of sales relative to revenue earned, companies ought to seek a *constant reduction in the total cost of ownership of the internal and external processes and relationships* that deliver their products and/or services.

Companies should normally highly value any operational activities that optimise or improve the efficiency and effectiveness of the processes and systems through which products and/or services are provided. Companies, therefore, normally highly value *improvements in capacity utilization* (i.e. in the use of their capital assets at 100% of potential use, or improvements in that direction that reduce downtime). They also ought to highly value *improvements in process cycle times* (i.e. in the internal and external timeliness or speed of supply, production and delivery), as well as *improvements in product and service quality* (i.e. reductions in internal and external defects, elimination of rework etc.).

Given also that companies must respond to customer wants and needs effectively, they ought to highly value *improvements in customer responsiveness* (i.e. in the ability of the company to act flexibly internally to changing customer preferences). Since they must often work closely with suppliers to engineer improvements in the supply of outsourced goods and/or services, companies also ought to highly value *improvements in supplier and supply chain responsiveness* (i.e. in the ability of suppliers and their supply chains to act flexibly in delivering increased value in response to customer changing preferences).

Taking these commercial and operational value characteristics together, it is possible to create an understanding of the objective commercial ends and operational means that all companies seek. Figure 11 demonstrates that sometimes there are circumstances when commercial ends and operational means coincide and *high commercial and operational value* for a firm (Quadrant B) occurs. Conversely there can be circumstances of *low commercial and operational value* (Quadrant C). In between these two extremes are Quadrant A, in which *high commercial value* is achieved but *low operational improvement* occurs, and

Quadrant D, in which there is *low commercial value* even though *high levels of operational improvement* occur.

Taking these indicators together it is possible to envisage three different transactional outcome scenarios for exchange parties in horizontal business relationships: a commercial win outcome occurs if *rents* are maximised with full market closure; a partial win occurs if *rents* are earned without being maximised or normal returns are earned with or without full market closure; and a lose outcome occurs if break-even or losses are incurred.

Similarly, on the operational side, if all of the operational improvements outlined in Figure 11 are achieved which might improve functionality (use value) for the customer and also close markets to competitors then an operational win is achieved. If some, but not all, are achieved then a partial operational win has been achieved, and if none of these operational means are achieved then a lose outcome has occurred operationally.

This is because in horizontal business relationships both parties generally have the same ideal operational and commercial goals (they normally want their relationship to result in operational market closure and above normal returns commercially). Despite this, it is possible that they will bring to the relationship different operational means, and what is achieved in the specific horizontal relationship will have different operational and commercial outcomes for them in their broader business circumstances outside the alliance or joint venture relationship. Thus, what will be an operational or commercial win, partial win or lose for one party may not be equally so for the other. This, plus the opportunity to free-ride on others in relationships, provides scope for opportunism even in strategic alliances and joint ventures (Watson and Sanderson, 1997; Das, 2004).

In vertical business relationships, conflict and tension is always much more prevalent than in horizontal exchange because the commercial goals of the buyer and supplier are not fully commensurable. Furthermore, while there may be no inevitable tension between the operational goals of the buyer and supplier, there is always the possibility of some tension. This is because suppliers can leverage buyers commercially if they are able to achieve operational improvements that allow them to create market closure, or if they fail to pass the maximum feasible improvements in functionality to the buyer (i.e. if they supply goods and/or services at below *x-efficiency*).

In such circumstances, even if a supplier can provide increased functionality to a buyer at a cost that is currently much lower than all its competitors, the operational benefit to the buyer may only come at the price of dependency on that supplier, who can earn *rents* at their expense. Given that the *rents* earned by the supplier are always a cost that is borne by the buyer, which could be passed to the buyer in the form of lower costs, it is inevitable that there will always be tension (if not always outright conflict) for buyers and suppliers in both the operational and commercial aspects of transactions.

These tensions are outlined in Figure 12 which shows that, while there may be operational means that provide market closure and above normal commercial returns that suppliers value, these may not be equally valued by the buyer. Suppliers fully achieve a complete win (cells F and I) when they achieve the maximum feasible *rents* from their exchange partner, while also achieving the maximum feasible share of the revenue

118   Win-Win?

available from the buyer due to full market closure against their competitors.

Figure 12: Commercial and Operational Trade-Offs for Buyers and Suppliers

	A BUYER WINS/ SUPPLIER LOSES	**B BUYER WINS/ SUPPLIER PARTIALLY WINS**	**C BUYER WINS/ SUPPLIER WINS**
FULLY ACHIEVED	Buyer receives the maximum feasible increase in functionality and the maximum feasible reduction in total costs of ownership/ Supplier makes a commercial loss or breaks even with a declining share of revenue.	Buyer receives the maximum feasible increase in functionality and the maximum feasible reduction in total costs of ownership/ Supplier earns rents (but not the maximum feasible) or normal returns, whether revenue is maximised or not.	**Not Feasible:** *This is because, irrespective of any increases in functionality, the maximum feasible reduction in total costs of ownership for the buyer must be at the expense of the ability of suppliers to earn the maximum feasible rents.*
	D BUYER PARTIALLY WINS/ SUPPLIER LOSES	**E BUYER AND SUPPLIER BOTH PARTIALLY WIN**	**F BUYER PARTIALLY WINS/ SUPPLIER WINS**
PARTIALLY ACHIEVED	*Buyer can receive all feasible functionality and total cost of ownership trade-offs, except the maximum feasible increase in functionality with the maximum feasible reduction in total costs of ownership at the same time, or a decrease in functionality with an increase in the total cost of ownership at the same time/ Supplier makes a commercial loss or breaks even, with a declining share of revenue.*	*Buyer can receive all feasible functionality and total cost of ownership trade-offs, except the maximum feasible increase in functionality with the maximum feasible reduction in total costs of ownership at the same time, or a decrease in functionality with an increase in the total costs of ownership at the same time/ Supplier earns rents (but not the maximum feasible) or normal returns, whether revenue is maximised or not.*	Buyer can receive all feasible functionality and total cost of ownership trade-offs, except the maximum feasible increase in functionality with the maximum feasible reduction in total costs of ownership at the same time, or a decrease in functionality with an increase in the total costs of ownership at the same time/ Supplier earns the maximum feasible share of revenue through full market closure.
	G BUYER LOSES/ SUPPLIER LOSES	**H BUYER LOSES/ SUPPLIER PARTIALLY WINS**	**I BUYER LOSES/ SUPPLIER WINS**
NOT ACHIEVED	*Buyer receives no, or a reduced, functionality and increased total costs of ownership/ Supplier makes a commercial loss or breaks even with a declining share of revenue.*	*Buyer receives no, or a reduced, functionality and increased total costs of ownership/ Supplier earns rents (but not the maximum feasible) or normal returns, whether revenue is maximised or not.*	Buyer receives no, or a reduced functionality and increased total costs of ownership. Supplier earns the maximum feasible rents with the maximum feasible share of revenue through full market closure.

VALUE CAPTURE BY THE BUYER (Value for Money): NOT ACHIEVED / PARTIALLY ACHIEVED / FULLY ACHIEVED

VALUE CAPTURE BY THE SUPPLIER (Value from Supply)

© Robertson Cox Ltd, 2004. All Rights Reserved.

The buyer fully achieves a win (Cells A and B) when they receive the maximum feasible increase in functionality from their suppliers given *x-efficiency*, at the same time as attaining the lowest, or maximum feasible reduction in the, total costs of ownership possible (preferably with suppliers as 'loss leaders', then at break-even or, finally, earning normal returns tending to zero). In this light what is a win, partial win and lose for the buyer is not the same as for the supplier and vice versa, as the nine cells in the matrix in Figure 12 clearly indicate.

Thus, *buyer wins/supplier loses* (Cell A) occurs when the buyer receives the maximum feasible increase in functionality possible (given *x-efficiency*) and the maximum feasible reduction in the total costs of ownership, and the supplier experiences a declining share of revenue and makes a commercial loss or only breaks-even. *Buyer wins/supplier partially wins* (Cell B) occurs when the buyer receives the same as above, but the supplier either makes *rents* (without achieving the maximum feasible levels) or only earns normal returns, whether revenues are maximised or not.

Buyer partially wins/supplier loses (Cell D) occurs when the buyer receives any of the feasible functionality and total cost of ownership trade-offs, except for either the maximum feasible increase in functionality with the maximum feasible reduction in the total costs of ownership at the same time, or reductions in functionality with increases in the total costs of ownership at the same time. The supplier here experiences a commercial loss or break-even, with a declining share of revenue.

Buyer partially wins/supplier partially wins (Cell E) occurs when the buyer experiences the same as in the previous outcome, but now the supplier receives either *rents* (without achieving the maximum feasible levels possible) or normal returns, whether revenues are maximised or not. *Buyer partially wins/supplier wins* (Cell F) occurs when the buyer experiences the same as previously, but now the supplier makes the maximum feasible *rents* and also the maximum feasible returns from the buyer, through full market closure against competitors.

Buyer loses/supplier loses (Cell G) occurs when the buyer receives no, or a reduced, functionality at the same time as increased total costs of ownership, and the supplier makes a commercial loss or break-even and experiences a declining share of revenue. *Buyer loses/supplier partially wins* (Cell H) occurs when the buyer experiences the previous losing outcome, but the supplier makes *rents* (without achieving the maximum feasible level possible) or normal returns, with or without maximising returns. *Buyer loses/supplier wins* (Cell I) occurs when the buyer achieves the same losing outcome as previously, but the supplier earns the maximum feasible *rents* and the maximum feasible share of revenue possible through full market closure against competitors.

It follows from this discussion that, as Figure 12 also demonstrates, Cell C *buyer wins/supplier wins* is not a feasible outcome in buyer and supplier exchange. The reason for this is self-evident. If a buyer is to receive the maximum feasible increase in functionality (given *x-efficiency*), and also receive the maximum feasible reduction in the total costs of ownership, then it is inevitable that these can only be achieved at the expense of the supplier.

This arises because the ideal for the buyer is to have the supplier constantly innovate with *x-efficiency* but never to make *rents*. In fact the buyer would prefer the supplier to innovate and provide any improvements in functionality to them as a 'loss leader' (i.e. at less than the costs of production and delivery). If this altruistic outcome is not achievable then a buyer normally prefers that any improvements in functionality be passed to them at break-even (i.e. at cost) or, failing that, with normal returns that tend as close to zero as possible.

It is axiomatic that such outcomes are only achievable at the expense of the supplier. The ideal outcome for the supplier is that they provide to the buyer only those functionality improvements in *x-efficiency* required to close the market to their competitors and also to be able to earn the maximum feasible *rents* that are possible from them. Clearly, this goal is in conflict with the desire by buyers to receive the lowest feasible total costs of ownership, and also to be able to switch easily to any supplier who may be able to provide an improvement in *x-efficiency* in the future.

In this sense, the objective interests of buyers and suppliers are not fully commensurable and, as a result, vertical business relationships must experience "contested exchange" (Bowles and Gintis, 1988; Cox, 2004c). This means, as we shall see, that relationship outcomes are always asymmetric, even when they occur as a partial win-partial win for buyers and suppliers. Although it might be thought that a partial win-partial win for buyers and suppliers indicates that a symmetrical outcome has occurred, in fact, this is not really the case because of the non-commensurability of interests in these types of business relationships.

Interestingly enough, recent research demonstrates that, although the objective interests of joint venture and strategic alliance partners may be fully commensurable (because both parties in horizontal business relationships can simultaneously achieve their ideal outcomes) they may not always be. This implies that asymmetric (as well as symmetric) relationship outcomes can also occur in horizontal business relationships (Das and Rahman, 2002; Das, 2004).

This is why, when putting these operational and commercial win, partial win and lose outcomes from horizontal and vertical exchange together, it is clear that the theoretically possible outcomes from business relationships are many and varied. There is, of course, an additional level of complexity in business relationships that arises from the fact that the operational and commercial ideals of those engaged in exchange are not the same when we consider horizontal and vertical business relationships.

This is because in horizontal business relationships the two parties are working together towards the creation of the same operational and commercial goal (the creation of a product and/or service that both will jointly own and share in its commercial business success or failure), even though they may fight over the ultimate sharing of value from this exchange relationship. In vertical business relationships the interests of the two parties are never commensurable even though they may coincide on occasion. This is because the buyer's ideal is to maximise functionality and costs reductions, which can only occur at the expense of the supplier. The supplier, on the other hand, seeks to maximise returns and market closure, which can only occur at the expense of the buyer. Given this, one has to consider carefully and separately the theoretically feasible options that can occur in horizontal as well as in vertical business relationships.

5.2 *Objectively Feasible Outcomes in Horizontal Business Relationships*

Figure 13 demonstrates theoretically that, not only is there a wide range of symmetrical and asymmetrical outcomes in

Commercial and Operational Outcomes 123

Figure 13: Symmetry and Asymmetry in the Commercial and Operational Outcomes from Horizontal Business Relationships

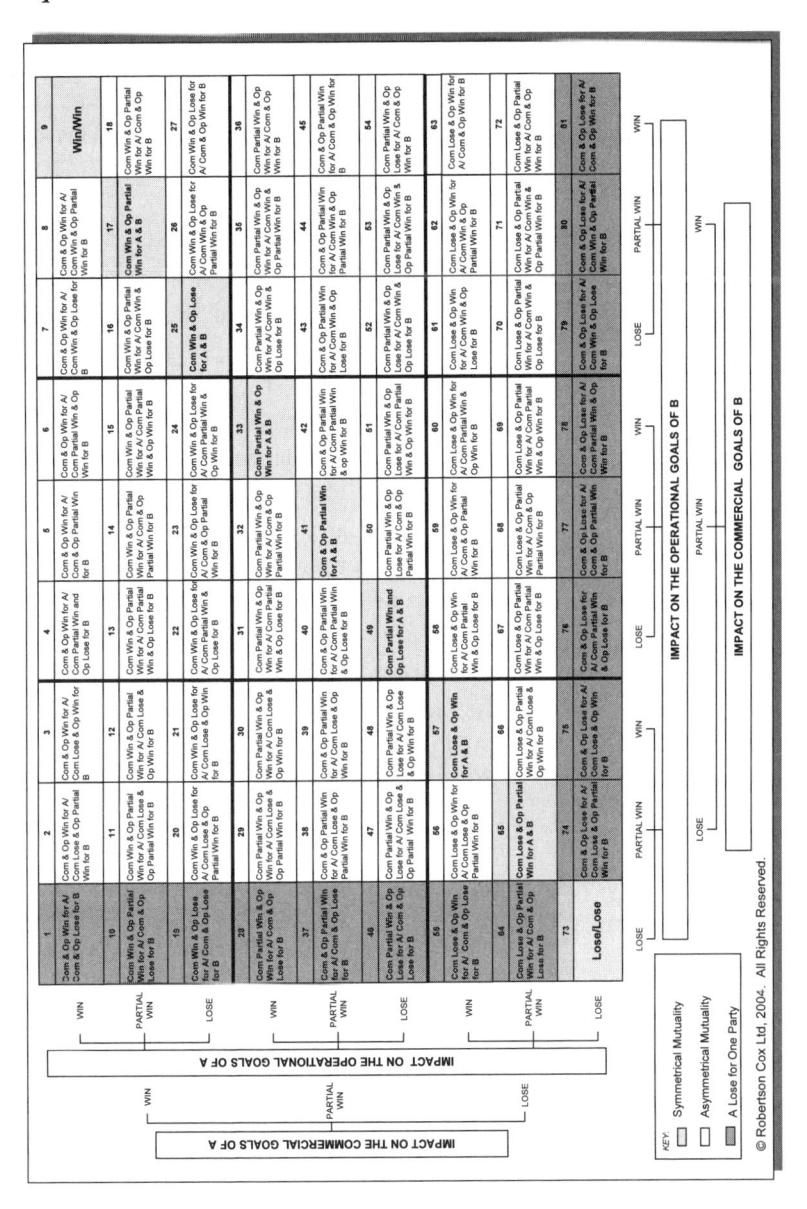

horizontal business relationships, but also that, as a result, the choices about how to manage business relationships are highly complex for both parties. Despite this complexity, as we shall see, when an objective (economically rational) approach is adopted not all of these outcomes defined theoretically here are actually available in practice to the participants in all types of business relationships.

By theoretically linking the three potential outcomes of win, partial win and lose with commercial ends and operational means, Figure 13 shows logically that there are eighty-one potential outcomes from horizontal business relationships. Of these, nine are *symmetrical outcomes* (cells 9, 17, 25, 33, 41, 49, 57, 65 and 73). This means that both parties to the exchange experience a similar outcome in relation to their ideal commercial and operational goals. The remaining seventy-two are *asymmetrical outcomes*, where one party achieves more than the other from the relationship, whether the outcomes are a combination of win, partial win or lose for each party.

All of the *symmetrical outcomes*, apart from cell 73 (which is a lose-lose), involve exactly the same type of commercial and/or operational win or partial win for both parties. What is interesting from this discussion is that there is only one outcome in which it can be said that a true win-win (*ideal mutuality*) can occur in theory. This is cell 9 where both parties simultaneously fully achieve both their operational and their commercial ends. This is a *symmetrical outcome* that delights both parties.

The remaining eight outcomes are also symmetrical, but they do not provide for the simultaneous achievement of everything that both parties might desire. As a result, although seven of these eight *symmetrical outcomes* are *forms of mutuality* (cell 73 is unique as a lose-lose), they are not, however, *ideal mutuality*. Thus, in cell 17 both parties simultaneously achieve a commercial win but only a partial win operationally. In cell 25 both parties simultaneously achieve a commercial win but no additional operational benefit. In cell 33 both parties simultaneously receive a partial win commercially and a win operationally. In cell 41 it is a partial win commercially and operationally for both parties. In cell 49 it is a partial win commercially with no additional benefit operationally for both parties. In cell 57 it is no commercial benefit with an operational win for both parties, and in cell 65 it is no commercial benefit but a partial win operationally.

It is possible to consider eight of these nine symmetrical outcomes as the basis for sustaining horizontal business relationships. This is because they all provide some form of operational and/or commercial benefit, and they are all based on some form of *symmetrical mutuality*, although only the outcome in cell 9 can be seen as *ideal symmetrical mutuality*. Despite this mutuality, as defined here, it is not necessarily confined to *symmetrical outcomes*. It is also possible to have *asymmetrical outcomes* in which mutuality occurs. This implies that mutuality is a complex phenomenon, but also that very many forms of symmetrical and asymmetrical exchange can sustain horizontal business relationships. It is not just *ideal mutuality* or *symmetrical mutuality* that is required for long-term horizontal business relationships to be sustained.

It is the case, therefore, that, since many *asymmetrical outcomes* involve degrees of mutuality (i.e. both parties achieve at least some form of win or partial win operationally and/or commercially, without both receiving exactly the same), these types of relationship outcomes can also sustain business relationships. This is because, if one party is receiving something of what they desire operationally and/or commercially, it is possible for them to want to sustain that relationship even if the other party is achieving more or less than they are. The key is always whether or not, for them, the current outcome is better than all currently feasible alternatives.

As Figure 13 reveals, there is, therefore, a range of potential outcomes—fifty-six—in which *asymmetrical forms of mutuality* can occur. This means that when managers and commentators use the concept of mutuality they must be extremely careful in defining exactly what it is that they mean by the concept. As the Figure shows, mutuality can encompass cell 9 (*ideal mutuality*), cell 8 (where A achieves all that they desire commercially and operationally, while B also achieves all they desire commercially but only partially what they desire operationally), and also situations like those in cell 65 (where neither A nor B achieves what they desire commercially but they both receive some partial operational benefit).

It follows from this that, when managers and writers use the concept of mutuality, they must be sensitive to the fact that it can have a wide range of meanings operationally and commercially, and that in horizontal business relationships it can encompass both *symmetrical* and *asymmetrical outcomes*. Interestingly enough, this is also true when one considers win-lose (*zero-sum*) outcomes. As Figure 13 indicates, while *zero-sum* outcomes are always asymmetrical they can also have degrees of meaning for the two parties to an exchange. There are sixteen cases in which some form of win-lose occurs in two party exchanges. Of these, however, only eight types are pertinent. This is because, while there are sixteen cases, there are only eight outcome types. This is because the only thing that changes is whether the winner or loser is A or B.

The eight *zero-sum* outcomes that can arise vary in the degree to which one party achieves a win, when the other loses. The worse case scenario must be, therefore, when one party achieves everything that they desire commercially and operationally and the other party achieves no commercial or operational benefit whatsoever (cells 1 or 81). After this, the winning party might be expected to prefer a commercial win with a partial win operationally (cells 10 or 80), followed by a commercial win without operational benefit (cells 19 or 79). Following this logic, in the partial commercial win category the preference is likely to be for outcomes in cells 28 or 78, followed by those in cells 37 or 77, and then by those in cells 46 or 76. In the no commercial, but operational, benefit category either party would normally be expected to prefer outcomes in cells 55 or 75 (an operational benefit) to those in cells 64 or 74 (only a partial operational benefit).

This discussion is clearly informed by a view that commercial ends should normally outweigh operational means when considering the rank ordering of preferences in horizontal business exchange. As we shall see later, however, when buyer and supplier exchange is considered in more detail, the decision about the primacy of commercial ends over operational means in rank ordering preferences can vary widely depending on the impact of operational improvement (increases in the functionality of supply) on overall corporate performance.

Nevertheless, what this discussion confirms is that one should not talk glibly about the need for win-win and mutuality outcomes in horizontal business relationships. This is because there is tremendous complexity of outcomes in exchange transactions. If this discussion has achieved nothing more than provide a way of thinking about the complex choices and trade-offs that two parties need to think about when they negotiate the terms of any business relationship then it will have served its purpose. There is, however, one final paradox that must be dealt with before we turn to the implications for managerial practice and current and future academic research.

It was argued earlier that, if we took an objective view of business relationships, some outcomes are not feasible in certain types of vertical relationships. In this final section we adopt the same perspective in relation to the outcomes that have been theoretically defined as possible when commercial ends and operational means are conjoined in horizontal, and then later for vertical, business relationships. As we shall see, from an objective point of view, there are also significant limits on the feasibility of outcomes in different types of horizontal as well as vertical business relationships.

As we saw, there are five basic forms of horizontal business relationships. These are *full-equity joint ventures*, *preferential-equity joint ventures*, *lump sum* and *mark-up*, *royalty-based* and, finally, *non-equity cooperative strategic alliances*. What is interesting about each of these types of horizontal business relationship is that, although they are similar in some respects, they are dissimilar in others. Thus, while all horizontal business relationships are similar in that they involve the two parties in the exchange working together operationally to create a jointly owned product and/or service from which they make a commercial return, it is possible (depending primarily on the remuneration structure) for opportunism to occur commercially, and in some relationships more than in others. Given this, as Figures 14, 15, 16, 17 and 18 show, some of the outcomes outlined in Figure 13 as theoretically possible, are not feasible in practice in horizontal business relationships.

Commercial and Operational Outcomes 129

Figure 14: Feasible Commercial and Operational Outcomes in Full-Equity Joint Ventures

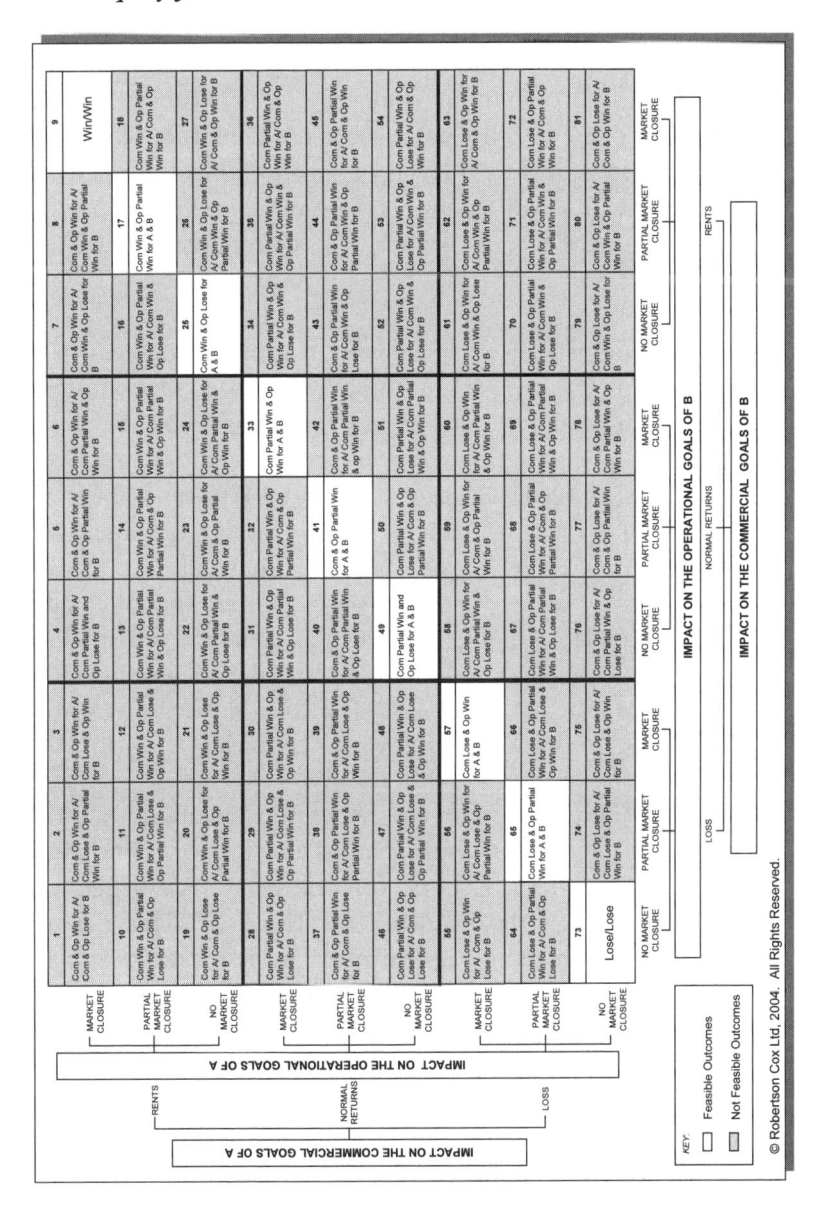

130   Win-Win?

Figure 14 demonstrates that in *full-equity joint ventures* only nine *symmetrical outcomes* are feasible when two parties enter into an exchange and operational and commercial benefits are conjoined. This arises because both equity partners are working towards the same operational outcome, which can either be that market closure is fully, partially or not achieved. Similarly, while there may be different levels of shareholding, both parties must experience the same commercial outcome of a win (*rents*), partial win (normal returns) or lose (no commercial returns at all).

Figure 15 demonstrates the eighteen feasible outcomes in a *preferential-equity joint venture*. In these types of joint ventures, only symmetrical operational outcomes are feasible because both parties are developing the same product and/or service. Despite this, because one party (A) can behave opportunistically against another (B) then asymmetrical outcomes commercially are also feasible. Thus, all nine of the outcomes feasible under *full-equity joint ventures* are feasible (cells 9, 17, 25, 33, 41, 49, 57, 65 and 73), but a further nine outcomes (cells 3, 6, 11, 14, 19, 22, 30, 38 and 46) are also feasible because of the possibility of operational symmetry for both parties and commercial asymmetry favouring A over B.

With *lump sum* and *mark-up strategic alliances* the situation is a little different. This is because both parties are on the same side operationally but there is scope for one party (A) to behave opportunistically against the other commercially. This means that, since A can guarantee a return before B makes one, it is not feasible that lose-lose can occur under this arrangement. This is because A always makes a return even though B may not. Despite this, as Figure 16 demonstrates, all the other eight symmetrical outcomes (cells 9, 17, 25, 33, 41, 49, 57 and 65) are feasible because A and B can both experience the same commercial and operational results.

Commercial and Operational Outcomes 131

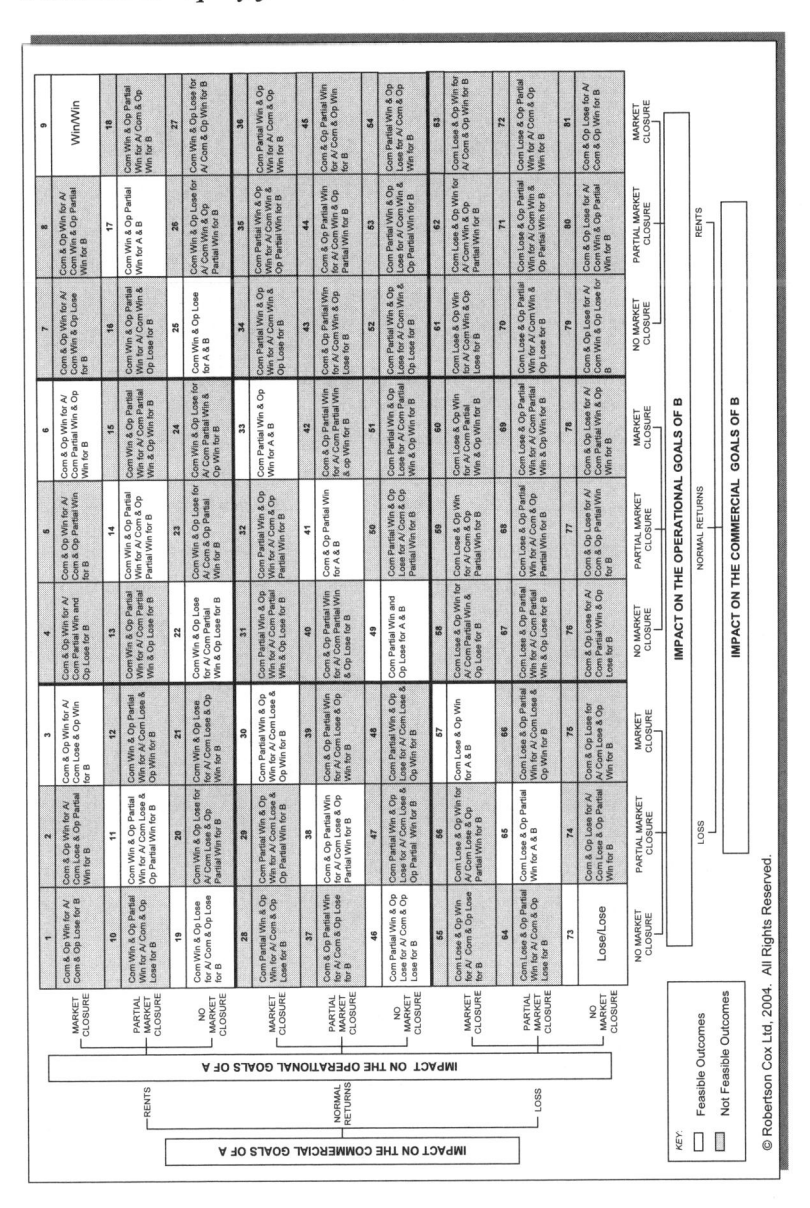

Figure 15: Feasible Commercial and Operational Outcomes in Preferential-Equity Joint Ventures

132   Win-Win?

Figure 16: Feasible Commercial and Operational Outcomes in Lump-sum and Mark-up Strategic Alliances

Furthermore, since it is possible for A to ensure that they never lose, all outcomes that could arise with a commercial loss for A and some commercial gain for B are not feasible, whatever the operational outcome. Despite this, it is possible for an asymmetrical outcome favouring B to occur. That is all win outcomes favouring B, where there is a partial win for A, but where there is operational symmetry of outcome. This arises because the *lump sum* or *mark-up* may provide A only with normal returns but B can make above normal returns. This means that outcomes in cells 36, 44 and 52 are feasible.

Similarly, as in *preferential-equity joint ventures*, all asymmetrical commercial outcomes that favour A, but that also have symmetrical operational outcomes, are feasible. This means that outcomes in cells 3, 6, 11, 14, 19, 22, 30, 38 and 46 are feasible. Overall this means that 20 outcomes are feasible for *lump sum* and *mark-up strategic alliances*.

Figure 17 outlines the range of outcomes that are feasible for *royalty-based strategic alliances*. The outcomes here have some but not all of the characteristics of both *joint ventures* and *lump sum* and *mark-up strategic alliances*. Thus, in these types of strategic alliances, as in the *full* and *preferential-equity joint ventures*, it is feasible for both parties to experience all of the nine symmetrical outcomes from win-win through partial win-partial win to lose-lose (cells 9, 17, 25, 33, 41, 49, 57, 65 and 73). A lose-lose is also possible here because, operationally, the two parties could create a product and/or service but fail to make sales sufficient to allow a profit to be made. In this case, A would not be able to ensure that they did not lose because the royalty would only be paid if sales were made. This is a different scenario to the situation when a *lump sum* or *mark-up* is paid to A before B makes any sales or return.

134   Win-Win?

Figure 17: Feasible Commercial and Operational Outcomes in Royalty-based Strategic Alliances

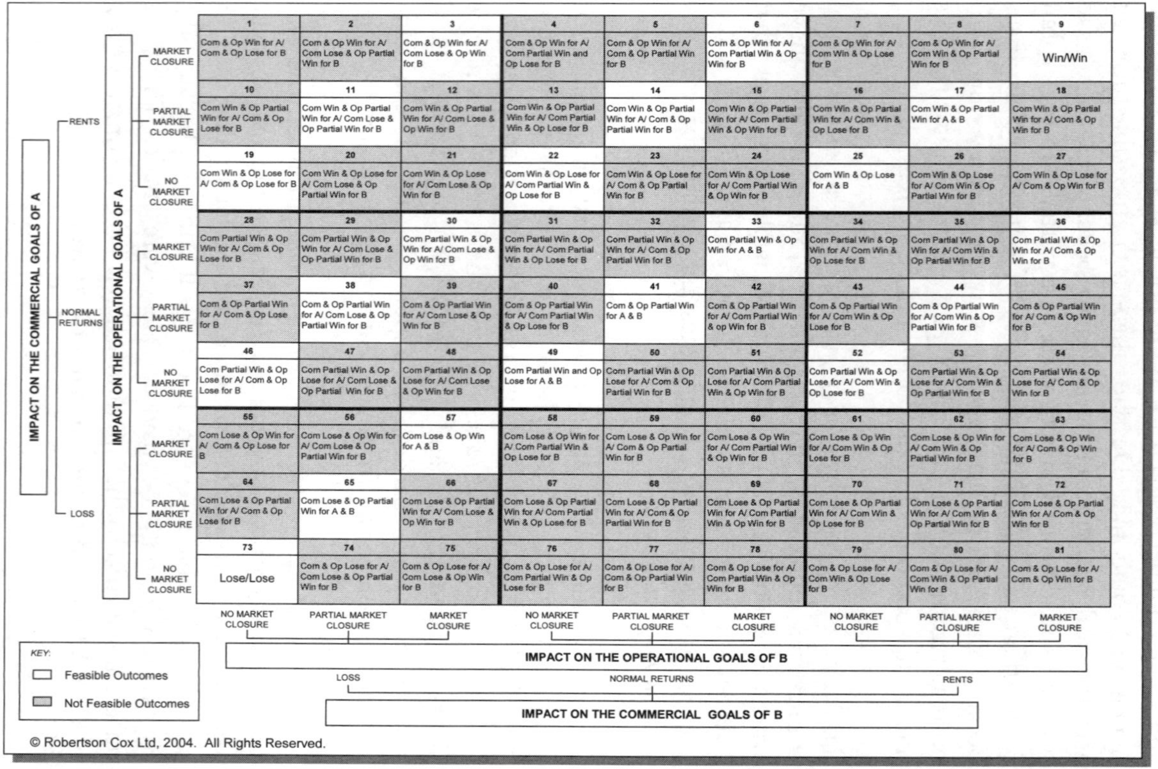

Despite this, and unlike the situation in *preferential-joint ventures*, partial win-win outcomes that favour B are also feasible. This is because, as in the case of *lump sum* and *mark-up arrangements*, the royalty payments might allow A only to make normal returns, but B is able to earn *rents* from their sales revenue. This means that not only are all of the nine symmetrical operational outcomes that favour A commercially feasible (cells 3, 6, 11, 14, 19, 22, 30, 38 and 46), but the three operationally symmetrical but commercially asymmetrical outcomes that favour B (cells 36, 44 and 52) are also feasible. This means that in this form of strategic alliance there are twenty-one feasible outcomes commercially and operationally.

There are even more feasible outcomes in *non-equity cooperative strategic alliances*. This is because in these types of arrangement, while there is operational symmetry as both parties are working to create and sell the same overall product and/or service in the market, the commercial consequences can be symmetrical or asymmetrical. This fusion of operational symmetry with commercial symmetry and asymmetry is outlined in Figure 18.

As this Figure shows, there are twenty-seven feasible outcomes in *non-equity cooperative strategic alliances*. These include the nine symmetrical commercial and operational outcomes (cells 9, 17, 25, 33, 41, 49, 57, 65 and 73); the nine operationally symmetrical outcomes that favour A commercially (cells 3, 6, 11, 14, 19, 22, 30, 38 and 46); and the nine operationally symmetrical outcomes that favour B (cells 36, 44, 52, 60, 63, 68, 71, 76 and 79).

This discussion of feasible horizontal business relationships demonstrates four things. First, a win-win based on *ideal mutuality* is objectively feasible in all joint venture and strategic alliance relationships. Second, and perhaps paradoxically,

Figure 18: Feasible Commercial and Operational Outcomes in Non-Equity Cooperative Strategic Alliances

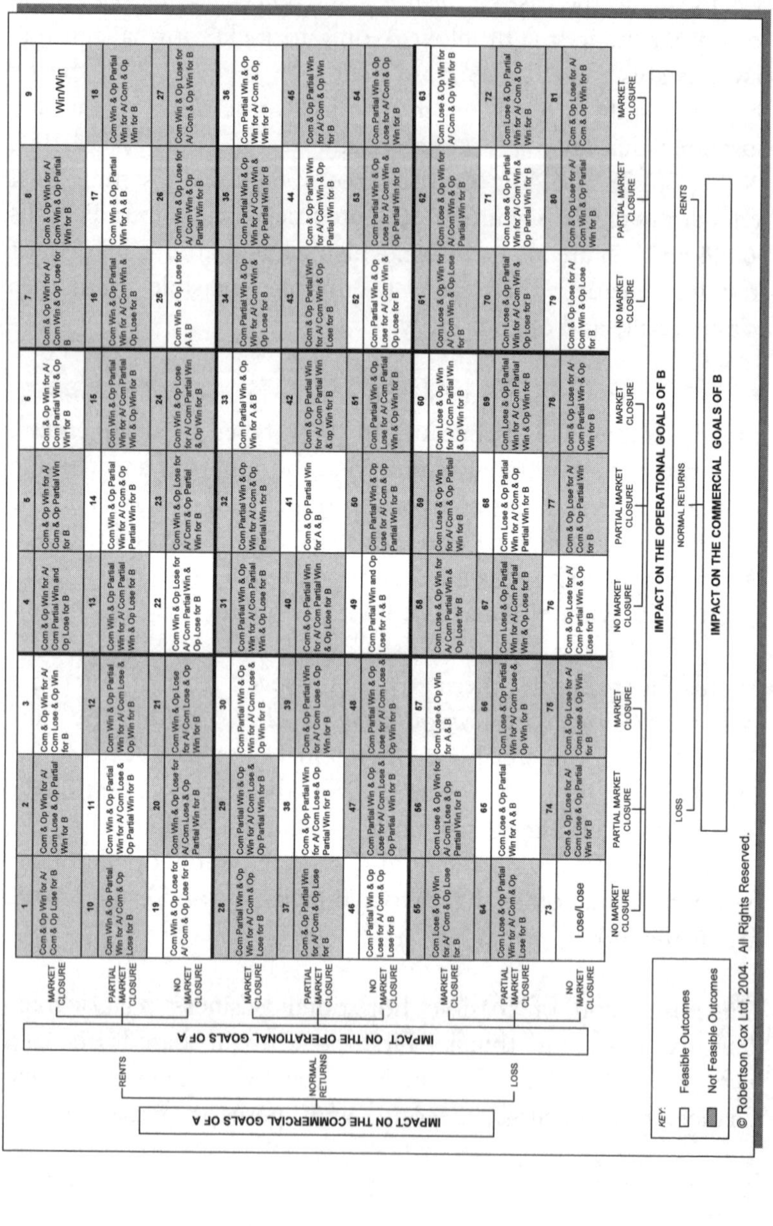

despite this, joint venture and strategic alliance relationships can be sustained in the absence of objectively defined win-win outcomes. This is because there is a wide range of feasible mutuality outcomes that, although falling short of an ideal win-win in which both parties fully achieve all of their operational and commercial goals, still allow these types of business relationships to be sustained.

Furthermore, and third, as we saw, the range of feasible outcomes varies across different types of horizontal business relationships, as does the scope for symmetrical or asymmetrical commercial outcomes. This variation is normally based on commercial rather than operational considerations. This is because, operationally, both parties are normally on the same side producing and selling the same product and/or service. The asymmetry in the relationship is typically based on the degree to which one party is able to protect their own commercial interests, so that they can guarantee their financial return while a higher proportion of the operational and/or commercial risk is borne by the other party.

This implies that even in joint venture and strategic alliance relationships there is scope for conflict and tension between relationship partners. This is because even in these relationships there can be symmetrical as well as asymmetrical commercial outcomes. Only in the case of *full-equity joint ventures* does it appear that asymmetrical commercial outcomes cannot occur. Although it is also the case that one party can own more of the full-equity shares than another, which can generate conflict and tension in the relationship.

What follows from this is the realisation that, since a win-win is not guaranteed, nor is it absolutely necessary to sustain horizontal business relationships, there are choices available to participants about how they should be constructed operationally and commercially. This means that there must be scope for conflict over operational and commercial outcomes, and an inevitable tension as the objective interests of both parties are more or less satisfied (Wathne and Heide, 2000; Das, 2004).

This implies that the ability to use commercial forms of power (i.e. the ability to achieve one's intended effects to generate asymmetrical outcomes when there is a clear and observable conflict of transactional interests between two parties) must be present in horizontal relationships, although it may not if win-win (*positive-sum* or *ideal mutuality*) and partial win-partial win (*nonzero-sum* or *symmetrical mutuality*) outcomes occur. As we shall see, if economic power can be used in horizontal exchange (where both parties are normally on the same side operationally, if not always commercially) its use in vertical exchange (where interests are not fully commensurable and exchange is contested) is inevitable.

5.3 Objectively Feasible Outcomes in Vertical Business Relationships

The first thing that must be recognised about vertical business relationships (when an objective, economically rational perspective is adopted) is that exercises of power between buyers and suppliers are inevitable. The primary reason for this is because, even when they find ways of sustaining business relationships, there is a continuous and observable transactional tension, and sometimes conflict of interests, between the buyer and the supplier over the commercial and operational aspects of exchange.

As Figure 19 shows, while it is possible theoretically to envisage situations where buyers and suppliers could simultaneously achieve their ideal goals, this is not possible in practice because of the objective non-commensurability of interests between the two parties. This is because the operational and commercial ideal for the buyer (the maximum feasible increase in functionality given *x-efficiency*, conjoined with the maximum feasible reduction in the total costs of ownership, with suppliers experiencing either a loss, break-even or normal returns) is in direct (and observable) conflict with the operational and commercial ideal for the supplier. The supplier, ideally, searches for the maximum feasible *rents*, conjoined with the maximum feasible share of revenue and full market closure against competitors.

The buyer counts a win commercially, therefore, as a situation in which they are always able to reduce the total costs of ownership to their lowest feasible level for any given level of operational functionally. Commercially this means that, at whatever level of operational functionality the supplier is capable of operating, the ideal situation for the buyer is that the supplier makes a loss, only ever breaks-even, or earns low or normal profits that tend to zero. This is because the supplier's profits are a direct cost to the buyer.

If this is the commercial ideal for the buyer, the commercial ideal for the supplier is clearly in conflict. This is because the ideal for the supplier operationally is, for whatever level of operational functionality they are required to supply, that they achieve market closure against their competitors (win 100% of the available customer and/or market revenue available) but at the same time earn above normal returns. These *rents* if achieved are, however, a direct part of the cost of ownership for the buyer, and this explains why this type of vertical

140 Win-Win?

Figure 19: Feasible Commercial and Operational Outcomes in Buyer and Supplier Exchange

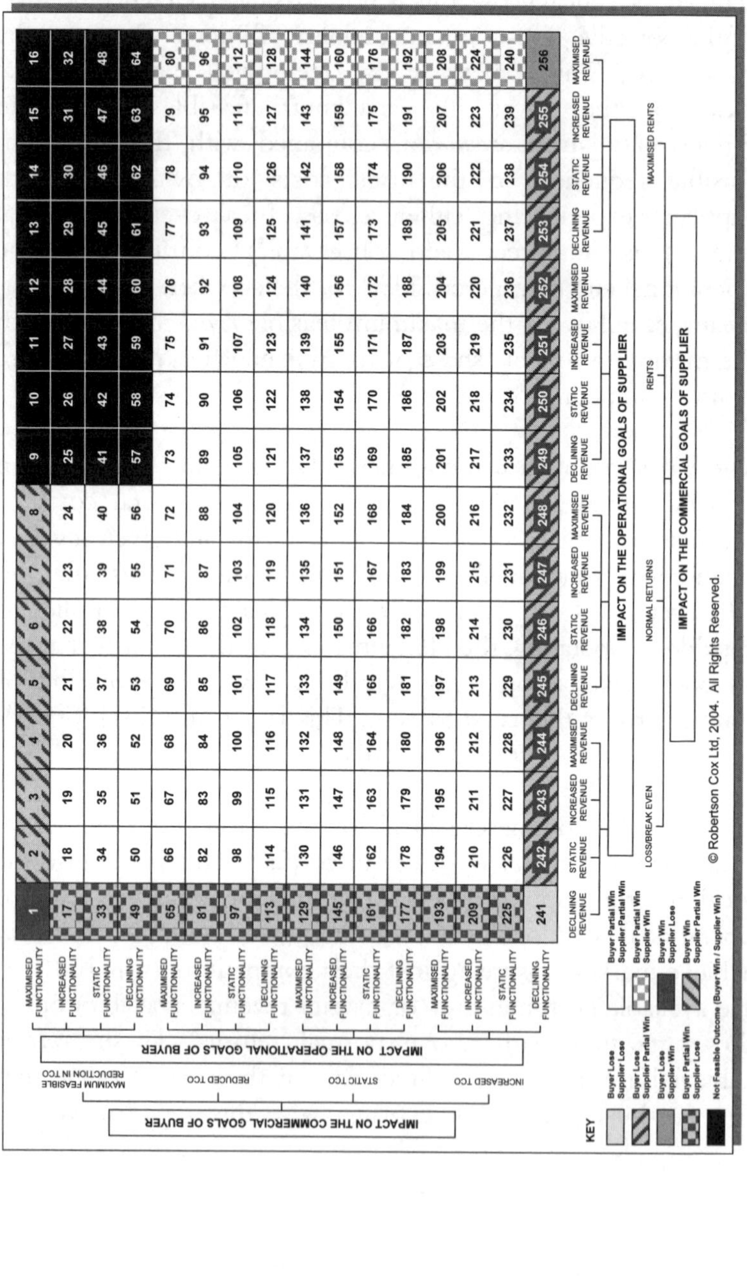

business relationship (unlike that in horizontal transactions) can never be fully commensurable operationally or commercially.

This means, as Figure 19 demonstrates, that, when one considers the full range of operational and commercial goals of buyers and suppliers, there are many more potential outcomes, in vertical than in horizontal business relationships. Furthermore, win-win outcomes based on *ideal mutuality* are simply not feasible and, because the objectives of the two parties are not the same commercially or operationally, *symmetrical mutuality outcomes,* in which both parties achieve exactly the same operational and commercial benefit, are also not feasible.

This means that, because both parties have non-commensurable interests (they are not pursuing the same operational and commercial goals or interests), the best that can be achieved will either be *zero-sum* outcomes (win-lose or partial win-lose for one party over the other) or *nonzero-sum* outcomes (a win-partial win for one party over the other or partial wins for both sides). In horizontal business relationships, therefore, *nonzero-sum symmetrical mutuality* outcomes are a common occurrence. In vertical business relationships, even when partial win-partial win outcomes occur, only *nonzero-sum asymmetrical mutuality* outcomes are feasible.

This is because, whichever partial win outcome occurs, there is nearly always a better alternative for both parties than the outcome that is currently being adopted. Furthermore, even in circumstances in which one party has achieved the most favourable partial win outcome that is feasible for them, there is always a superior alternative that their partner could be operating from. This implies, as we shall see in Figure 19, that in vertical business exchange all *nonzero-sum* outcomes are based on forms of *asymmetric mutuality*.

This means that in buyer and supplier exchange, even when *mutuality* occurs and relationships can be sustained, it is not possible (as it is in horizontal exchange) for both parties to experience exactly the same outcomes. Furthermore, whatever outcome is agreed upon, given that neither *ideal mutuality* nor *symmetrical mutuality* is feasible, there will always be a preferable outcome that both, or at least one, of the parties could aspire to than the arrangement that has been agreed upon. This explains why tension and conflict are inherent in all forms of buyer and supplier exchange, and not just in *zero-sum* outcomes.

To assist in our understanding of the inherent contested nature of buyer and supplier exchange, Figure 19 links the objective operational and commercial goals of buyers and suppliers when they enter into business transactions. This shows that both parties have divergent operational and commercial goals, and this is a clear difference when comparing vertical and horizontal business relationships. Ideally, the buyer is seeking operationally the maximum feasible increase in functionality (use value) that is possible from the supplier and, simultaneously, the maximum feasible reductions in their total costs of ownership commercially. On the other hand, the supplier is, ideally, seeking to maximise revenue for any given level of operational functionality that must be provided while, simultaneously, seeking to maximise profitability (Cox, 2004c; Cox, et al., 2004).

Given this, a buyer achieves a full or complete win if it is able to maximise increases in functionality (given *x-efficiency*) and also maximise the reduction in their total costs of ownership, with the supplier experiencing a loss, breaking even, or making only normal returns (that tend to zero). A partial win for the buyer occurs when a buyer receives any of the feasible functionality and total cost of ownership outcomes, except for maximum feasible increases in functionality with maximum feasible reductions in total costs of ownership at the same, or increased total costs of ownership with reduced functionality at the same time. A lose outcome occurs for the buyer when either no, or a reduced, functionality is received with increased total costs of ownership.

On the supplier's side, a full win occurs when both the maximum feasible *rents* and share of revenue are earned; a partial win occurs when *rents* (although not the maximum feasible) or normal returns are earned, with or without the maximisation of revenue share; and a lose occurs when a commercial loss, or break-even, is achieved, with a declining share of revenue from the transaction.

Applying these principles there are far more feasible relationship outcomes in vertical than in horizontal business relationships. Figure 19 shows, however, that the 32 *ideal mutuality* outcomes that involve a commercial win-win (cells 9, 10, 11, 12, 13, 14, 15, 16, 25, 26, 27, 28, 29, 30, 31, 32, 41, 42, 43, 44, 45, 46, 47, 48, 57, 58, 59, 60, 61, 62, 63 and 64) are not feasible in buyer and supplier exchange. This is because whatever the operational benefits to both parties, it is not feasible for both parties to simultaneously achieve the maximisation of their ideal commercial goals—maximum feasible reductions in the total cost of ownership for the buyer and maximum feasible *rents* for the supplier.

Despite the lack of practical feasibility for these 32 cases, it is clear that 224 commercial and operational outcomes are feasible in vertical relationships. Of these outcomes, some display forms of *asymmetrical mutuality* (*nonzero-sum* outcomes) while others result in winners and losers (*zero-sum* outcomes).

Apart from understanding that win-win outcomes are never feasible while lose-lose is a perfectly feasible outcome in vertical exchange, the first major distinction to make is between *zero-sum* and *nonzero-sum* outcomes. Based on the methodology used in Figure 19, there are 30 *zero-sum* outcomes that are feasible in buyer and supplier relationships. The most extreme forms of these are buyer wins/supplier loses (cell 1) and its converse buyer loses/supplier wins (cell 256). In both of these scenarios one party fully achieves everything that they ideally value, while their exchange partner receives either nothing that they value, or a decline in performance compared with the past. Clearly, these types of relationship outcomes are unlikely to be sustainable for very long unless there are countervailing transactions allowing one side to lose continuously with impunity.

The remaining 28 *zero-sum* outcomes (cells 17, 33, 49, 65, 81, 97, 113, 129, 145, 161, 177, 193, 209 and 225 favour the buyer; cells 242, 243, 244, 245, 246, 247, 248, 249, 250, 251, 252, 253, 254 and 255 favour the supplier) suffer from the same difficulties. While all 28 outcomes are less favourable to the buyer or the supplier than those in cells 1 and 256 respectively—because they only partially win and do not receive everything that they would ideally desire—one party is still experiencing a loss, and this implies that some countervailing support must be provided by the loser if the relationship is to be sustained over time.

Notwithstanding the desire by the loser in any of these relationships to sustain any of these *zero-sum* outcomes, it is also clear that some outcomes are likely to be more favourable to the interests of the winner than others. Despite this, the issue of which *zero-sum* outcomes are most favourable to buyers or suppliers is not necessarily a simple one—particularly in the case of buyers.

Assuming that the buyer is unconcerned about the sustainability of a relationship, or a supplier is able to provide a continuous 'loss leader', a buyer would normally prefer to achieve a win-lose (cell 1) to any of the other 14 partial win-lose outcomes that favour the interests of the buyer. This is because cell 1 provides the buyer with the maximum feasible reduction in the total costs of ownership *and* the maximum feasible increase in functionality, with the supplier making a loss or only breaking even with a declining revenue share.

Beyond this ideal outcome, however, the buyer often has to make some very difficult choices about alternatives. The buyer may understand what is ideal but, when a choice has to be made between maximising increases in functionality or reductions in the total cost of ownership, the buyer may be faced with very difficult choices indeed (Cox et al., 2004).

The reason for this is because particular buyers (and the organisations they represent) may require very different value propositions to be successful. What this means is that some buyers may need to prioritise reductions in the total costs of ownership above increases in functionality, while others may have to prioritise cost reductions over functionality improvements. If, therefore, both options cannot be maximised, it then depends on whether increases in functionality or reductions in the total costs of ownership are of relatively more or less significance for the buyer.

This is a problem that recurs for buyers in all vertical exchange transactions, and it cannot be defined away theoretically by saying that increases in functionality are always preferable to reductions in the total costs of ownership, or vice versa. The answer is that for particular buyers in specific organisations the relative importance of these two factors depends on circumstance and corporate strategy.

If cost leadership is the corporate strategy then reductions in the total costs of ownership may be preferable to increases in functionality. On the other hand, if differentiation is the corporate strategy then increases in functionality may be more important than reductions in the total costs of ownership. Unfortunately, it is rarely this simple when organisations have to think about these choices. This is because the relative importance of these two factors may vary across particular categories of spend within the same organisation.

This means that one cannot make categorical statements about which choices will be prioritised by buyers. All one can do is to make some general statements about rank order preferences, i.e. if the buyer prefers functionality over cost considerations and vice versa.

Assuming, therefore, that the buyer values an increase in functionality higher than a reduction in the total costs of ownership then their rank order preferences (after cell 1) will normally favour outcomes in cell 65, followed by those in cell 129 and then those in cell 193. This is because, while all of these outcomes maximise the increase in functionality, the first does so with reduced (if not maximally reduced) total costs of ownership, the second has static total costs of ownership, and it is only in the third option that the total costs of ownership increase.

Following this logic it is likely that the rank order preference of the buyer would then be for those outcomes that result in an increased (if not maximally increased) functionality relative to the total costs of ownership. That is outcomes in cell 17, followed by cell 81, then 145 and 209. Following the same logic the rank order preference would then be for static functionality outcomes in cell 33, then 97, 161 and 225. Finally, for this value proposition, it would be for those declining functionality outcomes that favour cost reduction opportunities in cells 49, then 113 and finally 177. The outcome in cell 241 does not figure in this context because it has a unique property. It is the least desirable relationship outcome that is feasible. It is the lose-lose (*zero-zero*) outcome for the buyer and the supplier in which neither party receives anything they value.

If, however, the buyer favours reductions in the total costs of ownership over increases in functionality then it is normal for the rank order preferences to change dramatically. In this case the rank order preference would place outcomes that provide for the maximum reduction in the total costs of ownership first, irrespective of the impact on functionality. The rank order preference would normally, however, favour first those outcomes that maximise cost reductions and also provide for some degree of improvement in functionality.

Thus, after cell 1 the rank order would normally be for those outcomes in cell 17, then 33, followed by 49, which all maximise cost reductions. Following this, those outcomes that reduce (without maximising the reduction of) costs would be preferred, with outcomes in cells 65, followed by those in 81, 97 and 113. The next preference would be for static costs of ownership in cells 129, then 145, 161 and 177. Finally, increased total costs of ownership outcomes would be mitigated by increases in functionality. In this way, the rank ordering of outcomes in cells 193, followed by 209 and, finally, by 225 would be normal.

This discussion shows that for buyers the trade-offs between functionality improvement and the total costs of ownership can have a marked impact on the choice of preferred outcomes. This is a significant fact in its own right, but of even greater importance when, as we shall see later, those who make buying decisions can use their own subjective preferences about outcomes, unconstrained by the objective logic of the organisations they represent. In this way, sub-optimal outcomes can easily occur because managers have subjective preferences of their own, or genuinely misconceive the objective requirements of their organisation for success.

This problem of subjective preferences and misconception also arises for suppliers when they think about rank order preferences, although it can be argued that it is normally less acute than for buyers. This is because, while suppliers also have to think carefully about the balance between commercial returns and operational revenue the choice is rarely as difficult to make. This does not mean that managers supplying goods and/or services do not make mistakes in these trade-offs—clearly they do—or that in some circumstances revenue issues may outweigh profitability considerations. On balance, however, the bottom line of profitability is nearly always the primary goal of business organisations and if this goal is not achieved satisfactorily, eventually, all else fails. Given this, the rank order choices of suppliers are normally somewhat easier to make.

Thus, it is obvious that cell 256 is the first priority of all suppliers when they consider *zero-sum* outcomes. In this outcome, the supplier maximises both the revenue and the *rents* that are achievable and fully closes the market to their competitors. Following this, since business is ultimately about making money rather than receiving revenue, then suppliers can normally be expected to favour outcomes that maximise commercial ends (profitability and returns) over operational means (revenue share). Thus, after cell 256, suppliers will normally prefer outcomes in cells 255, then 254 and 253. These all maximise *rents* but have variable outcomes relative to revenue shares.

Following these relatively benign options the supplier is likely to favour outcomes that provide *rents* (without maximising them) and prioritise the options once again based on the relative impact on revenue shares. Thus, outcomes in cells 252, then 251, 250, followed by 249 will be favoured. If *rents* cannot be earned the rank order preference will be for those outcomes that result in normal returns, but also have the greatest impact on revenue share. Thus, outcomes in cell 248 will be preferred to those in 247, followed by 246 and finally by those in 245. Finally, if a loss or break-even has to be endured outcomes in cell 244 will be preferred to those in 243 and, finally, to those in 242.

Obviously, if suppliers are experiencing short-term problems with revenue to run their business and value survival over profitability, if they have long-term strategies to provide 'loss leaders' to drive other competitors out of the market, or if they are using unbundled pricing strategies that create 'lock-in' with scope for opportunism post-contractually, then they will have very different rank order preferences—in the short-term at least. In these circumstances, revenue share without profits may be the primary short-term goal for the supplier. In such circumstances, the supplier can be expected to prefer all outcomes that maximise revenue rather than returns, although returns will still be a consideration.

In this situation the rank ordering can be expected to start again with cell 256 as the first preference because both revenue and returns are maximised. However, if the buyer will not provide all of the revenue with maximised returns then a supplier can be expected to offer the outcome in cell 252 (maximised revenue share with non-maximised *rents*), followed by 248 (maximised revenue with normal returns), and finally 244 (maximised revenue with a loss or break-even).

The second order preference in this scenario would then be cells 255, then 251, 247, and finally 243. These outcomes offer relatively declining returns in return for an increased share of revenue. The third option would be for outcomes in cells 254, then 250, 246, and finally 242 that offered declining returns for static revenue. Ultimately, the supplier might be forced to offer the fourth preference. These would be those outcomes in cells 253, followed by those in cells 249 and 245. These would offer declining returns for declining shares of revenue. Clearly, such supplier strategies are not sustainable in the long-term, and can only be countenanced in extremis when survival is paramount, or when countervailing profits are being made elsewhere to allow 'loss leaders' to be offered.

This discussion demonstrates that negotiating outcomes in buyer and supplier exchange is far more complex than in horizontal business relationships. This is because, with non-commensurable interests, and changing strategic emphases from both the buyer and the supplier, the scope for information asymmetry and bounded rationality by both parties about the intentions of the other is very high indeed. Both buyers and suppliers can clearly agree to very different outcomes—with markedly different consequences for their exchange partners—depending on the views they take about their respective short and long-term strategies and value propositions.

This problem is not confined to *zero-sum* outcomes because the same issues also arise in *nonzero-sum* outcomes. There are a limited number of these outcomes that are clearly asymmetrical and can be defined as a win-partial win for either the buyer or the supplier. The first group of win-partial win outcomes that are discussed here are the seven buyer win/supplier partially win outcomes. These are outcomes in which the buyer normally highly prizes in which it is possible to achieve maximum feasible improvements in functionality and the maximum feasible reduction in the total cost of ownership, while the supplier only achieves sub-optimal outcomes that only partially satisfy them.

Given that buyers can be expected to value both of these trade-offs, their rank order preferences are relatively simple in this case. The buyer can be expected to prefer the outcome in cell 2 first. This is because this provides for the maximum feasible functionality with the lowest feasible total costs of ownership (the supplier is making a loss or breaking even), and with the lowest relative dependency on the supplier (revenue is static and not being increased). This preference will normally be followed by cell 3 and then cell 4. While the outcome is the same (in functionality and cost terms), the difference relates to the relative dependency of the buyer on the supplier.

Following this logic, the buyer will then normally opt for outcomes in cell 5 followed by those in cells 6, 7 and, finally, 8. In these four outcomes the total costs of ownership are likely to be higher than in the previous grouping because the supplier is earning normal returns rather than a loss or breaking even. The rank ordering still follows the relative dependency logic with the buyer preferring outcomes that provide less rather than more dependency on the supplier.

Conversely, the views of the supplier about these outcomes are likely to be somewhat different. If they follow the logic of preferring returns over revenue, but seek to maximise revenue when they can, then they will prefer outcome 8 followed in order by 7, 6 and 5. This is because all of these options provide for above normal returns but some provide for more revenue than others. After this, suppliers are—in contrast to buyers—likely to prefer outcomes in cell 4, then 3 and, finally, 2. This is because, even when providing 'loss leaders' or breaking even, suppliers can be expected to prefer those options that maximise their revenue to those that do not.

If, on the other hand, the supplier prefers in the short-term to seek revenue more than returns then the suppliers rank order preferences for these outcomes would change. Now the supplier would prefer the outcome in cell 8 first, because it maximises revenue with normal returns. But after this they would prefer cell 4, which maximises revenue without a return. This might, for example, be desirable in cases were cash flow is essential to allow a company to survive. Following this logic the rank order preferences of the supplier would shift to outcomes in cells 7, then, 3, followed by those in cell 6 and 2. The outcome in cell 5 is from this perspective, the least desirable. This is because it only provides a declining revenue share even though normal returns can be made.

The same logic applies when considering the eleven buyer partial win/supplier win outcomes on Figure 19. Since these options are *asymmetric mutuality outcomes*, in which the supplier maximises *rents* and revenue, all of the outcomes are desirable, but some are more desirable than others. From the supplier's perspective it is clearly most desirable if when returns are maximised so are the costs that the buyer has to incur. This is because a cost increase generates higher revenue and, potentially, if the supplier's costs have not increased an even higher level of returns. At the same time the supplier would normally prefer not to pass value to the buyer in the form of maximised functionality (relative to *x-efficiency*) if they are able. This is because if they can hold some functionality improvements back they will be able to charge the buyer additional costs for any additional improvements in the future—thereby further maximising revenue and returns.

Given this logic, a supplier can be expected to prefer outcomes in cell 240. This is because in this circumstance the supplier can provide static functionality even though costs are increasing for the buyer and the supplier is still maximising revenue and returns. Following this, the supplier can be expected to prefer all other outcomes that increase the total costs of ownership for the buyer. This encompasses, first, outcomes in cell 224 followed by those in 208. If costs cannot be increased for the buyer then the supplier is likely to favour those outcomes that keep costs static. This means that the next rank ordering will be for those outcomes in cell 192 followed in turn by 176, 160 and 144. Finally, if costs have to be reduced the supplier will, in turn, prefer outcomes in cells 128, 112, 96 and, finally, 80.

The buyer in these circumstances does not have the same rank order preferences. If the buyer has to allow the supplier to make the maximum feasible returns and revenue share then the buyer can be expected to prefer outcomes that at least provide them with some of what they ideally desire. In this case the buyer would normally prefer the outcome in cell 80 first. This is because it allows them to achieve maximum feasible increases in functionality with reduced total costs of ownership. As we saw in the previous paragraph, this is the last preference in this grouping of outcomes for the supplier. This drives home the point that the objective preferences of buyers and suppliers are never the same in vertical business relationships.

Beyond this first preference for the buyer in cell 80, the problem arises once again that what outcome a buyer prefers depends on whether they value functionality improvements over reductions in the total costs of ownership. If a buyer prefers functionality to costs then the rank order preferences will run from outcomes in cell 80, through those in cells 144, 208, 96, 160, 224, 112, 176, 240, 128 to 192. If a buyer prefers costs reductions to functionality then the rank order preferences will run from outcomes in cell 80, through those in cells 96, 112, 128, 144, 160, 176, 192, 208, 224 to 240. It will be obvious that the rank ordering of preferences for these cost reducing outcomes for the buyer are the opposite of the preferences for the supplier described above.

These contrasting rank order preferences for buyers and suppliers, when they enter into negotiations over relationship outcomes, clearly demonstrates the contested nature of exchange in vertical business relationships. This analysis of win-partial win outcomes shows that buyers and suppliers can have very different preferences regarding relationship outcomes and the complex trade-offs over functionality, costs, revenue and returns. Furthermore, as a full analysis of the remaining partial win-partial win (*nonzero-sum mutuality*) outcomes that are feasible shows below, even though buyers and suppliers can agree to sustain relationships, unless one party finds itself in its most favoured position (given its current strategic needs, which may change over time) then there will always be more advantageous outcomes for one or both parties than the outcome currently agreed upon.

Interestingly enough, as Figure 19 demonstrates, there are far more partial win–partial win outcomes (175 in total) in vertical business relationships than any other potential outcomes. The 175 partial-win–partial win outcomes that are feasible far outweigh the other 18 win-partial win outcomes that make up the 193 total feasible *nonzero-sum* outcomes in vertical exchange. This implies that there should be many opportunities for buyers and suppliers to find accommodations that allow them to sustain business relationships with one another and avoid the 30 *zero-sum* outcomes of win-lose and partial win-lose.

Unfortunately, while this benign outcome may be feasible, the fact that partial win accommodations can be arrived at does not mean that they will be sustained. Indeed, given that partial win-partial win outcomes in vertical business relationships are always contested, it is more likely in practice that they will not be sustained than they will be sustained. There is one primary reason for this inherent instability in buyer and supplier exchange, and this is because, whatever partial win-partial win accommodation is arrived at, there is nearly always a preferable outcome for both, or for one, of the parties in the relationship. This implies that, unlike in horizontal business relationships, there is no *nonzero-sum* (or *positive-sum*) outcome that achieves *symmetrical mutuality*, where both parties can achieve an outcome that provides them with an equivalence of satisfaction.

Thus, even though one party may (given their current strategic requirements) have achieved their currently most advantageous partial win-partial win outcome, the other party will not be achieving either their ideal goal (cell 18 for the buyer if they value cost reductions more than functionality, or cell 66 if they value functionality over cost reductions/cell 239 for the supplier if they value returns over revenue, or cell 236 if they value revenue over returns).

This means that, unless the buyer or the supplier can find an exchange partner that is willing to accept the outcome that most favours them (a willing supplicant), their current exchange partners will only stay with them until a more conducive alternative can be found. This conclusion is also true even when one party is not able to achieve their most favourable outcome in the partial win-partial win category. For example, if a relationship outcome is currently located within cell 136 (static costs of ownership but maximum feasible increases in functionality for the buyer, with normal returns and the maximum revenues feasible for the supplier) there are always more desirable outcomes than this for both parties.

In this case the buyer would ideally prefer to find an exchange partner who would allow them to reduce the total costs of ownership in the direction of the maximum that is feasible, given *x-efficiency* now, and more importantly, in the future. The buyer would also prefer it if normal returns could be replaced by break-even or, if feasible, a supplier who was capable of providing this as a 'loss leader'. The supplier, on the other hand, would prefer to have a buyer who would allow them to increase the total costs of ownership so that they could make *rents*, but without having to increase functionality at all.

In such circumstances it is obvious that all vertical business relationships must be inherently unstable. This is because both parties are attempting to force outcomes in the direction of the ideal for them and, if this cannot be achieved, towards the most favourable position for their own interests that they can. Given this, it is clear that when *nonzero-sum* outcomes are considered buyers and suppliers will have very divergent views about rank order preferences, as the discussion below demonstrates.

Taking buyers first it is clear that their first preference for partial win-partial win outcomes will vary depending on whether they value functionality more than reductions in the total costs of ownership. Thus, if the buyer values functionality more then the most favourable outcome for them is cell 66 (maximised functionality with reduced total costs of ownership, with the supplier making a loss or breaking even, and receiving static revenue). This outcome provides the most favourable functionality outcome with the least dependency on the supplier, who is forced to operate without making any profits.

All outcomes that follow this logic will then be rank ordered according to whether or not they allow more or less dependency on the supplier. Thus, cell 67 will be preferred to cell 68 because the relative dependency on the supplier is less. The preferences of the buyer will then follow logically the pattern of preferring outcomes that provide for the same maximisation of functionality, but with limited dependency on the supplier in revenue terms relative to the profits being earned. Thus, after cell 68 the preference ordering will be for cells 69 through 79. But, given that maximising functionality improvement is key here, the rank ordering jumps after this to the series starting with cell 130 (that is static costs of ownership with maximum feasible improvements in functionality) and the rank ordering runs from cell 130 horizontally through to cell 143.

After this series, the buyer normally prefers the series that begins with cell 194 (increased total costs of ownership with maximum feasible improvements in functionality). The sequence would then follow the preference ordering of cell 194 horizontally through to cell 207. Buyers then normally prefer all outcomes that increase functionality but rank those outcomes that reduce total costs of ownership higher than those that do not. Thus, the remaining rank ordering for buyers who value functionality is cells 18 through 24, followed by 82 through 95, followed by 146 through 159, followed by 210 through 223, followed by 34 through 40, followed by 98 through 111, followed by 162 through 175, followed by 226 through 239, followed by 50 through 56, followed by 114 through 127 and, finally, 178 through 191.

If, on the other hand, the buyer values cost reductions more than functionality improvements then the rank ordering changes dramatically. Now the buyer will first seek out all outcomes in which cost reductions can be maximised and functionality improvements, while still important relatively, will be secondary when rank ordering. The first series that will be preferred will be those outcomes that maximise cost reductions with cell 18 being the preferred first choice outcome. The series here will run horizontally from cell 18 to 24 and be followed by cells 34 through 40 and then by cells 50 through 56. All of these outcomes provide for the maximum feasible reductions in the total costs of ownership, but are also ranked according to their ability to achieve functionality improvements and also to reduce the profits that suppliers earn and the buyer's relative dependency on the supplier.

Following this logic the buyer will then normally prefer all of the outcomes that reduce the total costs of ownership (without maximising this reduction). The series now runs horizontally from cell 66 to 79, followed by cells 82 through 95, followed by 98 through 111, followed by 114 through 127. The third series are those where the costs of ownership remain static and the rank ordering runs horizontally from cell 130 to 143, followed by 146 through 159, followed by 162 through 175, followed by 178 through 191. Finally, the series that involve increases in the total costs of ownership are ranked in relation to their ability to provide countervailing improvements in functionality. The series runs from cell 194 through 207, followed by 210 through 223, and finally 226 through 239.

This previous discussion demonstrates that the rank order preferences of buyers will change dramatically if they value functionality more than cost reduction and vice versa. The same logic applies to suppliers in partial win-partial win outcomes. The point to reflect upon here is, however, twofold. First, suppliers have very different rank order preferences if they value revenue more than returns and vice versa. Secondly, the rank order preferences of buyers and suppliers are never the same whatever value propositions they value most.

Suppliers who value returns over revenues (which is normally the case) will choose as their first preference outcome cell 239. This is because in this cell not only are *rents* maximised but revenue is increased and the buyer receives only a static level of functionality with increased costs of ownership, which may improve the revenue received by the supplier. This implies that, although this is not the supplier's ideal (the ideal outcome is cell 256 if relationships do not need to be sustained/cell 240 if they need to be sustained), it is the most favourable outcome within the *nonzero-sum* choices available.

Given this logic, it is inevitable that a supplier will then rank order all outcomes according to their ability to maximise returns, while limiting the demands of the buyer to reduce total costs of ownership and improve functionality. Revenue, while still important, will be a secondary consideration. Given this, the rank order preferences of the supplier who values returns

160   Win-Win?

over revenue will be for outcomes in cell 239 followed by 223, 207, 191, 175, 159, 143, 127, 111, 95 and 79, followed by 238, 222, 206, 190, 174, 158, 142, 126, 110, 94 and 78, followed by 237, 221, 205, 189, 173, 157, 141, 125, 109, 93 and 77. The rank order will then follow the logic of rank ordering the outcomes vertically in each column in Figure 19 starting with cells 236 to 76, followed by 235 to 75, followed by 234 to 74, followed by 233 to 73, followed by 232 to 24, followed by 231 to 23, followed by 230 to 22, followed by 229 to 21, followed by 228 to 20, followed by 227 to 19 and, finally, from 226 to 18.

If, however, the supplier values revenue more than returns then the rank order changes and the first preferred outcome is in cell 236. This is where the supplier maximises revenue and achieves normal returns, and the buyer receives static functionality and an increase in the total costs of ownership. This is clearly the preferred option because it is the outcome that allows the supplier to maximise revenue, while also increasing the costs incurred by the buyer, without having to incur costs on improving functionality.

All other options are then rank ordered based on this logic. The second preference is the outcome in cell 220. This is similar to the outcome in cell 236, but now the supplier has to incur costs on improving functionality. The rank order in this series also runs vertically through the columns depicted in Figure 19 until the buyer is able to force the supplier to reduce the costs of ownership, which reduces the revenue received.

The logic here, therefore, rank orders the outcomes vertically in each column in Figure 19, starting with outcomes in cell 236 to 76, followed by all of those outcomes that maximise revenue. That is outcomes in cells 232 to 24, and 228 to 20. This series is then followed by all of those that increase revenue without maximising it. This means outcomes in cell 239 to 79, followed by 235 to 75, followed by 231 to 23, followed by 227 to 19. After this, all outcomes that result in static revenue will be rank ordered using the same logic. Thus, outcomes in cells 238 to 78, followed by 234 to 74, followed by 230 to 22, followed by 226 to 18. Finally, all those outcomes that result in declining revenue, but which have countervailing improvements in returns, will be rank ordered. That is cells 237 to 77, followed by 233 to 73, followed finally by 229 to 21.

The discussion here shows that there are many choices available to buyers and suppliers when they enter into relationships, and that their preferences vary widely. This underlines the central argument of this book. This is that horizontal and vertical business relationships have some similar but also some very different properties, and that buyer and supplier exchange is always contested due to an objective non-commensurability of interests. No clearer demonstration of these differences, and of the inherent conflict and tension in buyer and supplier exchange, can be made than the conclusion arrived at here, that neither *ideal mutuality* nor *symmetrical mutuality outcomes* are feasible in vertical business relationships.

The most graphic demonstration of these conclusions is the fact that even when buyers and suppliers engage in *nonzero-sum* outcomes their rank order preferences are never the same. Ultimately, therefore, all vertical business relationships are unstable due to the constant pressure of objective commercial logic on both parties to find superior relationship outcomes than those that they have currently achieved.

As we saw, however, even in cases when one party is able to achieve its ideal or most favoured outcome it is unlikely that this will remain a sustainable outcome for long. This is because for one party in the relationship to accept the ideal, or the most favourable, relationship outcome for another implies that they are not pursuing their own objective interests to the full. Such outcomes can, however, be sustained in the real world because individuals can subjectively misconceive their own and/or their organisation's objective economic interests. Furthermore, they can decide that the ideal is unattainable and become permanent willing supplicants to dominant buyers or suppliers (i.e. turn necessity into a virtue and accept only low returns like Wal-Mart and Toyota have done as suppliers). These issues are discussed in more detail in the next chapter.

The arguments presented here also raise important questions about how to manage vertical business relationships effectively. The analysis here shows that, while writers can write about transparency, trust and mutuality as the basis for sustaining business relationships, such arguments may be dangerous if they are used unthinkingly. This is because if there is inherent conflict and tension in business relationships then power (the ability to leverage value for oneself from others in circumstances of observable conflicts of interest between two parties) must also exist. Given this, current thinking about the inherent value of trust and/or transparency as *the* means by which business relationship alignment can be achieved must be questioned.

There is, however, a final problem, which was discussed briefly above and also in Chapter 1. This is the concept of economic false consciousness, which is discussed in the next chapter. Business relationships—especially those involving buyers and suppliers—often succeed (both parties are happy with the outcome) even though they should not. The reason for this is because individuals often do not fully understand the difference between objective and subjective perceptions of reality in business exchange. In the next chapter the problem that occurs for commercial value appropriation from a misunderstanding of objective and subjective interests is discussed in more detail.

6

False Consciousness in Business Relationships: The Problem of Subjective and Objective Interests

The discussion so far has been informed by the idea that it is impossible to define a win-win (*ideal mutuality*) unless an objective definition of this is provided for particular types of business relationships. Only by doing so is it possible to rescue the win-win concept from its current highly subjective, confused and tautological meaning. In doing so it has been argued that win-win (a *positive-sum* outcome) may not be feasible in all types of business relationships and, paradoxically perhaps, that mutuality (a *nonzero-sum* outcome) is not always necessary to sustain some types of relationships.

Despite this, many readers may be still unconvinced by the arguments presented here. This is because most people still believe that a win-win (a *positive-sum* outcome) is always feasible. This is primarily because of the problems of economic or commercial false consciousness, associated with a misunderstanding of the difference between objective and subjective interests in business exchange.

This lack of conceptual clarity is explained in more detail in this penultimate chapter. The discussion explains why it is that many commentators and practitioners are guilty of a form of economic or commercial false consciousness. That is, they subjectively misconceive the objective economic or commercial situation within which they are operating. The discussion that follows is informed by an analysis of the problem of subjective and objective interests in relation to the operational and commercial value trade-offs experienced in horizontal and vertical business relationships.

6.1 The Problem of Objective and Subjective Conceptions of Commercial and Operational Value

It is often said that: "all that glitters is not gold". Just because something can be done operationally does not mean that it has any commercial value. This is a truism but many practitioners, and those who advise them, fail to understand this simple fact of life. Take, for example, the millions of words written and man hours devoted to lean approaches to production and supply management. While no one can doubt the operational benefits that companies have achieved in reducing unnecessary waste and inefficiency in their internal and external processes from the adoption of lean tools and techniques, one might still question the overall commercial benefit of this activity.

The reason for doing so is that it is not clear that car assemblers (the firms in which these operational practices were first developed) have derived any significant overall commercial value from implementing them. Given that the car industry still earns only very low returns in the 0% (or worse) to 3% range annually, with many western car manufacturers facing junk bond status, one might wonder what the commercial value is for companies utilising these tools—especially when all of the improvement in commercial and operational value appears to be passed to end customers, and is not retained by the innovating companies in the market or supply chain. As a result, one might argue that these operational approaches are, relatively speaking, nothing more than a treadmill to commercial oblivion or poor performance. That is, firms survive with losses, break-even or make low normal returns at best, but can never hope to earn *rents*.

The problem is even worse than this in some cases. In the car and other mature manufacturing industries one might at least be able to argue that if a company does not use lean tools and techniques they could find themselves out of business altogether. In this case there must be some commercial benefit from the use of this operational approach, even though these commercial benefits are small. In some industries—like construction, food and fmcg retailing, shipbuilding and farming—it is clear, however, that the adoption of these principles operationally has only limited commercial benefit for many participants in the chain.

In the construction industry it has long been apparent that the adoption of lean production and supply principles are only of limited value, and for only a few participants in the chain. This is because of the project and ad-hoc nature of demand that makes the implementation of lean operational practices beyond the internal boundary of the firm almost impossible, except for those supply chain actors with a high level of continuous and standardised demand (Cox and Townsend, 1998).

Morevoer, many suppliers now see the adoption of vendor-managed inventory in the retail sector as a recipe for post-contractual 'hold-up' by buyers (Milgrom and Roberts, 1992). This is a process by which the supplier operationally manages the inventory system for the buyer in as lean a manner as possible. Unfortunately, because of its dependence on the buyer for business, the supplier also takes all of the commercial risk in the process, and normally earns only low returns even after developing close collaborative operational working relationships with the buyer.

In the shipbuilding and farming industries the problem is potentially even more acute. Recent attempts by the DTI and MOD in the UK to improve efficiency operationally through the adoption of lean management techniques appear to have had only limited impact on the commercial profitability of the majority of those operating within these chains (Sanderson, 2004; Cox, Chicksand and Palmer, 2004).

This evidence of commercial myopia about the benefits of operational activities is mirrored by the example of IBM in the IT industry. IBM managed to record two of the largest commercial losses in corporate history in 1992 and 1993, while still being able to claim that operationally they had more patents than any other company in the world. IBM simply did not understand that just because they had achieved something operationally this practice might not have much commercial value at all. This is to confuse operational means with commercial ends.

Similarly, in a recent consulting engagement, with a now defunct insurance company, it was discovered that the company had been able to attract more customers than any of its competitors by the use of direct selling methods (i.e. using television advertising and internet-based methods to win customers without using brokers as intermediaries). The company, however, while having the largest number of customers in the market, made no profit from handling their business. When asked why the company was pursuing this recipe for corporate disaster (they were clearly operating in commercially lose-win or lose-partial win outcomes with their customers) the senior managers explained that selling direct was now industry standard practice and they were simply doing operationally the same as everyone else.

It is hardly surprising that this company was eventually taken over by a much better managed insurance company. This new company understood that, just because direct selling in the UK insurance market had helped Direct Line to make money initially, once everyone started doing it and competing on price to win the business, this technique did not necessarily provide a way of making acceptable returns for anyone. The new company retained direct sales but stopped competing for business that did not make a profit.

What follows from this discussion is the realisation that one must be careful in assuming that, just because something can be done operationally, it will have a commercial value that warrants the necessary investment of time and effort in the innovation (Cox et al., 2003). Furthermore, even if an operational improvement in one company in a particular industrial and commercial context does lead to success, this does not mean that the same operational innovation will also lead to success for those who copy it in a completely different operational and commercial context (Cox, 1997a).

It is important, therefore, to understand which operational improvements lead to commercial benefits and those that do not. Furthermore, when it comes to working closely with exchange partners (especially in vertical business relationships between buyers or suppliers), it is important to recognise that what may be operationally and/or commercially beneficial for one party may not be equally so for the other partner in the exchange relationship. This means that the trade-offs over operational and commercial value that occur in horizontal business relationships must be differentiated carefully from those in vertical business relationships.

What this means is that business relationships of any type (horizontal or vertical) cannot exist unless there is some form of operational interaction (although this can be relatively arm's-length or highly collaborative for both horizontal and/or vertical relationships). When there is operational linkage of this type it is possible—and especially in more collaborative relationships—that there can be operational gains from exchange even though commercial gains for one or both parties may be low, and in some instances non-existent.

When this occurs the possibility arises that managers on either side of a relationship may come to value the operational more than the commercial gains from exchange—or perhaps lose sight of the commercial ends in pursuit of operational means that satisfy their own personal goals rather than those of the organisations that they represent. For those involved extensively in competence development in business it is painfully apparent that this is a common problem. All too often serious misconceptions about the basic principles of business (forms of commercial myopia) can be discerned amongst managers.

First, managers often do not understand, from an economically rational point of view, what *ideal* outcomes are commercially (i.e. they do not understand the difference between profits and *rents*, and what causes the latter to occur). This means that they have a subjective misunderstanding of the logic of commercial exchange. The second problem is that, because they do not understand commercial exchange, they tend to value operational benefits—things that make their life easier or their job simpler—without fully understanding the impact of any particular operational initiatives on commercial outcomes.

Third, because managers do not understand the relationship between operational means and commercial ends, they are often guilty of path-dependency (Dosi, 1995). Path-dependency means that managers and their organisations collectively learn how to undertake certain operational activities that may have led to success in one commercial circumstance, but do not develop an ability to unlearn old ways of working when circumstances change commercially. As a result, path-dependency can lead companies to fail because managers, like old dogs, cannot learn new tricks.

Finally, most managers are never trained in entrepreneurship or the principles of commercial and operational leverage. This is for two major reasons. Business Schools do not necessarily train managers in the principles of commercial and operational leverage because many management academics themselves have had limited experience in the real world of business and do not understand transactional exchange commercially. Indeed, management academics often believe that win-win outcomes are always feasible and/or believe that business should adopt social as well as commercial goals.

Given this, it is hardly surprising that those trained in management schools are often unready for the reality of commercial and operational exchange in business transactions. More worrying perhaps is the glaring problem that most managers entering companies do not even attend Business School and have never been trained in the principles of business management or economics. Indeed, most managers have studied anything but business or economics related subjects, and learn the reality of transactional exchange on the job—if, that is, they are lucky enough to be exposed to it when they enter business.

Furthermore, very few induction programmes for new entrants in organisations have training elements focused directly on learning about the realities of business and economic exchange. This is clearly one of the most glaring competence and training gaps in modern organisations. This is because in western countries many young people live an economically cosseted life far removed from the harsh realities of business exchange and leverage.

As a result, in many large organisations, especially where there has been a history of structural dominance in markets, it is not surprising to find very senior managers who have no real understanding of the commercial principles of business and who have risen to the top by dint of their ability to play internal political games. Given this, it is not surprising that many senior, as well as, junior and middle managers fail to demonstrate any real understanding of the objective realities of transactional exchange when confronted with the principles discussed here. Nor is it surprising, therefore, that there is often considerable evidence of serious commercial incompetence within companies at all levels of management.

Given the lack of appropriate commercial training, plus the lack of time and resources that are normally available within companies to develop the competence of their staff, or to allow them to undertake the level of work necessary for them to fully comprehend the transactional motives of their relationship partners, it is hardly surprising that managers tend to rely on the pursuit of their own subject conceptions about value and interests, when they have to make decisions about what to do and how to do it. Experience in numerous consulting engagements shows that a high proportion of managers simply do not understand the basic principles of commercial and operational leverage in business.

Despite this, experience shows that they do have ways of overcoming this problem. In practice, however, most managers have personal rules of thumb that allow them to make decisions about what they should do operationally and commercially when involved in internal and external transactions. Given the lack of proper understanding amongst managers about the commercial consequences of operational actions (and the lack of robust and rigorous tools and techniques within organisations to force myopic individuals to make the correct decisions), most managers appear to use a proxy when deciding what should be done. This proxy is nearly always what the manager believes is in his or her own subjectively perceived best interest.

Commercial false consciousness (or subjective myopia about the realities of commercial and operational exchange) arises in business, primarily, because managers normally think, first, about how any operational activity will affect their career and/or status within an organisation, and only in the most indirect way about the relative significance of any operational activity to the overall commercial well-being of the company as a whole. This helps to explain, for example, why it is that the greatest obstacle to innovation in buying is the perceived risk of any innovation to the career development of the buyer and not to the performance of the company. What this means is that any innovation by a buyer in finding new suppliers will be first factored against the potential risk that any sourcing innovation poses to the career and standing of the buyer (particularly if anything goes wrong), and only second against the potential commercial and operational benefits of this course of action to the company for which they work.

This superimposing of subjectively perceived personal interests onto the objective interests of the organisation is a common problem. It is not, however, a form of irrationality by human beings. It is, in fact, a perfectly rational response by individuals who have never been properly trained in the objective principles of commercial and operational exchange, and who are experiencing very high levels of environmental uncertainty. This predilection also helps to explain why it is that so much operational practice in business is not innovative but is, in fact, based on benchmarking or catch up thinking (Cox, 1997a).

Since managers do not want to take risks with their own careers, or with their standing in organisations, they tend to favour actions that achieve acceptable commercial requirements (and especially those that minimise any personal risk to their own careers) rather than those actions that carry heavier personal risk but which might maximise commercial returns to the organisation. This is another way of saying that managers tend to be risk averse.

The argument here is not that they are necessarily driven to be risk averse by the requirements of the organisation, but rather by their own personal predilections for career advancement. This means that, paradoxically, while all organisations say that they wish to reward innovation and risk taking, most organisations unwittingly incentivise risk aversion. This is because risk taking for most individuals in most organisations is a one-way bet. If a risk with uncertainty is taken, and it succeeds in providing successful innovation, then the manager knows that their boss will probably claim credit for it. If, on the other hand, it fails most managers know that they will be blamed and that they will potentially lose their job, or at the very least their prospects of rapid advancement in the company. All managers understand completely the aphorism that "success has many fathers; but failure is an orphan".

In these circumstances, managers will tend to be risk averse in relation to their own careers, and this reinforces the natural tendency to superimpose what is subjectively (and also arguably in the short-term objectively) good for them on to what is also objectively good for the company. If these subjective perceptions of value and interests by managers are also based on a subjective lack of understanding of commercial reality then the propensity for organisational false consciousness (or commercial and operational myopia) will be very high indeed.

These tendencies within organisations also help to explain why it is that innovation only ever really occurs in established companies when commercial reality (normally some form of external shock from competitors or occasionally governments and/or regulators) fundamentally challenges the organisation's survival. In such circumstances individual personal preferences, and the historic internal and external power structures and operational ways of thinking and acting that have been created to support them, are often fundamentally challenged. In the new commercial and operational reality those individuals, whose subjective predilections stand in the way of economic rationality, are either swept away or the company—by clinging to objectively irrational ways of working and thinking—will not survive.

It is clear, therefore, that for all of these reasons many managers in business suffer from economic false consciousness. This means that they do not really understand the objective reality of transactional exchange. This commercial and operational myopia is reinforced also by the tendency to superimpose subjective preferences onto the objective goals of the organisation, and also by the fact that those engaged in transactions of all types also suffer from bounded rationality as a result of the conscious and unconscious use of information asymmetry (Simon, 1955; Akerlof, 1970; Molho, 1997).

Indeed, when managers who do understand the objective reality of transactional exchange better than their relationship partners are able to indulge in the conscious use of information asymmetry, they normally achieve superior outcomes commercially and operationally than they ought to (given the structural resources available to both parties). When this happens then opportunism—self-seeking interest with guile—is clearly in play in transactions (Williamson, 1993). This use of opportunism grounded in information asymmetry, as we shall see in the final chapter, is one of the key power resources available to transaction partners when they indulge in business relationships, and one that makes the unthinking and non-calculative use of trust and transparency in business relationships fraught with danger (Williamson, 1985, 1996).

Managers are often, therefore, guilty of economic false consciousness, or a subjective misunderstanding of the objective reality they are experiencing. They often do not understand the objective principles of business commercially, and they frequently value operational gains without fully understanding their objective commercial benefits. As we shall see, this problem is most acute in vertical rather than horizontal business relationships. This is because both parties are more often on the same operational and commercial side in horizontal business relationships. This is not the case in vertical business relationships where legally separate organisations must first pursue their own commercial and operational goals in an environment where there is an objective conflict of commercial and operational interests.

What follows from this is that, in practice, even though it is possible to define objectively what a commercial and operational win-win means, most managers appear to believe that a win-win occurs if they subjectively value (find reasonable or acceptable) whatever is done operationally or commercially with their exchange partners. Thus, if both parties are satisfied that they have received some form of operational and/or commercial benefit, then most managers would see the outcome as a win-win.

This way of defining a win-win is clearly tautological. This is because the concept becomes whatever the manager involved subjectively (or for that matter any omniscient academic observer) believes it to be. This way of thinking can lead to bizarre outcomes. In one case the senior managers in a company explained to the author that they had just experienced a win-win with a major consultancy company because, although the strategies that the highly paid consultants had provided to restructure the company strategically had failed to deliver any real commercial value, they themselves had not been sacked for the failure. The reason for this was that, having paid very prestigious consultants to develop their strategy, they could not be blamed if it had not worked. They had bought the best—and paid a premium price for doing so. If these consultants could not come up with a successful strategy then the managers who had employed them (and also their superiors in the company) felt they could not really be blamed for failure.

On closer inspection, we can see that what may have been in the subjective interests of the managers was not necessarily in the objective interest of the company they represented. While the managers involved had experienced, from their subjective perceptions, a win—they had received operational benefit (a strategy) and protected their jobs—they had not received anything of tangible commercial value for the company they represented. This was because the strategy had failed to deliver.

In this sense the organisation they represented (and its shareholders) was, objectively speaking, the commercial loser. It had paid for something operational that was of no real commercial value. The supplier in this case, however, was clearly the winner. They had provided something operational that did not deliver the expected commercial return, but they had received a fee that provided them with above normal returns (*rents*).

Obviously, the consulting firm might lose in the long-term if it developed a reputation for constantly failing to deliver commercially successful operational strategies. On the plus side for the consultancy company was the fact that in implementing strategies there are so many intervening variables that militate against a clear delineation of causality that it is always difficult to assign exact blame for failure to any one cause. The consultants could argue that, rather than it being due to their poor strategising, the failure occurred because of unforeseeable changes in market forces, or due to the failure internally by managers to implement exactly what the consultants had recommended.

This inability to clearly define causality means that sometimes it is possible for both parties to an exchange to subjectively believe that a win-win has occurred when in fact, objectively speaking, it has not. Using the approach recommended here to analyse this case we can see that it was not, therefore, a win at all from the buyer's perspective (meaning the company and not its senior managers). Objectively speaking, it was a commercial lose. This is because the company did not receive any real improvement in functionality—it did not receive an improved strategy—and the total costs of ownership were very high, allowing the supplier to make above normal returns.

Subjectively, however, from the managers' perspective, it was a win-win. This was because the managers in the buying company received what they wanted operationally (a strategy without risks to their own careers), and they could pass the commercial failure off onto other factors. The suppliers achieved everything they desired operationally and commercially, so for them it was a subjective as well as an objective win (assuming of course that their reputation was not seriously affected by the failure of their proposed strategy— which it was not given that they are still used regularly by the company in question for the majority of their strategy work and also by many other blue chip companies).

As a result of this, it is clear that, because of economic false consciousness and their ability to superimpose subjective interests on to the objective interests of organisations, managers can make quite serious errors in their judgements about whether or not they are, or are not, objectively experiencing a win, partial win or lose outcome from a business relationship. Furthermore, if this can happen then there must be scope for continuous sub-optimality and error in the way in which managers operate in business transactions. As we shall see below, this is why managers often subjectively misconceive what they are engaged in operationally with others as a win-win, when objectively what is happening is far from this reality commercially and operationally.

6.2 *The Seeds of False Consciousness: Understanding Subjective Conceptions of Commercial and Operational Trade-Offs in Business Relationships*

The discussion above shows that companies experience operational and commercial trade-offs. When these occur it is clear, however, that—since business is ultimately about making money—commercial outcomes should always be more important than operational outcomes, although they are always inextricably linked. Thus, it is operational innovations that provide the basis for commercial gains from trade. This means that managers have to be cognisant of the impact of operational improvements on commercial realities all of the time.

Objectively speaking, therefore, managers ought only really to value those operational outcomes that occur in cells B and A in Figure 11 in Chapter 5. This is because only these operational activities provide the basis for high levels of commercial return. In cell C, the operational activities do not improve and neither does commercial performance. Paradoxically perhaps, in cell D, operational improvement does not increase commercial performance and so is a waste of time, unless the improvements can be used in other interrelated relationships to generate higher commercial returns. If this does not occur then the operational improvements are of little value commercially.

Unfortunately, while Figure 11 provides an indication of the objectively rational rank ordering of outcomes that ought to occur in business relationships, it is possible for managers to have subjective views about what should count as a commercial gain and also as an operational improvement. Thus, it is possible, as we saw above, for managers to believe that an operational improvement is important because it provides them personally with an easier life, even though it does not really generate improved commercial returns for their organisation.

This type of outcome could occur, for example, if a manager decided that he or she should employ several assistants to do their work so that they could play golf more often. As a result, the cost of operations would rise without any improvement in commercial gain. It would also occur if a manager outsourced the activities of the organisation to another company with no discernible improvement in operational practices and commercial performance. In other words, it is more than possible for managers to do things that they highly value operationally, but which have no objective commercial value whatsoever.

Similarly, if an operational improvement is implemented that does impact on commercial performance in such a way that an objectively discernible improvement is achieved, but this falls short of the creation of *rents*, and makes only a small improvement in profitability, a manager could still perceive this as a win commercially, even though it is less than ideal. This would occur if a manager spent a considerable amount on an operational innovation (say process improvement work with consultants) that provided some reduction in operating costs without impacting significantly on corporate overall performance. An example might be internal cost reductions that provided a small improvement in bottom line performance to raise profits annually from 1% to 1.25%. This would be a commercial gain but, objectively speaking, the company would still be achieving only a partial win (low or normal returns) rather than a true win (*rents*).

This problem of intra-organisational economic false consciousness (where managers are able to set their own subjective performance standards against which a win outcome is measured internally) is one thing, but it can be exacerbated significantly when inter-organisational relationships occur—and especially in vertical business relationships. If it is possible for managers to subjectively misconceive what a win means internally with respect to their own company's performance, this problem is multiplied when considering the impact of any operational activities on the performance of legally independent parties to an exchange.

Obviously, this problem of subjective misconception of the commercial consequences of operational practices exists, but it is arguably less acute in horizontal rather than in vertical business relationships. This is because in most, although not all, horizontal business relationships the two parties to the exchange cannot ultimately avoid the commercial consequences of what they do operationally together. In this sense most horizontal business relationships are very similar to intra-company relationships, in that what is being done operationally will eventually be objectively visible to all parties—although the problem of disentangling what is the objective causal relationship between any particular operational intervention and commercial outcomes internally within the *joint venture* or *strategic alliance* entity still remains.

Inter-organisationally, however, this problem of internal false consciousness is duplicated. This is because there can be subjective misconception of what a win-win outcome is on both sides of an exchange. Thus, in both companies it is possible for managers to have a false perception of what the relationship is between operational activities and commercial outcomes, as well as a complete misunderstanding of what the objectively ideal goals are for each company when they enter into exchange relationships. This means that, when managers interact across corporate boundaries, both parties can have their own subjective definitions of what commercial and operational gains are. This makes the win-win concept extremely difficult to disentangle and sustainable business relationship alignment so difficult to achieve (Cox et al., 2004; Cox, 2004c).

Given this problem of the subjective perception of interests, Figure 20 demonstrates the subjective reality of business relationships when two parties to an exchange interact in ignorance of objective reality. As the Figure shows, when managers can subjectively decide what level, or type, of operational and/or commercial gain is to count as a win then, rather than only one theoretically possible win-win outcome being possible (see Figure 1 earlier), it is possible for managers to consider nine outcomes as a potential form of win-win. This is because, subjectively speaking, each party perceives that they are achieving something that they subjectively value operationally and/or commercially.

From a subjective point of view, therefore, the nine win-win outcomes (all of which can be regarded as forms of mutuality in this way of thinking) are cell 2 (*commercial and operational win for A/operational win for B*); cell 3 (*commercial and operational win for A/commercial win for B*); cell 4 (*commercial and operational win for A and B);* cell 6 (*commercial win for A/operational win for B*); cell 7 (*commercial win for A and B*); cell 8 (*commercial win for A/commercial and operational win for B*); cell 10 (*operational win for A and B*); cell 11 (*operational win for A/commercial win for B*); and, finally, cell 12 (*operational win for A/commercial and operational win for B*).

Figure 20: **Subjectively Perceived Commercial and Operational Trade-Offs in Business Relationships**

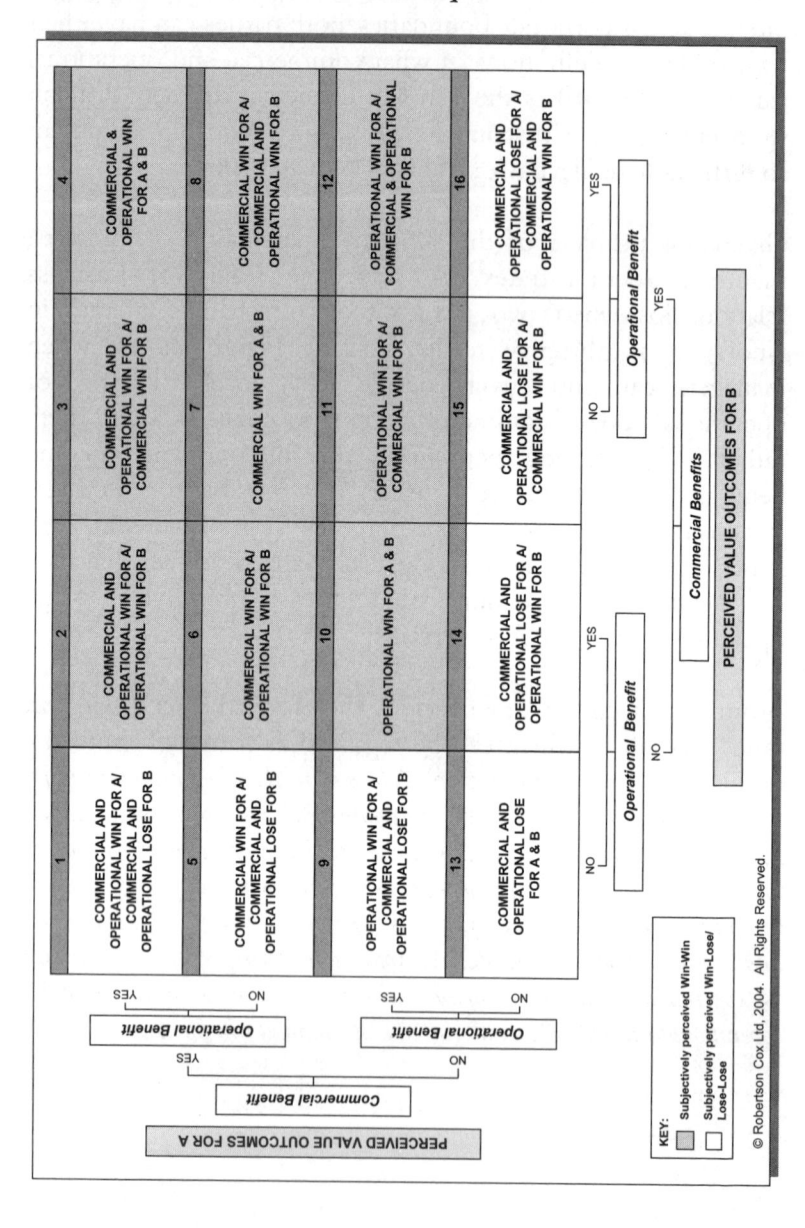

This subjective perception of the gains from trade also leads to the delineation of seven potential lose outcomes rather than the five analysed objectively in Figure 1. These are the outcomes in cell 1 (*commercial and operational win for A/ commercial and operational lose for B*); cell 5 (*commercial win for A/ commercial and operational lose for B*); cell 9 (*operational win for A/ lose for B*); cell 13 (*commercial and operational lose for both A and B*); cell 14 (*commercial and operational lose for A/ operational win for B*); cell 15 (*commercial and operational lose for A/ commercial win for B*): and, finally, cell 16 (*commercial and operational lose for A/ commercial and operational win for B*).

It is clear that when managers interact in business relationships that it is these sorts of subjective considerations that inform their judgements about whether or not a win-win outcome has occurred. Managers normally assume that if they receive something operationally and/or commercially that they subjectively value from a relationship then they have achieved a win and, if the other side has also achieved something that they subjectively value, then it is possible to talk about a win-win relationship.

This way of thinking recognises, of course, that it would be best if both parties could achieve all of the benefits that they subjectively value operationally and commercially (cell 4). Nevertheless, when this cannot be achieved, this way of thinking assumes that relationships will be more sustainable if individuals on both sides are achieving more, rather than less, of what they subjectively value. Thus, it is likely that, after cell 4, where both parties maximise their subjective commercial and operational goals, there would be a somewhat different rank ordering of preferences over outcomes by both parties.

Thus party A might be agnostic about cells 2, 3 or 4 in the sense that they are achieving everything they desire, whatever the other party achieves. Obviously, however, if relationships need to be sustained (and are not one-off games) then it is likely that A would normally favour cell 4 followed by cell 3 (because B ought to value commercial more than operational gains) followed by cell 2 and then by cell 1. In all of these outcomes A achieves everything they desire.

The second series of rank order preferences is for those outcomes that provide A with a commercial rather than operational gain. Thus, other things being equal, A ought to prefer outcomes in cell 8, ahead of those in cell 7, followed by those in cell 6 and, finally, those in cell 5. This is because in each of these cells A is achieving a commercial gain. The rank order simply indicates that if the relationship is to be sustained then it is better to operate in an environment in which B achieves more rather than less of that which they subjectively desire.

Following this logic A should, where it is unable to make a commercial gain, rank order those outcomes in which they achieve an operational gain that most favours B. This means that A would rank order its preferences as cell 12, followed by cell 11, cell 10 and cell 9. Finally, one might expect A to be completely agnostic about cells 13, 14, 15 or 16 since they all represent lose outcomes for them. If they were vindictive, however, they might subjectively rank order their lose preferences as 13, first, followed by 14, then 15 and, finally, 16. The rationale for this rank ordering is based on the view that if A is losing then B should as well.

It follows that the rank ordering preferences of B would be slightly different. This is because B is likely, after cell 4, to pursue their own subjective interests, not those of A. This indicates that there is still scope for tension in business relationships, even when subjective perceptions of outcomes is considered. After cell 4 it is likely, based on the logic outlined for A above, that B would rank order their preferences as cell 8, followed by cell 12 and then cell 16. Following this series they would then normally prefer cell 3, cell 7, cell 11 and cell 15. In the third series they would then favour cell 2, followed by cell 6, cell 10 and, finally, cell 14. While being generally agnostic about the final four choices that are lose outcomes, they might be expected to prefer cell 13 outcomes and then cell 9 followed by cell 5 and, finally, cell 1.

The problem with this way of thinking is that, while it seems logical at first sight from an economically rational point of view, the assumptions it is based on may be very dangerous indeed. The first problem is that, if the definition of a win or a win-win is purely subjective, then managers may adhere to none of the rank order preferences that have been outlined above. This is because a manager could decide that they are uninterested in commercial gains from trade and simply pursue an operational objective that they personally valued. In doing so, they might fail to consider any of the commercial consequences of their decision for their own company, or for their partners or suppliers returns.

This type of action is a particular risk in vertical rather than in horizontal business relationships because, in many of the latter, the consequences of any operational activity are, eventually, visible to all parties commercially. In vertical relationships this may never be the case because of the lack of transparency over the commercial consequences of particular operational activities within the other party's business.

However, there is a more significant problem than this. While managers make all sorts of decisions regarding what they subjectively perceive as a win or win-win, this can force managers into very poor thinking about the objective outcomes from exchange relationships. As was argued earlier, if an objective view of commercial reality is adopted (based on ideal, economically rational thinking) it is clear that many of the cells in Figure 20 may not be feasible in all types of business relationships, but also that the choices available to managers are more complex than those presented in Figure 20.

6.3 *The Paradox of Subjective and Objective Interests in Vertical Business Relationships*

We saw in chapter 3, that, when an objective commercial view of interests is adopted, a win-win is feasible for all parties in horizontal business relationships. Thus, in all types of *joint ventures* and *strategic alliances* it was argued that it is feasible for both parties to an exchange to simultaneously achieve everything that they would ideally desire operationally (full market closure) and commercially (maximum feasible *rents*). This means that, while both parties may not achieve the same total share of commercial value from their relationships, it is possible for them both to achieve their ideal operational and commercial goals.

This reasoning means also that in horizontal business relationships the outcomes defined in Figure 20, and especially those outcomes in cells 3, 7, 8, and in particular cell 4, where both parties achieve their subjectively defined commercial (as well as their operational) goals, are feasible. This means that in horizontal business relationships the subjective and objective interests of both parties to the exchange can be commensurable, although they may not be in practice if one or both parties are using opportunism. The same cannot be said for vertical business relationships between buyers and sellers. This is because, while both the buyer and supplier may subjectively perceive that they are experiencing a win-win outcome, objectively speaking this is not possible. This is because, as we saw earlier, the objective interests of buyers and suppliers are not fully commensurable (Cox, 2004c).

This problem of the non-commensurability of interests in buyer and supplier exchange can be explained quite simply by reference to the feasibility in practice of the theoretically possible outcomes outlined in Figures 12 (see Chapter 5) and 20. The argument presented here is that, while in practice it is possible for managers in vertical business transactions to believe subjectively that they are operating in cell 4 in Figure 20, objectively speaking it is not feasible in theory or practice for them to operate in cell C in Figure 12. The explanation for this is straightforward.

A supplier could enter into a transaction with a buyer that provides for them an outcome that, subjectively speaking, is of a very high commercial and operational value (they stay in business, they achieve a growing market share, or they increase their profitability, etc.). The buyer, at the same time, could receive from the supplier operational and commercial benefits (in the form of differentiated products and/or services and lower costs of ownership) that are also highly valued subjectively. Clearly, in this case, both parties would, subjectively speaking, be operating in cell 4 of Figure 20. Despite this, it is not possible in theory or in practice for buyers and suppliers to operate in cell C in Figure 12 (*ideal mutuality*).

The reason for this is that the ideal goal of a buyer is to have their suppliers pass value to them in the form of the maximum increase in functionality with the maximum feasible reduction in the total costs of ownership. At any moment in time a buyer can only achieve this ultimate ideal (i.e. fully achieve their objective goals) if the supplier is only ever allowed to make a loss, break-even or make normal returns rather than *rents*. In such circumstances, buyers and suppliers in this case must be operating in cell B (*the buyer wins/the supplier only partially wins*), but not in cell C in Figure 12.

Conversely, if suppliers are to achieve their ideal commercial goals it is essential that they close markets to others and become permanent or temporary monopolists, such that they are able to determine the trade-off between use value and cost in the market and earn the maximum feasible *rents*. If this is the case then it is impossible for buyers to be fully successful (in an ideal sense) and operate in cell C in Figure 12. On the contrary, if the supplier is able to earn the maximum feasible *rents* then the transaction must operate in cell F (*the supplier wins/the buyer only partially wins*) rather than cell C (*ideal mutuality*).

Despite this, in practice (paradoxically) it is still possible for a buyer and a supplier to believe that they are operating in cell 4 in Figure 20 (*high commercial and operational value for both the buyer and the supplier*). This is because Figure 20 is based on subjective rather than objective reality. Thus, it is possible for a supplier to be a monopolist and still be able to provide for buyers both a lower cost of ownership and an increase in existing use value, while still earning *rents*. In such a circumstance both the buyer and supplier may subjectively highly value the commercial and operational improvements from the transaction (cell 4 in Figure 20).

Objectively, however, the buyer in this example is not operating in cell C in Figure 12, but in cell F. This is because, even if the operational improvement in use value is high in this circumstance, the buyer could receive substantially reduced costs of ownership if the supplier was forced to reduce profits (*rents*) and make losses, break-even or earn normal returns through regulatory or competitive pressures. This explains the paradox of mutuality in buyer and supplier exchange and its highly complex nature both commercially and operationally.

There is, however, a further level of complexity in understanding the objective tensions in the buyer and supplier relationship. Notwithstanding the earlier argument about the subjective rank order preferences of buyers and suppliers (as outlined in Figure 20), this insight about the objectively ideal interests of buyers and suppliers substantially modifies the way in which buyers and suppliers ought to think about their subjective preferences.

As we saw, it was argued that buyers and suppliers intuitively might feel that the best way to sustain a business relationship is to find outcomes in which both they and their partners in the exchange achieve high levels of commercial rather than operational gain. Thus, after cell 4 in Figure 20 (where both parties achieve high levels of commercial and operational gain), buyers might normally be expected to have rank order preferences for cell 3 outcomes over cell 2 and then cell 8, followed by cell 7 and then cell 6. Conversely, suppliers (after cell 4 as their first choice) might be expected to rank order their preferences for outcomes in cell 8, then cell 12, followed by cell 3, then cell 7 and, finally, cell 11. This indicates that both buyers and suppliers can be expected to think about their own interests first, but that they must also think about what the other party to the exchange desires if they are to sustain the relationship.

Unfortunately, if the previous discussion about objective rather than subjective interests is accepted, this may not be a safe assumption to make for either party to an exchange. If the objective commercial interests of buyers and supplies are not fully commensurable in theory or practice, then it cannot be assumed that it is always 'safe' (commercially speaking) for a buyer or a supplier to allow the other party to achieve high levels of commercial value from a transaction. This is because the other party may be achieving returns from the relationship at their expense, which objectively speaking should not be allowed. In these circumstances the rank order preferences of buyers and suppliers have to be modified to reflect the underlying objective tension in business relationships commercially.

In this light, the subjective rank order preferences of a buyer in Figure 20 ought to be cell 2 (*buyer achieves high commercial and operational gain/the supplier only achieves operational gain*), followed by cell 6, cell 3, cell 7, cell 4, with cell 8 as the least desirable commercial outcome. For the supplier the ideal rank ordering objectively becomes cell 12 (*the supplier achieves high commercial and operational gain/the buyer achieves only an operational gain*), followed by cell 11, cell 8, cell 7, cell 4, with cell 3 as the least desirable commercial outcome.

Despite this objective reordering of buyer and supplier preferences, there is one further level of complexity in understanding transactional exchange. The analysis above describes the rank order preferences of buyers and suppliers when they seek to maximise their commercial gains from exchange, based on the assumption that it is not possible objectively for both parties to achieve their ideal (highest value) outcome if the other party is able to achieve their ideal. Notwithstanding this objectively rational view of the non-commensurability of these two ideal positions in vertical business exchange, it is possible for relationships to operate subjectively in cell 4 of Figure 20 (*high commercial and operational gain for both parties*).

This subjective outcome could occur, for example, if a buyer was in a transaction with a supplier who was prepared to pass continuous use value and reduced costs of ownership to the buyer, and also accept only normal commercial returns as their ultimate goal, but also perceived this to be of high commercial gain for themselves. The supplier in this case would not be pursuing their objective ideal commercially (*rents*), but would be accepting a less than ideal outcome (normal returns), which they personally highly valued.

On the other side of the equation such a subjectively optimal rather than ideal outcome is also possible for a buyer. In this case a buyer might receive a significant increase in use value from a supplier operationally (in the form of differentiated products and/or services) that allowed the buyer to improve their differentiation and earn for themselves *rents* rather than normal returns. The buyer would subjectively perceive this to be a highly valuable commercial outcome. At the same time, the supplier might also be able to earn *rents* from providing the products and/or services to the buyer. Clearly both parties would subjectively perceive this to be a situation of high commercial and operational gains for both parties (cell 4, Figure 20).

The problem with this subjective interpretation of reality is that although both parties in the two examples above are operating subjectively in cell 4 of Figure 20, objectively speaking, at least one side in each exchange is operating in a non-ideal manner. Thus, suppliers in the first case perceive themselves to be achieving high commercial gains, when in fact they are objectively earning only basic returns and passing a high level of commercial value to the buyer. In fact, objectively speaking, the exchange is taking place either in cell B (*buyer wins/supplier partially wins*) or in cell E (*buyer partially wins/supplier partially wins*) in Figure 12.

In the second case, while both parties may clearly be content with the arrangement subjectively, it is obvious that if a more contested and/or regulated environment existed for the supplier then the costs of ownership of the buyer would decrease (with potentially higher commercial benefits overall for the buyer). This is because the supplier would be required to operate with normal returns rather than *rents*. In this case it is the buyer who is unable to operate in the ideal situation and, objectively speaking, the exchange is taking place in cell F (*buyer partially wins/supplier wins*) of Figure 12.

These two cases demonstrate that in the real world of business both buyers and suppliers may subjectively misconceive the objective value they receive from transactions. This problem of subjective and objective interests is well understood in social and political science thinking but, surprisingly, not much remarked upon in the business management literature (Gallie, 1955-6; Balbus, 1971; Connolly, 1972; Lukes, 1977; Cox, Furlong and Page, 1985).

Given this, it seems sensible to conclude that business managers—and especially those involved in vertical business relationships—would be significantly assisted if they were taught how to recognise the differences between objective and subjective interests when they engage in business relationships. If this was achieved business relationship management could be significantly improved, and especially by those organisations able to significantly reduce the current levels of economic false consciousness (about the commercial consequences of operational exchange) amongst their managers.

Having outlined why there is a significant difference in the meaning of win-win and mutuality when an objective rather than subjective view is taken of interests in business exchange, we turn in the final chapter to a discussion of the implications of this insight for management practice and current and future academic thinking in business economics and management.

7

On Interests, Power and Mutuality in Transactions: Towards a Science of Business Economics and Management

In this final chapter the broader implications of this discussion are analysed in relation to current academic thinking about best practice in business relationship management. It is argued that current thinking about best practice is potentially dangerous. This is because many writers do not appear to understand what *mutuality* actually means in practice, and deny that economic forms of power are prevalent in business relationships.

The book concludes by supporting the view that effective business relationship management can only be achieved if power (and/or the threat of its use) is recognised as a major factor that can occur in all types of business relationships. Effective relationship management in business, therefore, requires that managers and commentators embrace the reality of power in dyadic exchange transactions, and accept that in many business transactions irresolvable conflict and tension will always exist.

Only by doing so, and accepting that the use of pre- and post-contractual opportunism by exchange partners are not forms of market or transactional failure, but legitimate tools to be used by managers as a power resource in all types of transactional exchange, will it be possible to develop a science of business economics and management. Such a science requires a comprehensive understanding of the operational bases of commercial power and leverage in different forms of internal and external business transactions, and the recognition of the role of human beings in this process.

This final chapter focuses, therefore, primarily on the problem of power and how it can be conceptualised in business transactions. This requires a discussion of recent writings about power in economics and business, as well as a brief review of the counter-arguments made by those who deny that the concept has any utility for understanding business or economic exchange. This also requires a discussion of the challenge by the Coasean perspective to the political economy (or power) explanation for the existence of the firm. These reviews are followed by an analysis of the political economy school of 'contested exchange', which provides a starting point for a more rigorous operationalisation of the concepts of power, interests and transactions in business and economic exchange. A final section focuses on the implications of this conceptualisation for future academic research and for managerial action.

7.1 *Power, Transactions and Interests in Business Relationships*

For those interested in the concept of power in business relationships it is as if there is a dialogue of the deaf in the academic study of business relationships. What this means is that, while there has been a continuous history of writing about the concept of power, and even though managers constantly use it as part of their daily discourse, the majority of academics in the economics and business management disciplines either do not discuss the concept at all, or reject it as a basis for thinking about ways to understand and improve business performance. This is surprising because the literature on power in the social sciences, and also in some branches of business management and economics thinking in particular, has been extensive. Despite this, there has been little rigorous debate about the meaning or utility of the concept for business management practice.

The literature on power in economics can be dated in the modern era, initially at least, to the Physiocrats and to Marx. Quesnay in 1758 argued that wealth arose not primarily from money but from exchange value or 'power in exchange': this was the ability to command the commodities and services of others in exchange relationships (Commons, 1934). Marx, in the nineteenth century, developed his labour theory of value. This theory focused on the power of the owners of the means of production and exchange to appropriate value from the labour of others (Marx, 1967).

As a result, there have been two broad strands of thinking about power in business management and economics. The first has focused on the power relationships between two legally autonomous actors engaged as buyers and sellers in external exchange transactions, where goods and/or services are passed from one party to another in return for money. This external transactional or contractual focus on power clearly owes its lineage to Quesnay and the Physiocrats.

The second approach has tended to focus on the power relationships between owners and employees within organisations. This approach has tended to emphasise the ways that owners (and also preferred employees) are able to create hierarchies of status and reward that allow them to appropriate for themselves the lion's share of the value that the organisation earns from engaging in production and exchange. This internal transactional and contractual focus on power owes its lineage to Marx and the labour theory of value.

In more recent business management and economics (as well as social science) thinking there have been many commentators who have written about aspects of internal and/or external power. Writers on these two aspects of power include: Robertson (1928); Chamberlain (1933); Robinson (1933); Coase (1937); Brady (1943); Bain (1956); French and Raven (1959); Emerson (1962); Harsanyi (1962); Blau (1964); Baran and Sweezy (1966); Nagel (1968); Zald (1970); El-Ansary and Stern (1972); Goldman (1972); Walmsley and Zald (1973); Jacobs (1974); Benson (1975); Lustgarten (1975); Etgar (1976); Cook (1977); Salancik and Pfeffer (1977); Stolt and Emerson (1977); Cook and Emerson (1978); Pfeffer and Salancik (1978); Porter (1980); Stern and Reve (1980); Bacharach and Lawler (1981); Pfeffer (1981); Wilkinson (1981); Achrol et al., (1983); Arndt (1983); Gabel (1983); Campbell and Cunningham (1983); Cook et al., (1983); Frazier (1983); Galbraith and Stiles (1983); Mintzberg (1983); Schul., (1983); Anand and Stern (1985); Cowley (1985); Cox, Furlong and Page (1985); Granovetter (1985); Cowley (1986); Dwyer and Summers (1986); Gaski (1986); Thorelli (1986); Dwyer and Sejo (1987); Hunt et al., (1987); Bowles and Gintis (1988); Heidi and John (1988); March (1988); Yamagishi et al., (1988); Frazier and Rody (1991); Scott and Westbrook (1991); Buchanan (1992); Finkelstein (1992); Bowles and Gintis (1993); Gundlach and Cadotte (1994); Hadeler and Evans (1994); Provan and Gassenheimer (1994); Ramsay (1994, 1996a, 1996b); Brown et al., (1995); Frazier and Anita (1995); Kumar et al., (1995); Williamson (1995, 1996); Hakansson and Gadde (1997); Rajan and Zingales (1998); Aghion and Tirole (1997); Cox (1997a, 1997b, 1999b, 2001); Bowles and Gintis (1999); McDonald, (1999); Cox, Sanderson and Watson (2000); Maloni and Benton (2000); Olson (2000); Cox et al., (2002, 2003, 2004a, 2004b); Cox (2004b, 2004c); and Kim et al., (2004).

Despite this history of interest, there has never been any final clarification of the power concept in business management or economics. This lack of rigorous epistemological discussion of the concept, despite the extensive writing about power within and between organisations, is clearly perverse. Its cause may have something to do with the fact that in western academic thought and practice there has never been a rigorous or holistic approach to epistemology in social science training. Rather, there has been the creation of disciplinary boundaries that focus intellectual thought and practice on specialised aspects—economics, business management, psychology, sociology and politics—of the total human condition.

As a result, there has developed an unhealthy and unhelpful cult of the specialist in the social sciences, and this is particularly true in the economics arena where the concept of power has, arguably, found its most barren ground. The primary reason for this is that the project that most mainstream economists appear to be focused on is one that sees power (normally in the form of opportunism and/or market failure) as the evil that must be eradicated through the development of perfectly competitive markets. As a result, the problem of who wins and who loses in the allocation of material scarcity, and how, has been largely ignored.

In its place had grown up an academic community of scholars who believe that the ideal outcome for wealth creation for all human beings is a situation in which competition forces all suppliers in exchange transactions to continually pass use value to buyers, and only to earn normal returns (profits) that tend to zero. It is hardly surprising, therefore, that there is limited interest within economics faculties in the concept of power. This is because the ability by individuals or organisations (when they act as suppliers) to close markets to their competitors and create monopoly power is regarded as market failure. This is the very evil that most economists believe that they are on earth to eradicate.

Ironically, while academics in business management cannot be so conveniently labelled (because they are normally an heterogeneous group of individuals, operating with a wide range of disciplinary and sub-disciplinary traditions), those in the strategy and marketing sub-disciplines have, in recent years at least, begun to recognise that their primary role is to understand the circumstances that allow individuals and organisations to undertake the very market closure that mainstream economists believe they should be eradicating. The dominant school of thinking within the business strategy and marketing is today the resource–based approach (Penrose, 1959; Wernerfelt, 1984; Barney, 1991; Grant, 1991; Peteraf, 1993; Foss, 2003).

This resource-based school seeks to dimensionalise the internal resource and capability configurations through which individuals and organisations can find *ex ante* (pre-contractual) and *ex post* (post-contractual) mechanisms for the generation of sustainable above normal returns (*rents*). In other words, although the resource–based school does not really focus on the concept of power, it is focused unequivocally on understanding the internal resources and capabilities that allow individuals and organisations to create market closure on a sustainable basis. If this is not an exercise of market power through the deployment of internal means that is focused on achieving competitive leverage in exchange, then it is not clear what the resource-based project is focused on at all.

What this short discussion demonstrates is that, while mainstream economists and the resource-based school rarely discuss the concept of power in exchange transactions, everything they study is focused on this topic. If economists are successful in finding ways to create perfect markets then they must be diminishing the ability (power) of, or means by which, individuals and/or organisations (when they act as suppliers) can earn sustainable *rents* from exchange transactions with buyers/consumers. In this way, any interventions that diminish the power of suppliers to earn sustainable *rents* must augment the ability (power) of buyers/consumers to make suppliers pass value to them, while only ever earning normal returns.

Conversely, every mechanism that resource-based writers isolate (through which individuals and/or organisations can close markets to competitors) must provide a mechanism that augments the ability (power) of those individuals and/or organisations to earn sustainable *rents*, and to control the level of use value that must be provided to buyers. In this way, it becomes clear that mainstream economists and resource-based thinkers are in fact never likely to be able to agree on anything. They will continue to talk past one another because they are working to illuminate two very different sides of the same coin. That coin is the exchange transaction. Mainstream economists are focused on dimensionalising the objective interests of buyers, either as consumers or in business-to-business relationships; while the resource-based school is focused on dimensionalising the objective interests of suppliers.

The reason that these two schools of thought find it so difficult to communicate with one another is because they have not recognised that the unifying elements for the social sciences as a whole, and for the economics and business management disciplines in particular, are the concepts of the exchange transaction and its relationship with power. All of human existence is based ultimately on exchange and, as a result, transactions must form the basis for any science of human existence. However, because human existence occurs in circumstances of absolute and relative scarcity (Cox, 1997a), not everyone is able to achieve their ideal goals (whether these are objectively or subjectively defined)—and, as argued here, this is particularly true in vertical, as opposed to horizontal, business relationships.

Given this, all outcomes from vertical forms of transactional exchange must result in relative winners and losers and, in such circumstances, there must be resources and capabilities that allow the individuals and/or organisations involved to appropriate more rather than less of what they desire. In such circumstances, the causes of any symmetric or asymmetric outcome must be the power resources used (either wittingly or unwittingly) by the parties in exchange transactions.

This means that power—the ability to achieve one's intended outcomes when there is a conflict of interest between two exchange parties—must be the primary causal concept in social science (and therefore economics and business management) thinking. In this light, the primary explanatory concept through which human existence must be understood is the exchange transaction (Commons, 1924; Homans, 1958).

While this seems obvious, ironically, most social science academics do not necessarily share the view that there should be a unified approach in the social sciences. This is primarily because of the disciplinary boundary problem discussed earlier, but it is also a function of the failure to undertake any systematic grounding in the epistemology of the social sciences when the sub-disciplines of the social sciences are taught. The result is that academics can have extremely prestigious careers in their sub-disciplines without ever confronting the difficult idea that their field of enquiry might be incredibly limited in focus, or that there might be contending views about causality and the meaning of concepts.

Whatever the cause of this academic malaise there is little doubt that the lack of interest by many academic writers in one of the central concepts in human existence (the ability of one party to achieve their outcomes at the expense of another, when there are conflicts of interest between two parties to an exchange) is surprising to say the least. Furthermore, there is the additional problem that when writers have in the past focused on the concept of power in business relationships they often use the concept without rigour and without a robust conceptual definition. This leads to subjective, vague and woolly uses of the concept that are difficult to substantiate (March, 1966, 1988; Williamson, 1995, 1996).

As a result of this failure by academic writers to develop an objective, scientifically rational and universally accepted definition of the concept, many academic writers see little value in it at all. It is also because of this lacuna that many writers on business relationship management find it possible to use purely subjectively (and often tautological) rather than objectively defined definitions of success and failure in business exchange.

It is interesting to note, in this regard, that most of what has passed for advice on best practice in business relationship management thinking in recent years has been based on a desire to eschew any consideration whatsoever of the concept of power. Indeed, many recommendations for managers appear to be based on the idea that trust and mutuality are the most effective ways of managing business relationships. It is often argued, therefore, that if both parties do not trust one another and adopt transparency in their business dealings with one another then, by definition, this cannot be an ideal or optimal relationship.

Hopefully the analysis here has shown that this line of reasoning can be extremely dangerous for managers when they enter into business relationships. There are three major reasons for this conclusion. The first is that a win-win or *ideal mutuality (positive-sum)* outcomes may not always be achievable in all types of business relationships, and not at all in buyer and supplier exchange. The second is that while there are *symmetric mutuality* and *asymmetric mutuality (nonzero-sum)* outcomes in horizontal business relationships, *symmetric mutuality* outcomes are not feasible in vertical business relationships. This is because in buyer and supplier exchange all outcomes are asymmetric.

Third, if there is inherent conflict and tension in most, if not all, business relationships over who gets what from the exchange, then encouraging managers to achieve the ideal or optimal outcome for themselves by recommending the use of trust and transparency (when opportunism, bounded rationality and information asymmetry are a fact of life) is a potential recipe for disaster. This is particularly true in vertical business relationships because, as we saw in Chapter 5, there are nearly always more favourable outcomes for either party to any exchange, when compared with the current accommodation arrived at. In these circumstances, trusting others and providing transparency about operational and commercial consequences may simply provide an opportunity for the other party to take advantage of the situation.

7.2 *Critics of the Power Concept in Economic and Business Management Thinking*

Given this, it is interesting to note that one of the foremost theorists of the uses of opportunism in exchange transactions, where bounded rationality and information asymmetry are constant dangers, argues that trust is not a useful basis for the effective management of business exchange, but also denies that power exists in business relationships. Oliver Williamson has argued that:

"One of the implications of opportunism is that "ideal" cooperative modes of economic organization, by which I mean those where trust and good intentions are generously imputed to the membership, are very fragile. Such organizations are easily invaded and exploited by agents who do not posses these qualities" (1985, pp.64-65).

Despite these structures against the use of trust in business relationships, due to the problems of pre- and post-contractual opportunism, he has also argued, as has March (1966, 1988), that power is a disappointing concept and that:

"…many dependency issues can be addressed in efficiency terms, whereupon power considerations largely vanish" (1996, p.39).

Furthermore, and somewhat paradoxically, even though he denies that trust and power are useful concepts in understanding effective business relationship management he still believes that mutuality is the best way of managing business relationships:

"Credible contracting is very much an exercise in farsighted contracting, whereby the parties look ahead, recognize hazards, and devise hazard mitigating responses—thereby to realise mutual gain" (Williamson, 1999, p.1090).

These quotes demonstrate two things. First, that Williamson understands many of the operational mechanisms available to buyers and suppliers, and that trust and transparency alone are very poor mechanisms to guarantee *mutuality*. Second, despite this understanding of operational means, he does not accept that power exists in business relationships, nor does he fully define what mutuality means in transactional exchange (Williamson, 1995). This is because, for Williamson, all failures to create mutually acceptable outcomes must be based on inefficient contracting rather than on the objective non-commensurability of commercial and operational interests.

Despite the otherwise excellent account by Williamson of the operational means for leverage by buyers and suppliers of their ideal commercial ends, the analysis presented here shows this rejection of power as a concept may be misguided. This is because, while one can fully agree with Williamson's analysis of the problems of opportunism in business relationships, one must take fundamental issue, both with his rejection of power as a useful concept, and his view that all business relationships can be based on mutually acceptable outcomes that eradicate (or provide order for) the underlying conflict and tension within them (Williamson, 2000).

The analysis presented here demonstrates that it is perfectly possible to provide a rigorous and robust definition of power in business relationships. This is based on, first, understanding the ideal (economically rational) commercial goals of the parties to exchange relationships and, then, the extent to which they are able to achieve more or less of that which they ought to ideally value at the transactional level. Obviously, however, if this is not undertaken based on an objective definition of commercial and operational outcomes then one is left with a purely vague and subjective definition of interests (March, 1966).

In other words one has to accept Williamson's challenge to those who write about the concept of power:

"...*power tends to be myopic (transactions are not examined 'in their entirety') and ...it is tautological. Power needs to be operationalized, whereupon refutable implications that accrue to this perspective can be derived.*" (Williamson, 1995, p.21)

"*Power will not shed its tautological reputation until a unit of analysis has been named and dimensionalized. Conceivably the transaction is the unit of analysis in the power arena as well. If so that needs to be stated. Whatever the unit of analysis, the critical dimensions with respect to which this unit differs in power respects need to be identified...Finally, power needs to develop the refutable implications that accrue to this perspective and demonstrate that the data line up.*" (Williamson, 1995, p.34.)

The analysis presented here hopefully begins the process of responding to Williamson's challenge. Building on the work of Commons (1924) and Homans (1958) on transactions and exchange theory, the resource dependency school (Emerson, 1962; Cook, 1977; Pfeffer and Salancik, 1978), the governance perspective (Williamson, 1975, 1985, 1986) and the political economy school (Porter, 1980; Bowles and Gintis, 1988, 1993, 1999), it is argued that the basic unit of analysis for the power perspective in business economics and management thinking (as well as in all social science thinking more generally) must be the different forms of exchange (transactions) that underpin all human relationships.

This is because, while the study of business management and economics encompasses many aspects of intra- and inter-organisational activity, the ultimate purpose of business, and why the firm as an organisation exists in the first place, is to provide a mechanism through which individuals can appropriate value (in the form of profit) for themselves (as owners and/or controlling managers) from any and all internal and external forms of transactional exchange. In other words, the firm exists as an operational mechanism—with variable degrees of ownership and control of resource endowments—to leverage value (in the form of profit) for individuals from any *critical assets* that can be exploited commercially in all, and any, types of internal and/or external transaction (Cox, 1997a). This definition, therefore, takes issue with the view that the firm exists primarily to economise on the costs of transactions (Coase, 1937; Williamson, 1975, 1985).

7.3 *A Political Economy and Power Critique of Coase and the Theory of the Firm*

It is interesting to reflect at this point on the utility of transaction cost economics. This extremely influential and insightful approach to organisational make/buy and purchasing decisions suffers from a number of analytical weaknesses. The first of these is that the answer provided by Coase to the question of why the firm exists appears to be somewhat simplistic. Or to put the matter another way, Coase raised a singularly important question which cannot be answered satisfactorily by classical economists or by transaction cost economists, but which had already been explained more than satisfactorily by Marx.

The issue that Coase raised was why anyone needed to create a firm if, as individuals, they could just as easily appropriate value (make profits) for themselves from the exchange of goods and services in the marketplace. The answer to this question proposed by Coase is that, because there are costs to managing and coordinating transactions with others, in order to economise on the costs of transactions it is sometimes better to manage and coordinate these transactions internally rather than to manage them through external contracts.

The Marxist answer to this problem is more straightforward. The reason any entrepreneur creates a firm is in order to find ways of appropriating more value for themselves from transactional exchange than they could if they acted independently. In other words, the firm is an operational mechanism for extracting value rather than for economising on the costs of transactions. This is because a firm can exist with, or without, a high level of vertical integration. The level of insourcing or outsourcing of required resources and capabilities by a firm—while affected by the relative costs of transactions—cannot, therefore, explain why a firm exists. Transaction cost economics, therefore, can only explain the size and shape of the firm, not its reason for existence.

Thus, even though entrepreneurs and firms do make decisions about insourcing, based on the relative costs of transactions, they also make decisions to outsource using exactly the same relative transaction cost assumptions. The point here is that a decision to insource cannot explain why a firm exists because firms still exist when they decide to outsource a significant share of their current internal activities in order to economise on the relative costs of transactions. A firm must, therefore, own and control some *critical assets* if it is to earn a return. In other words, a firm (and its managers) cannot appropriate value from exchange relationships (transactions) unless at least some key resources and capabilities are insourced, over which they possess enforceable property rights (Grossman and Hart, 1986; Hart, 1989, 1995; Hart and Moore, 1990).

This also means that, since an individual can legally own and control a firm, the Coasean argument about the distinction between market and hierarchy is rendered somewhat meaningless. This is because the Coasean problem is to explain why internal hierarchy replaces market exchange. On reflection this may be a false dichotomy because, when there is hierarchy (high levels of vertical integration), this always coexists with market relationships. The Coasean project may, therefore, be simply to understand the changing size and shape of the firm (i.e. which organisational boundary and contracting strategies are the most appropriate for economising on transaction costs so that the owners and controllers of *critical supply chain assets* can maximise returns).

It follows, therefore, that it is not possible to argue that the firm exists primarily to economise on the costs of transactions. This is to confuse a tactical decision about the boundary of the firm, and the most effective ways of managing external sourcing decisions, with the strategic purpose of the firm. While the relative costs of transactions will certainly affect the degree of vertical integration by a firm (how much of, and how many types of, supply chain resources will be insourced), as well as potentially contributing to competitive advantage and overall corporate profit performance if they are lower than costs incurred by others, they do not define its purpose or its reasons for existing.

It can be argued, therefore, that the primary purpose of all firms is to earn profits. In this light, the firm serves no higher purpose, even though there can be legitimate arguments about the levels of profit that are morally and/or ethically desirable; about the non-commercial benefits that should be provided by the firm to customers and society; and about the nature of the constraints that should be imposed on firms by governments and regulatory authorities because of the social, environmental, cultural and political externalities that arise from the commercial and operational activities of the firm.

This means that the transaction cost economising perspective provide answers to two very important questions—namely: how should managers within the firm make decisions about its boundary; and once they have decided to outsource, how should relationships be managed effectively with suppliers pre- and post-contractually? The Coasean framework does not, however, provide any answer to the question of why the firm exists in the first place. The answer to this question, as discussed above, is that the firm exists to allow those who own and/or control its activities to appropriate value (in the form of financial returns) for themselves.

From this value appropriation perspective it is possible to understand the historical processes through which primarily individual market-based transactions were replaced by relationships dominated by joint-stock limited liability companies. As we shall see, the primary reason for the existence of the firm lies not in the desire to economise on the costs of transactions, but to provide a technical or operational solution to the problems that faced individuals, as they sought to appropriate value for themselves in rapidly changing technological and economic circumstances.

It can be argued that the ability of an individual to earn profits from transactional exchange is always constrained by their capability and capacity to produce, sell and supply particular goods and/or services to customers. In other words, individuals (or a group of individuals) have to have resource endowments that lead to the creation of goods and/or services that are valued by buyers/consumers. Furthermore, these individuals (or group of individuals) must be able to own, control and exchange the goods and/or services that they legally own.

This means that they have property rights over particular resources that guarantee, through the legitimate authority and force of the state, that their owner and/or controller can appropriate all, or a guaranteed proportion, of the value achievable from exchange. The ability by individuals (or a group of individuals) to appropriate value in this way is, however, ultimately constrained by their personal capacity to create, sell and supply goods and/or services that are valued by others and owned and/or controlled by them.

Throughout history, therefore, the major economic problem for individuals seeking to appropriate value from exchange has been the physical limits on their own ability to appropriate value. Unless individuals can find some legitimate operational way (means) to create, sell and supply even more of the valuable goods and/or services to others, than is possible from their own labour, then there will always be physical limits to value appropriation by individuals. Entrepreneurial human beings have, throughout the ages, found that the simple operational answer to this problem of a limit to value appropriation is to create exchange transactions with others to allow them to appropriate a share of the value that the labour of others creates.

Historically, the normal exchange transaction between individuals has been that the principal in the exchange relationship (normally the entrepreneurial individual who knows how to create, sell and supply a particular valuable resource) provides their agent with money and/or shelter in return for their labour. In these circumstances there is always a negotiation between the principal and agent about the terms of trade, normally in the form of how much labour for how much money and/or shelter (Grossman and Hart, 1983).

Once the deal has been struck the principal then has to coordinate the activities of their contracted agents, and take risks on providing supply inputs for their agents to work on, before they can be sold, hopefully at a profit. These are the risks that entrepreneurs always have to take when they engage in trade. The only reason any sensible entrepreneur would take these risks is because they anticipate that, by doing so, they will also be able to appropriate a significant share of the difference between the total costs of all supply inputs (including labour) and the eventual selling price.

Economists call this surplus, or difference between the costs of sales and the revenues eventually received, profits. These are the returns that most economists would argue are legitimately due to entrepreneurs for their foresighted risk-taking with uncertainty, and efficiency and effectiveness in managing transactional exchange between buyer and sellers (Knight, 2002). These types of transaction will normally occur either through internal contracts (the agent produces the goods and/or services that the principal owns and/or controls on the principal's property) or through external contracts (the agent produces the goods and/or services that the principal owns and/or controls on the agent's own property, or that of a third party).

Marx, while recognising that this entrepreneurial process operates, referred to these types of profits as surplus value. By this, Marx meant that the surplus created from the gap between the wages paid to agents for their labour by principals (entrepreneurs) and the value of the finished goods and/or services was a form of exploitation of labour. This was because entrepreneurs were appropriating a disproportionate share of the value created in the production process, and it was possible for them to pay agents more from the surplus value that their labour was able to generate (Marx, 1967).

Marx, thereby, downplayed the uncertainty management and risk-taking role of the entrepreneur and attributed most of the value created in production and exchange to the labour of agents. As a result, he argued that entrepreneurs were abusing their power as principals (owners and controllers of the means of production) in business relationships by exploiting agents (labour).

Here is not the place to try to resolve this debate about the causes of value creation, but it is clear that Marx was an early proponent of the view that power exists in business relationships. Marx argued that it was the power of capitalists (through their ownership and control of the means of production and exchange) that allowed them to appropriate a disproportionate share of wealth (value) from exchange transactions (both internally within firms and externally through trade with buyers and sellers). This power, according to Marx, enabled capitalists to encourage labour to leave the land to enter factories in return for a dependent life as wage slaves.

What is perhaps more important than the realisation that Marx was an early proponent of the view that power is an inextricable factor in business management and economics, is the fact that he also provided a simple answer to the question posed by Coase about the reason for the existence of the firm. Marx wrote extensively about the problems that the rising class of capitalist entrepreneurs experienced during the early stages of the industrial revolution, when limited liability joint-stock companies (firms) were being created. What is apparent from this period is that the rise of the firm was a particular operational solution to a range of technical and commercial problems facing entrepreneurs.

The first major problem that had to be resolved by entrepreneurs was that the opportunities for value appropriation were changing, as the predominant forms of production and exchange shifted, from a primarily agricultural and land based system of trade, to one based increasingly on the manufacturing of, and trade in, commodities. The new means of production and exchange created additional problems for entrepreneurs because the size of the market for commodities was not constrained (as it had been in the past) by physical limits to production from the land. Now the limits to value appropriation were bounded only by the constraints on consumption within markets for commodities.

In this environment entrepreneurs faced the twin problems of having to raise increasingly large amounts of capital to invest in the production of capital-intensive means of production and exchange, and also a need to break down existing social and political barriers to trade. It is in this context that one must understand the rise of the firm. The creation of the modern firm was not, therefore, as Coase and the transaction cost economising school appear to believe, a solution to a problem of market inefficiency. Rather, it was the logical solution to a series of value appropriation problems associated with risk and uncertainty facing entrepreneurs in search of profit.

Given the new means of production and exchange, and the potential global scope of these commercial transactions and activities, entrepreneurs needed to raise capital in increasingly large amounts in order to create the new machinery, factories, railways, turnpikes and canals, as well as to create and stimulate increasingly global networks of production and trade, through which value could now be appropriated on an historically unprecedented scale. It follows that the scale of capital required significantly increased the levels of personal risk and uncertainty for entrepreneurs, and this required an operational solution. This was a legal mechanism that encouraged risk taking but also limited personal liability, while also allowing the maximum opportunity for entrepreneurial value appropriation.

The joint stock limited liability company (the firm) was a perfect solution to this problem. It allowed individuals to pool their limited resources, and to raise capital from others who themselves did not have the personal means of creating, selling and supplying commodities, but who wished to participate in new ventures and, also, by taking some risk with their capital, to appropriate value from the innovations of entrepreneurs. By this means, and also because the liabilities were limited, the firm proved to be an extremely successful mechanism for providing entrepreneurs with the levels of capital required to create, own and take commercial risks with the new means of production and exchange.

Interestingly enough, the desire by entrepreneurs and investors for commercial limits on the downside of risk taking, but with limited restrictions on the upside potential for value appropriation, also coincided with the need for greater control of agents by principals. The need to organise labour and the highly capital-intensive physical means of production in factories, rather than through the 'putting-out system' of workers supplying goods and/or services autonomously, using the principal's supplied raw materials in their own properties, also acted as a stimulus to vertically integrated firms. Clearly, this development was based as much on the need to discipline and control labour as on the relative productive (or transaction costs economising) efficiency of organising the means of production internally rather than externally.

For all of these reasons it is clear that the Coasean answer to the question of why the firm exists is partial. While there is historic support for the fact that the costs of economising on transactions did have an impact on the boundary of the firm, it is debatable that this was the primary reason why the firm was created in the first place. In truth, the decision to create joint stock limited liability companies must have arisen for strategic commercial reasons associated with the drive by individuals to appropriate value. The issue of the boundary of particular firms, and the relative transaction costs of insourcing or outsourcing particular aspects of supply, may have dictated the size and form of some firms, but it is stretching credulity to argue that these make/buy decision were, or ever are, the primary reason why the firm exists in the first place.

The reason for arguing this way is because, in the contemporary period, a similar process of technological and economic change is taking place in western capitalism as a function of the ending of the Cold War, the technological innovation of the internet economy, and the rapid economic development of emerging economies in China, India, South-East Asia and parts of the former Soviet Empire. In this new historical conjuncture it is clear that the formerly highly vertically integrated business model of many western companies is now being challenged by an outsourcing revolution.

This outsourcing of formerly insourced production and support activities to lower cost economies—especially to India and China—is having a profound impact on the boundary of the contemporary firm. This is clearly due, as the work of Coase and Williamson shows, to the significance of cost economising decisions on the boundary of the firm. Despite this, western firms still exist even though they have, and will continue to, outsource a considerable share of their formerly insourced activities.

This shows that, while the Coasean perspective provides an extremely useful way of thinking about make/buy and external sourcing decisions, it does not provide a comprehensive explanation for why the firm exists in the first place. Today, western companies are outsourcing because they believe this is the best way to stay in business and meet current competitive challenges. Presumably, if, during the early stages of the industrial revolution, outsourcing had been the most cost economising way of managing transactions, then sensible and economically rational entrepreneurs would have chosen this option rather than vertical integration. In other words, outsourcing today is seen as the best way of ensuring high levels of value appropriation, just as insourcing into vertically integrated factories was seen as the most effective way of ensuring value appropriation in the early stages of the industrial revolution.

The most rational explanation for the development of the firm is, therefore, that it was as an operational solution by entrepreneurs to a series of significant technical and commercial challenges to their strategic ability to appropriate value. Firms arose as an operational mechanism to resolve commercial problems that entrepreneurs faced in raising capital and taking risks with uncertainty, and also in controlling and coordinating their agents (labour). This required at that time—given the means of production and exchange that provided the mechanisms for wealth creation—a move towards a more vertically integrated approach to transactional exchange than had been the case in the past. Now labour needed to be coordinated in large factories in order to maximise productive efficiency.

What this discussion shows is that the creation of firms is always driven by the desire of entrepreneurs to find operational ways of owning and/or controlling *critical assets* through which they can appropriate value from transactional exchange. In this light, the Coasean perspective suffers from a problem of logical incoherence. This is because it is guilty of the problem of *'post hoc, ergo propter hoc'* reasoning. What this means is that, while there is no doubt that firms (once they have been created) do spend a considerable amount of time and effort considering the need to economise on the costs of transactions, this normally only occurs after the initial decision to create them.

This needs to be explained because many economists influenced by the Coasean logic do not appear to understand the motives of entrepreneurs. It is rare (although not impossible) for entrepreneurs to believe that they should create a firm solely in order to economise on the costs of transactions. Rather, entrepreneurs create firms in order to appropriate value for themselves. Transaction cost economising simply provides a way of thinking about the most appropriate boundary and shape of the firm that they own and/or control.

The first consideration for entrepreneurs is, therefore, whether or not they can create, sell and supply a particular product and/or service profitably. Their next concern is then, normally, whether or not they have the ability to create a differentiated supply offering or, if it is not differentiated, then one that allows them to appropriate an acceptable level of profit from its creation, sale and supply to customers. The first concern is nearly always with the ability to own and/or control the necessary supply inputs (*critical assets*) to allow the goods and/or services to be created, sold and supplied so that an acceptable return (profit) can be made.

The concern of entrepreneurs is, therefore, first with the availability of resources to own and/or control, not on their cost. It can also be argued that, whether or not the supply inputs are owned internally or externally will be, in part, a function of the costs of supply (on which an entrepreneur will normally seek to economise on costs), but also a function of the ability of the supplier of supply inputs (as agent) to resist cost economising attempts by entrepreneurs (as principals) to force them to work for them at wages or prices determined by the buyer. Thus, whether or not an entrepreneur can insource supply will be in part a function of an agent's ability to defend their own property rights against the leverage of the entrepreneur, in order that they (as principals in their own right) can appropriate a greater share of the value from exchange than they would if they were managed as employees within a firm.

Thus, the question of make/buy is not just driven by the costs of transactions but also by the relative bargaining position (power resources) of both the principal and agent when the two sides enter into transactional and contractual negotiations. Once the availability of required resources (*critical assets*) is assured then the second consideration for entrepreneurs (as principals) is the ability to sell the created and supplied goods and/or services to customers. Only then, it can be argued, once a sustainable mechanism for managing and controlling exchange transactions is in place, will entrepreneurs begin to focus on the total costs of supply and the need to economise on the costs of transactions.

Coasean logic is, therefore, guilty of failing to understand the practical reasons for firm formation (the desire to appropriate value), and also of reifying a second order problem for the entrepreneur—how to economise on the costs of transactions once sustainable value appropriation processes have been created—into the reason for the creation of the firm in the first place. The truth of this conclusion is only too evident for those who work on make/buy and sourcing decisions with major firms in the global economy. The make/buy and sourcing functions in most major firms are normally some of the most poorly resourced and have the lowest status positions within organisations. Given this, it is somewhat surprising to find that transaction cost economists believe that these decisions determine the existence of the firm.

In fact most firms, rather than seeing transaction cost economising as critical to their activities, in reality see this as very much a second order concern. In other words, transaction cost economising is normally only of importance when the more entrepreneurial and customer-focused strategies to differentiate internal product or service offerings, or find new ways to sell to customers, fail to generate sufficient revenue and/or profit. This forces firms to think about outsourcing expensive internal headcount and/or the leverage of supplier input prices, as mechanisms to reduce costs in the short-term in order to improve bottom line performance.

This is hardly a strategic role—rather transaction cost economising is for most firms an essentially tactical way of dealing with short-term profitability issues. Thus, while transaction cost economising can certainly assist the firm with improving value appropriation and, conceivably in some circumstances, achieving a competitive advantage through relative superior competence in economising, it is hardly the reason why firms exist in the first place—even though this may be for some firms the only way for them to survive.

Given this critique of the Coasean and transaction cost economising approach in general, one cannot doubt the major contribution that this approach has made to a more rigorous understanding of business management and economics. There is no doubt that, while the fundamental cause of firm creation can be found in the search by entrepreneurs to appropriate value for themselves, the transaction cost economising approach has provided an extremely rich and detailed way of thinking about the logical problems that face individuals and firms when they operate as buyers in transactional exchange relationships with their own employees and suppliers.

Despite this, the transaction cost approach, while strong on the interests and tactics that should be used by firms when they act as buyers, is less successful in explaining the interests and tactics of firms when they act as suppliers. This is why, despite Williamson's call for the strategising approach of the resource-based school to find common cause with the governance perspective around the explanation of transactional exchange, there has been something of a dialogue of the deaf (Williamson, 1991, 1999). This debate has yet to develop fully, although there are signs that some strategic management writers are beginning to develop an interest in this project (Oxley, 1999;

Foss and Foss, 2000, 2001; Foss, 2003; Lippman and Rumelt, 2003a, 2003b; David and Han, 2004).

7.4 Contested Exchange: A Mechanism for Understanding Power, Interests and Transactions

Although the governance or transaction cost economising perspective may not have resolved all issues in the theory of economic or business exchange, Williamson appears to be correct in arguing with Commons (1924) that the transaction is the basic unit of analysis for an understanding of business and economic relationships. Furthermore, since this requires—notwithstanding Walrasian economic arguments to the contrary—an understanding of human relationships, it may be that the exchange transaction is the basic unit of analysis for the social sciences as a whole (Homans, 1958).

There are, however, two major problems for the development of a science of transactional exchange in business management and economics. First, there must be the recognition within the two disciplines of economics and business management that exchange transactions are the basic unit of analysis. Second, there must also be a recognition that the objective interests of exchange partners may, but they may not always, be fully commensurable.

It is this recognition that the interests of exchange partners may be harmonious (and result in *ideal* or *symmetrical mutuality* outcomes), or conflictual (and result in *asymmetric mutuality* or *zero-sum* outcomes), which explains why exchange is often contested, and why power is a key analytical concept in economics and business management. It can also be argued that it is only by recognising that the objective interests of buyers and suppliers are not fully commensurable that the fusion of the strategising and governance perspectives can be satisfactorily completed.

This is because in fusing these two approaches (a development Williamson (1999) has argued must occur) one must recognise that the project is not about seeking to find transactional outcomes that always result in *ideal* or *symmetrical mutuality* outcomes. Rather, it is about explaining the tactics and levers that both exchange partners can use to maximise their own value appropriation interests when engaged in transactions with others where non-commensurable outcomes are feasible.

This way of thinking provides the basis for a robust clarification of the role of power in economics and business management. This is achieved by recognising that the *dependent variable* (that which has to be explained) in transactions is the extent to which the outcome from an exchange meets the objectively defined ideal interests (the ends) of the parties involved. The *independent variable* is the operational means (the structural and cognitive resources that either party brings to the transaction that allow them to achieve their objectively defined ends).

As Figure 21 indicates, therefore, power can be said to exist when, given the objective interests (ends) of the exchange partners, asymmetric outcomes occur that favour one party more than the other in a transaction. Asymmetric outcomes can be *nonzero-sum* (i.e. all of the outcomes that result in win-partial win, partial win-win and, only for vertical exchange, partial win-partial win), as well as *zero-sum* (i.e. all of those outcomes resulting in win-lose, partial win-lose, lose-partial win or lose-win).

Interests, Power and Mutuality 227

Figure 21: **The Nature of Transactional Exchange**

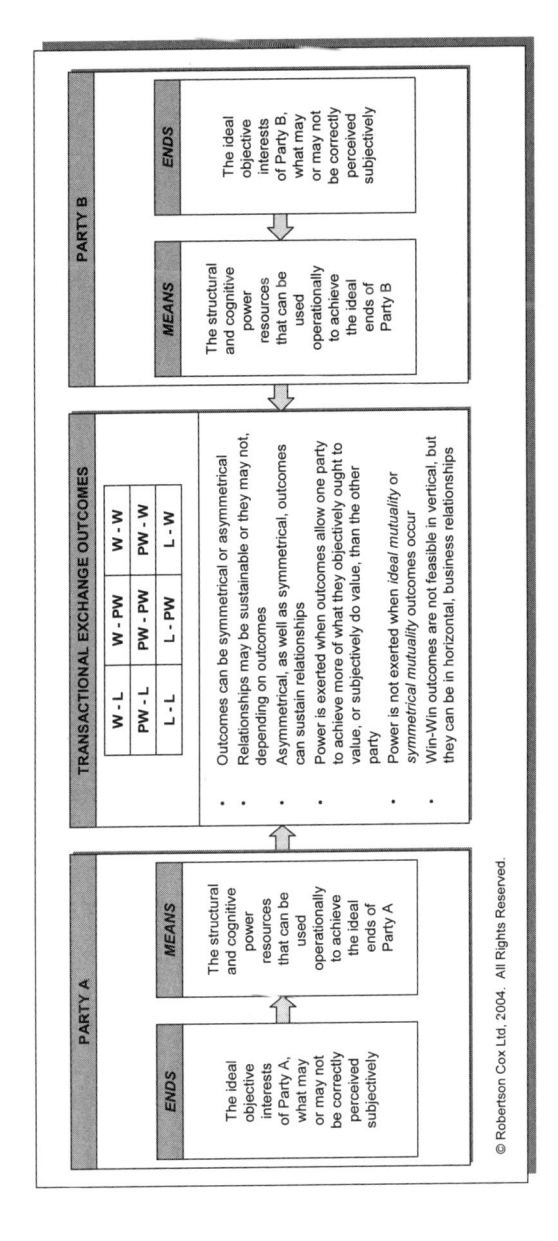

PARTY A

ENDS: The ideal objective interests of Party A, what may or may not be correctly perceived subjectively

MEANS: The structural and cognitive power resources that can be used operationally to achieve the ideal ends of Party A

TRANSACTIONAL EXCHANGE OUTCOMES

W - L	W - PW	W - W
PW - L	PW - PW	PW - W
L - L	L - PW	L - W

- Outcomes can be symmetrical or asymmetrical
- Relationships may be sustainable or they may not, depending on outcomes
- Asymmetrical, as well as symmetrical, outcomes can sustain relationships
- Power is exerted when outcomes allow one party to achieve more of what they objectively ought to value, or subjectively do value, than the other party
- Power is not exerted when *ideal mutuality* or *symmetrical mutuality* outcomes occur
- Win-Win outcomes are not feasible in vertical, but they can be in horizontal, business relationships

PARTY B

ENDS: The ideal objective interests of Party B, what may or may not be correctly perceived subjectively

MEANS: The structural and cognitive power resources that can be used operationally to achieve the ideal ends of Party B

© Robertson Cox Ltd. 2004. All Rights Reserved.

Power does not exist, therefore, in exchange transactions when both parties can simultaneously achieve their ideal ends (i.e. *ideal mutuality* a win-win in which each party achieves their objectively defined interests) or when *symmetrical mutuality* occurs (i.e. when both parties achieve exactly the same non-ideal outcome). If in a partial win-partial win outcome one party achieves slightly more than another then an asymmetrical outcome has occurred in the partial win-partial win category, and power has been exerted by the one party against the other. This means that *ideal* and *symmetrical mutuality* are only feasible in horizontal, and not in vertical, business relationships. In buyer and supplier exchange all partial win-partial win outcomes are asymmetric (see the discussion in Chapter 5 about Figures 13 through 19).

Using this approach, while also recognising that in the past the power concept has been poorly defined (March, 1966; Williamson, 1995, 1996), the basis for a more robust and rigorous operationalisation of it may be possible. By following Williamson's argument that the transaction may be the basic unit of analysis for the power concept (Williamson, 1995), and by understanding the interplay of the objective and subjective interests of actors in transactions, it may be possible to redeem the power concept in business management and economics thinking.

Furthermore, it may also be possible to provide a more thorough operationalisation of the power and leverage resources available to transactional exchange partners. This can be achieved by understanding the ways in which individual subjective conceptions of economic reality provide cognitive resources or power levers to one or to both parties in a transaction. This allows us to define a series of *cognitive power resources* that allow exchange partners to appropriate value for themselves at the expense of others. These power resources arise due to the resource endowments that flow to some individuals because they subjectively understand their own, and their exchange partners, objective economic interests better than their exchange partners (Cox et al., 2004).

If one party has the cognitive ability to subjectively understand their own and their exchange partner's objective economic interests we refer to this as *nous*. If both parties to an exchange simultaneously possess *nous* then it is unlikely that any *cognitive power resource* will flow to either party—although either party may still retain *structural power resources* that arise from market exchange based resource endowments.

But, if one party to the exchange has a superior cognitive ability compared with the other this will provide one party with a potential lever (a resource endowment based on information asymmetry), through which they can appropriate more value from exchange than they ought to given their relative structural resource endowments. Value appropriation levers based on *nous* occur, therefore, when one party in an exchange relationship has superior knowledge and understanding about their own, and their partners, objective economic interests and the other party subjectively misconceives their own objective economic interests and suffers, as a result, from a form of economic or commercial false consciousness or myopia.

By adopting this approach it is possible to identify and differentiate between the *cognitive* (subjective) and *structural* (market-based) *power resources* that are at play in transactional exchange. *Structural power resources* relate to the power levers available to economic and business exchange partners as a result of their ability to own and/or control and deploy market-based resources. These are the resources that arise out of the interplay of demand and supply variables in perfectly competitive or imperfect markets (Porter, 1980).

The *structural power resources* that arise from these market interactions are those that enhance the ability of exchange partners to leverage outcomes that favour their objectively defined (although they may also impact on subjectively defined) economic interests. These resources allow an exchange partner to appropriate more of what they ideally value from a transaction, and to achieve an asymmetrical outcome that favours their interests at the expense of their exchange partners. In the context of horizontal business relationships between joint venture and strategic alliance partners these are resources associated with superior endowments of capital, tangible and intangible assets, distinctive capabilities, intellectual property and know-how.

In the context of vertical business relationships these are the resources that flow to buyers and suppliers from superior dyadic resource endowments. For suppliers these are the same resources based on superior endowments of capital, tangible and intangible assets, distinctive capabilities, intellectual property and know-how. In other words, all of the resource endowments that create isolating mechanisms that provide suppliers with opportunities to create imperfect markets (Rumelt, 1987). This means all of those resource endowments that allow suppliers to close markets to their competitors so that monopoly or oligopoly outcomes occur, so that they can fix quality and price standards for buyers, and appropriate above normal returns (*rents*).

For buyers the structural resource endowments that provide power and leverage opportunities over suppliers are those, such as monopsony and oligopsony, low sunk and switching costs, regular market contestation, buying consortia and appropriate governance structures to eradicate ex-ante and ex-post opportunism in situations of incomplete contracting, and bilateral dependence. These dyadic resources allow buyers to set quality standards and fix prices, such that functionality is increased and the total costs of ownership are reduced on a continuous basis, with suppliers making only normal returns or worse.

This operationalisation of the power concept is based squarely on the argument that asymmetry in structural resource endowments between exchange partners provides the basis for one party to exert power over the other in the achievement of outcomes that favour their objective interests at the expense of those of their exchange partners. It is important, however, to recognise that this resource dependency argument has been roundly criticised by Williamson (1995):

"Resource dependency is very much a power perspective….resource dependency theory holds that the dependent party…is at the mercy of the other. Working as it does out of a myopic perspective, the theory holds that dependency is an unwanted and usually unanticipated condition. The recommended response to a condition of resource dependency is for unwitting victims to attempt, ex post, to reduce it. Transaction cost economics regards dependency very differently because it works out of a farsighted rather than myopic contracting perspective. Not only is dependency a foreseeable condition but, in the degree to which asset specificity is cost effective, dependency is (i) deliberately incurred and (ii) supported with safeguards. Thus, although less dependency is always better than more, ceteris paribus, deliberate recourse to asset specificity will be undertaken in the degree to which net benefits (due allowance having been made for safeguards) can be projected." (pp. 34-35)

At one level this is a forceful critique of the resource dependency argument but, even though it is, this does not invalidate the argument that resource dependency is one aspect of power, or that power is a useful concept in understanding exchange outcomes. There are a number of reasons for making this claim. First, while it is one thing for Williamson to argue that resource dependency is an outcome that exchange partners may seek willingly, this does not preclude the possibility that asymmetric outcomes can occur in exchange relationships in which both parties willingly accept asset specificity.

Thus, it can be argued that, even though one party accepts dependency in a relationship and becomes a willing supplicant, power is still being used against them. This conscious acceptance of the power of others occurs even though they have foresight and they are aware that it is happening to them. This is because the structural resource endowments of one party (the master or principal) force the other party in the relationship (the servant or agent) to accept the inequity of the exchange relationship. The fact that one party knows that it is being dominated and that it must accept this, because it has no better alternatives, does not mean that power has not been exerted against them.

Slaves have always known that power is being exerted against them. The problem for them is, however, always the same. They can willingly accept their dependency (knowing that there are objectively better alternatives they would ideally desire— they would prefer to be masters in their own right) or they can rebel and seek freedom. If the choice is between slavery with survival, and freedom with death or even less material wealth than they currently receive, then slavery is likely to appear a preferable outcome to freedom. The acceptance of slavery does not, however, imply that the slave is content, only that they currently have no better feasible alternative than to accept the power of the master.

In situations of market exchange, where none of the exchange partners are slaves, parties appear to enter freely into contracts. In such circumstances, Williamson implies, power cannot exist. This is because both parties willingly enter into the exchange and can use foreseeable foresight to accept asset specificity and resource dependency and mitigate the hazards of these by crafting credible commitments pre-contractually. Credible commitments involve both parties posting hostages as safeguards against post-contractual opportunism. If the risks of opportunism post-contractually are so high, Williamson argues, buyers will eventually supplant external contracting with insourcing (vertical integration) (Williamson, 1995).

The problems with this line of reasoning are manifold. First, Williamson does not appear to recognise that he is only talking about the safeguards or governance structures that are available to buyers, and does not discuss at all the safeguards that are available to suppliers in exchange relationships. Nor does he discuss safeguards in the context of horizontal business relationships. More importantly, perhaps, Williamson does not seem to recognise that power may still arise from the disjuncture of the ideal interests that both parties might wish to pursue and achieve, and the current imbalance in the structural resource endowments that both parties possess.

This means that, since there clearly are business relationships in which there is a high level of asset specificity and a need for bilateral dependency post-contractually, considerations of mutual net benefit in these circumstances must also include aspects of power. This is especially true when the exchange itself leads to asymmetrical outcomes for both parties in relation to their ideally desired objective outcomes. Thus, even with the ability for exchange partners to be far-sighted rather than myopic, the resource endowments of the two parties may result in one party achieving more of what they ideally desire than the other. All that the contractual safeguards ensure (if they are enforceable and all encompassing) is that the existing structure of exchange asymmetry (i.e. the power of one party over the other due to superior resource endowments) is being sustained.

Williamson's problem is that he does not recognise the concepts of subjective and objective interests in his analysis. He assumes interests are always subjectively defined, and does not appear to accept that there can be a disjuncture between what is subjectively perceived to be ideal and what is objectively ideal. Furthermore, because he focuses primarily on the buying side in the exchange relationship, he does not appear to accept that exchange can be contested, or that interests may not be fully commensurable in buyer and supplier exchange. As a result, one can understand why he argues that power disappears from consideration when both parties willingly enter into relationships based on net benefit calculations, even though one cannot agree with him.

This is because, if market exchange is freely entered into, then, in his schema, parties will only contract together for efficiency reasons based on calculations of net benefit. This may be a convenient argument, but it is not one that stands up when one introduces the concept of interest into the equation. It may be efficient for slaves to accept slavery over freedom, especially in circumstances in which freedom entails risks and uncertainty, but this does not negate the fact that slaves, given a choice between all feasible alternatives, would choose freedom every time if they could be guaranteed a better alternative than they currently have. The same logic can be applied to market-based exchange.

Just because one party willingly accepts supplicancy (a situation of asymmetric exchange in which they do not achieve their ideal goals, when the other party achieves all, or the majority of theirs) as it is currently the most efficient outcome available to them, does not mean that power is not being exerted against them. On the contrary, if there are (in theory and in practice) much more favourable outcomes that are feasible, then it is logical to expect them to opt for those outcomes if the circumstances allowed. Given, therefore, that current exchange relationships are always contracts to manage and codify existing power circumstances, it is possible to argue that power is being exerted against one exchange party to the extent that the current contractual arrangements allow one party to achieve their objectively ideal goals, while also ensuring that the other party does not attain their objectively ideal ends.

Relatedly, it is clear that Williamson has not grasped the significance of subjective and objective interests as power resources in exchange transactions. This is surprising, given that he has written so eloquently about the problems for buyers of opportunism (self-seeking interest with guile). Williamson has recognised that exchange partners can be opportunistic and use bounded rationality and information asymmetry to their advantage, but he appears to have chosen to ignore this cognitive dimension to exchange and deny that it can be a power resource for exchange partners. Instead, Williamson appears to have ignored this reality in pursuit of defining the ideal governance structure to ensure that this does not occur (primarily for buyers) through the creation of pre-contractual safeguards (credible commitments).

The problem is that Williamson's view of *homo economicus* is somewhat heroic. Williamson seems to be arguing that, since opportunism is a frequent part of business life, then a rational economic actor should guard against it occurring to arrive at mutually beneficial outcomes that are efficient for both parties (i.e. they are the best available given all of the other currently feasible alternatives). Unfortunately, while contracts can be rendered efficient, given the current power circumstances, this does not mean that they are ideal. Thus, while one party may accept their current supplicancy as the most efficient outcome, given all of the feasible choices currently available to them, this is not the same as saying that they are fully satisfied with the outcome.

Furthermore, since many transactions involve exchange relationships in which interests are not fully commensurable—and especially in those vertical business relationships that experience incomplete contracting where Williamson is so concerned about providing contractual safeguards against opportunism—it is inevitable that the conflict and tension over outcomes will arise. In these circumstances the use of opportunism (to achieve outcomes that improve on what ought to be achievable given the structural resource endowments of both parties) can either be seen as an evil to be eradicated (Williamson's position) or a legitimate tool for exchange partners to use in their struggle over value with others (the power and leverage position).

This means that in the power perspective cognitive and structural resource endowments are not a problem to be eradicated. On the contrary, they are resources to be nurtured so that asymmetric outcomes that enhance one's own value appropriation goals can be achieved. On the other hand, they are also a resource endowment to be guarded against when others possess them. In other words, they are not a problem if I possess them, but they are, and must be guarded against, if my exchange partner has them. The reason for this is because in business exchange it is sensible for each party to use all of the resource endowments–cognitive and structural—that are available to them. This is simply to understand the rules of the game of exchange (Cox, forthcoming).

Part of understanding the rules of the game is also recognising that some people understand business better than others. This means that some people have *nous* and others do not. This is because many economic actors experience false consciousness, or a subjective myopia about the reality of commercial exchange, due to the problems of bounded rationality and imperfect information. False consciousness on the part of one party about the relationship between what is done operationally and what the other party in an exchange receives commercially is, therefore, one of the key resources that provide opportunities for entrepreneurs and/or firms to appropriate value from others. This is the meaning of the aphorisms:

"There's one born everyday"

and,

"Never give a sucker an even break".

Information asymmetry and bounded rationality, therefore, render the creation of contractual safeguards through far-sighted contracting extremely hazardous for the uninformed. Managers often do not know what they do not know, and this makes it very difficult for them to deal with incomplete contracts and bilateral dependency. This problem is particularly acute when one side has more information about pre- and post-contractual outcomes than the other.

In these circumstances the power perspective recognises that imbalances in cognitive resource endowments are legitimate levers to be used by parties to an exchange, in order to achieve superior outcomes than might have anticipated by reference only to the *structural power resources* available to both parties in the exchange. In this light, power is not a problem to be removed from analysis by recourse to arguments about contractual efficiency. Rather, it is a concept to be embraced as the reflection of the means by which exchange partners achieve their objective goals in circumstances when interests are not fully commensurable in transactions.

Despite Williamson's critique it can be argued, therefore, that, while the proponents of the power concept have in the past failed to meet his challenge, a more robust operationalisation of the concept can be achieved and power can be redeemed as a useful analytical tool. The power concept has value, therefore, but only if analysis of the concept starts with an understanding of the objective interests (ends) of the parties to any exchange, which must then be linked to an understanding of what has been received by both parties to the exchange in relation to these objectively defined interests.

This provides a way of understanding which of the interests of the two parties have been more or less satisfied by any exchange outcome. By adopting this approach it is then possible to understand the circumstances under which power has, or has not, been exerted in a transaction. This, in turn, deals with one of the major criticisms made of the power approach—that it cannot explain when power has, and when it has not, been exerted.

The approach developed here also provides additional insights into the power concept. This is because it does not rely solely on structural resource endowments and/or dependencies to explain the ability by exchange parties to achieve asymmetrical outcomes that favour one party at the expense of the other. By recognising and embracing the concept of economic or commercial false consciousness, it is possible to provide an additional way of thinking about power resources than that developed within the resource dependency literature.

The fact that individuals often subjectively misconceive the objective reality that they are in is well understood in social psychology. Indeed, one can argue that the concept of bounded rationality, pioneered by Simon (1955), is one of the most important insights in social science thinking. The realisation that some human actors (in internal exchanges within firms and when representing organisations externally) often fail to understand their own, or their organisation's, objective (economically rational) interests, while others may not, provides an explanation for why information asymmetry is one of the most important resources that those engaged in exchange can use to further their own interests at the expense of others. It is through information asymmetry and bounded rationality that opportunism is operationalised as a *cognitive power resource* in transactional exchange.

This insight allows us to recognise that, while there may be *structural power resources* (associated with market closure and monopsony, etc) that parties to transactions can use to further their own interests to achieve asymmetric outcomes, there are *cognitive power resources* as well. These are all of the mechanisms that have been isolated—such as lying, cheating, obfuscating and withholding of salient information—by which one party can make it difficult for an exchange partner to make an informed decision about appropriate ways of working. This power resource is in such common use in the real world of social and economic exchange that all human beings have been known to say to themselves at some time in their lives:

"If I had known then what I know now, I would have done things differently."

Unfortunately in life there is also the problem that sometimes we do not have the benefit of the luxury of hindsight. This is because sometimes we do not know what we do not know. This means that, if we never find out that what we did not know, others could have taken advantage of us and we would never know about it. In such circumstances, although we cannot observe the exercise of power, there is no doubt—if an asymmetric outcome has occurred that favours our exchange partner's objective interests at the expense of ours, and we would have acted differently if we had known—then an exercise of power has occurred.

In this light, power in business, as in politics, can have many dimensions (Lukes, 1977). *The first dimension of economic or business power* occurs, therefore, when there are non-commensurable objective economic interests between exchange parties, and the asymmetry of outcomes is clearly observable to both parties, both before and after they have used the *structural power resources* available to them in the market.

The second dimension of economic or business power arises in situations of non-commensurable interests, when *cognitive power resources* are utilised to supplement *structural power resources* to ensure that the party suffering from false consciousness or myopia does not make the most appropriate choice available to them but, eventually, the true nature of the asymmetric outcome arrived at becomes apparent to both parties. The ability of the disadvantaged party to rectify this situation is then a function of the *structural power resources* currently available to them to create more favourable exchange outcomes for themselves with this, or another, exchange partner. There may, therefore, be circumstances in which the disadvantaged does or does not have redress post-contractually.

For example, time, linked to *cognitive power resources*, can allow one exchange partner to take advantage of another. Thus, a supplier may provide a 'loss leader' to a buyer such that the buyer achieves their ideal outcome. Unfortunately, the buyer may not understand that the supplier is only providing this outcome in the short-term because they want to eradicate competitors from the market. Once these competitors have been excluded from the market, the buyer will find—in time—that functionality declines and the total costs of ownership increase, allowing the supplier to earn the maximum feasible *rents*.

These types of time-based swings in the winners and losers from exchange are not confined to vertical business relationships, but are also common in horizontal business relationships as well (Das, 1990, 2004). In such circumstances, however, the buyer may, or may not, have the *ex post structural power resources* to allow them to redress the situation.

The third dimension of economic or business power occurs when there is a situation of non-commensurable interests, when *cognitive power resources* are used to supplement *structural power resources* to ensure that the party suffering from false consciousness or myopia does not make the most appropriate choices available to them, but this never becomes apparent to the disadvantaged party. In this situation the *cognitive power resources* are so deeply embedded, and the costs for the other party of removing information asymmetry and bounded rationality so high, that there is little chance that the opportunist will be caught out.

In such circumstances the disadvantaged party may have better alternative exchange choices, but they will never know about it, and their *structural power resources* will be redundant. In such circumstances power is being exercised, but the disadvantaged is simply not aware of it, and is normally happy in their ignorance. It is for these last two scenarios, and especially the third dimension outcome, that the old saying *"ignorance is bliss"* has been coined.

Thus, when assessing the power resources of parties to an exchange it is necessary to understand the structural resource endowments that each party brings to a transaction and the resource dependency this creates. The way this has been operationalised in this way of thinking is to understand the *relative utility* and *relative scarcity* of the resource endowments that both parties bring to a transaction, and how these factors shape exchange outcomes in relation to the objective economic interests of both parties.

This is not, however, the only resource endowment that must be factored into the dyadic equation. The approach developed by the power and leverage perspective also includes *opportunism* (based on information asymmetry and bounded rationality) as a key cognitive resource endowment in understanding power resources (Cox, 1997a, 1997b, 1999b, 2001; Cox, Sanderson and Watson, 2000; Cox et al., 2002, 2003, 2004a, 2004b; Cox, 2004b).

The power and leverage approach is, therefore, able to deal with Williamson's critique of the power concept and its overreliance on resource dependency arguments. This questioning of the governance critique of power is similar in many respects to the 'contested exchange' school of political economy writing developed by Bowles and Gintis. The approach developed here, however, while broadly supportive of that school, also takes issue with it in some important respects.

The approach developed by Bowles and Gintis assumes that all exchange is contested, while the approach adopted here does not. The problem with arguing that all exchange is contested is that this is tautological. This is because it denies the possibility of the counterfactual that there are exchange transactions in which there is an absence of contested exchange. In other words, if all exchange is contested then power must always be exerted. This denies that there is ever a circumstance in which power is not exerted. The approach adopted here contends that, while exchange is often and perhaps most of the time contested, it also may not be.

'Contested exchange' is, however, likely to be highly significant in most business and economic transactions. This is because individuals pursue their own economic self-interest first and, in the context of economics and business, individuals (and the firms they create or represent) seek to appropriate value. Nevertheless, not all transactions are contested.

This is because in horizontal business relationships the interests of both parties in an exchange are potentially (although they may not always be) fully commensurable—both in theory and practice both parties can simultaneously achieve the same *ideal mutuality* outcome of the maximum feasible above normal returns (*rents*). Similarly, there are outcomes that are non-ideal and both parties do not earn the maximum feasible *rents*, but both parties still earn exactly the same from the exchange (*symmetrical mutuality*). This means that there are exchanges in which no conflicts of interest occur and, as a result, one party does not exert power over another.

However, if one accepts the logic presented here then, even in horizontal business relationships, it is perfectly possible to argue that, while power may not exist in circumstances where both parties receive the same ideal commercial outcomes, there can be asymmetric (*zero-sum*) outcomes in which one party achieves all of that which they ideally desire, while another does not. In such circumstances an exercise of power by one party over another has occurred.

Thus, in horizontal relationships, since the ideal commercial goal for both parties is to achieve the maximum feasible *rents*, if one party achieves this and the other does not, then power has been exerted in the relationship. This would also be true if neither party earned the maximum feasible *rents* but one party was able to earn more than the other. In other words, any *asymmetrical nonzero-sum mutuality* outcomes in horizontal business relationships, in which one party achieves more than another, must have experienced an exercise of structural and/or cognitive power.

Similarly, in vertical business relationships between buyers and suppliers, since *ideal* and *symmetrical mutuality* outcomes are not feasible and only *asymmetric nonzero-sum* or *zero-sum* outcomes can occur, exercises of power will be constant. Thus, if the buyer is able to achieve their commercial and operational ideal (maximum feasible reductions in the total costs of ownership and increases in functionality, with the supplier making only losses or low returns) then a power situation of *buyer dominance* will have occurred in the relationship (Cox, Sanderson and Watson; 2000, Cox, 2001, 2004b; Cox et al., 2002).

While this may not always be fully achievable, if the buyer is able to ensure that the relationship outcome favours their interests more than it favours those of the supplier, then a situation of power favouring the buyer has occurred. Conversely, if the supplier is able to achieve their ideal outcomes (full market closure and the ability to maximise *rents*), then *supplier dominance* has occurred. While this may not always be possible, if the supplier can ensure that the relationship outcomes favour their interests more than those of the buyer then power has been exercised in favour of the supplier.

This operationalisation of the power concept, therefore, is similar to the 'contested exchange' thesis developed by Bowles and Gintis:

"We refer to this relationship as "contested exchange" because, unlike the transactions of Walrasian economics, the benefit the parties derive from the transaction depends on their own capacities to enforce competing claims" (Bowles and Gintis, 1993, p.85).

Despite this, the definition of power used here is somewhat different to that developed by Bowles and Gintis. Their definition of power is based on the assumption that power can only be exercised in conditions where contracts are incomplete (Bowles and Gintis, 1988, 1993, 1999). This limits exercises of power to *ex post* transactions between buyers and suppliers where opportunism exists because contracts are incomplete. Power clearly exists in these circumstances, as we argued above, but the problem with this definition of power is that even Williamson argues that opportunism can also be exercised *ex ante* and many writers recognise that structural power resources exist *ex ante* as well as *ex post* (Emerson, 1962; Cook, 1977; Pfeffer and Salancik, 1978; Porter, 1980; Williamson, 1985). Thus, power cannot be defined only in ex-post terms.

Furthermore, as Bowles and Gintis have themselves recognised, buyers and sellers can enter willingly into transactions even though they know the other side has *structural power resources* that allow them to achieve asymmetric outcomes that favour themselves. This means that power (defined as asymmetric outcomes) must exist when complete, as well as incomplete, contracts are in place. This is because buyers sometimes have to accept that suppliers can be price and quality fixers, just as buyers can sometimes fix prices and quality for suppliers (Stiglitz, 1987).

If this is the case—and if we use the objective interests of buyers and suppliers (or even those of horizontal business partners) as the purpose for exchange transactions—then even when a comprehensive clause contract is agreed upon (in which all potential scope for post-contractual opportunism has been covered) an exercise of power can still occur. This would arise if, in a comprehensive clause contract, one party was able to realise all of their ideal commercial goals and the other party was not.

Similarly, even if a comprehensive clause (complete) contract has been signed, if the buyer or the supplier is myopic and incompetent, it is possible for an exchange partner to take advantage of the other both *ex ante* and *ex post*. The pervasive *ex ante* failure by buyers to use rigorous market analysis, and to rely instead on "three bids and a buy, with the usual suspects", or their failure to use rigorous performance measurement and management tools post-contractually, allows suppliers scope to indulge in *ex ante* and *ex post* opportunism against buyers even when comprehensive clause contracts have been signed. The impact of *cognitive power resources* on time-based strategic moves by suppliers and by horizontal business partners discussed earlier also supports this critique.

On the other side of the exchange relationship, it is also perfectly possible for buyers to lie (use *cognitive power resources*) about the level of demand they may have in the future and, thereby, encourage suppliers to reduce their current prices, even though there is no intention of working with the supplier in the long-term. Furthermore, it is perfectly possible for buyers in a long-term relationship to leverage the 'hold-up' they have over the supplier through bilateral dependency and asset specificity, to force the supplier to pass value to them way beyond the original contractual terms agreed. This arises because the fungibility of assets is not necessarily the same for both parties in any transaction. The party that has more fungibility than another normally possess a *structural power resource* that they can use *ex post* against the other.

The perspective on power, interests and transactions adopted here contends, therefore, that the definition of the use and scope of power utilised by Bowles and Gintis is too limited. Power can be operationalised *ex ante* and *ex post*, and it can occur in complete and incomplete contracts. Also, it may not occur at all in some exchange transactions. It is also necessary to take issue with the definition of the exercise of power developed by Bowles and Gintis (1993):

"...we can offer a relative uncontroversial sufficient condition for the exercise of power, namely the ability of furthering one's own interests by imposing (or credibly threatening to impose) sanctions on another agent when the converse is not also true" (p.88).

This definition of an exercise of power appears to be focused primarily on *the first-dimensional view of power*. This is because Bowles and Gintis see the exercise of power only in terms of dominance, where there are clear and observable conflicts of interest between two parties to an exchange. Their definition tends to focus on the ability to "impose sanctions" or to ensure "obedience to commands" (Bowles and Gintis, 1999, p. 18), or to "enforce competing claims" (Bowles and Gintis, 1993, p.83).

The problem with this way of defining power is that it does not allow for exercises of power in two very important circumstances. The first is in transactions where opportunistic *cognitive power resources* (based on information asymmetry and bounded rationality) are used, and the exercise of power only becomes apparent over time, although enforcement may or may not be possible due to the possession of *structural power resources* by the disadvantaged (*the second-dimension of economic or business power*). In these circumstances *ex post* structural power resources may allow the disadvantaged to redress the power balance in their favour. On the other hand, they may not.

The second case arises when the exercise of opportunism is never revealed and, even though the disadvantaged does possess *ex post structural power resources* with which to redress the balance in their favour, the use of *cognitive power resources* by the opportunist is never disclosed so that redress never occurs (*the third-dimension of economic or business power*). Obviously, there could be an additional case within the third dimension in which the disadvantaged do not posses the *ex post structural power resources* to redress the power balance. But, since the use of *cognitive power resources* is never disclosed, it is a moot point whether it matters very much to the disadvantaged that they do, or they do not, have the *ex post structural power resources*.

This failure to recognise the need to make *cognitive power resources* a central element of their definition of power is somewhat surprising because Bowles and Gintis have implicitly recognised the significance of opportunism:

"Typically endogenous enforcement arises as a result of asymmetric information in an exchange, one party but not the other being privy to valuable information concerning the good or service to be exchanged." (1999, p.24).

This means that they accept information asymmetry exists, but do not appear to accept that opportunism about information is a key lever that can be used to exercise power over others in exchange relationships. They appear to insist that enforcement through the threat of sanctions, or through obedience to commands, are the only ways that power can be enforced. This definition must be partial because it does not provide for exercise of power based on the ignorance by one party of what is being done to them by another.

It can be argued, therefore, that while Bowles and Gintis outline the contested nature of exchange, they have not fully operationalised what is being contested, or the means (structural and cognitive) by which exchange partners can achieve their non-commensurable ends. Furthermore, Bowles and Gintis appear only to operate at *the first dimension of economic or business power* and do not fully integrate *cognitive power resources* into their schema.

They also tend only to focus on only one mechanism—*contingent renewal*—that buyers can use to assert their interests against suppliers. While there is no doubt that this is a powerful lever in the hands of far-sighted buyers it is not the only lever available to them. Obviously, if the suppliers ability to appropriate value disproportionately is a function of opportunism (based on bounded rationality and information asymmetry), then attempts by buyers to remove information asymmetry (while normally very costly in transactional terms), may also be efficient in power and leverage terms.

It is interesting also to reflect on the fact that the approach adopted by Bowles and Gintis does not really reflect at all on the levers available to suppliers to create power in business relationships over buyers. Like Williamson before them Bowles and Gintis, like most economists, appear to approach transactional exchange only from the perspective of the consumer or the buyer, or from the perspective of labour in relationship with the owners and/or controllers of capital.

There is also a final concern with the view expressed by Bowles and Gintis about the limited application of the exchange and transactions approach to business and economics:

"We do not consider the contested exchange model to be a general model of the exercise of power in market economies." (1999, p.24)

The approach developed here takes issue with this view and contends that the exchange transaction is the basic unit of analysis for all business and economic (and indeed for all social science) relationships, but that not all exchange is contested. When exchange is contested this means that power must have been exerted by one party to achieve an asymmetrical outcome that favours their interests at the expense of the other party in the transaction. This can occur in both *nonzero-sum* or *zero-sum* outcomes. Both of these types of outcome are feasible in both horizontal as well as in vertical business relationships.

If this interpretation is accepted then it is possible to develop an approach to the definition of power that provides a coherent way of thinking about ends, means and outcomes in exchange transactions. This way of thinking recognises that, while power may, or may not, be exerted in horizontal business relationships (where both harmonious and contested exchange outcomes are feasible), it is always exerted in vertical business relationships, where exchange is always contested. Figures 22 and 23 (which are derived from the initial analysis undertaken earlier and presented in Figure 21) provide a diagrammatic representation of transactions for both horizontal and vertical business relationships.

As Figure 22 shows, the ends and means pursued by both party A and party B in horizontal business relationships are congruent. By this one means that both parties share the same ends and seek the same means to achieve that end. This means that interests are fully commensurable in the sense that, given the coincidence of interests about means and ends, it is possible for both parties to achieve their ideal economic interests—the maximum feasible *rents*. It also follows that, if *ideal mutuality* is feasible, so is a failure to achieve this goal and to receive *symmetrical mutuality* outcomes that are based on a partial win-partial win or lose-lose. In all three of these circumstances it can be argued that power is not exerted in the relationship and exchange is harmonious.

Despite this, as Figure 22 demonstrates, it is also possible for asymmetric outcomes—'contested exchange'—to occur in horizontal business relationships. If one party in a joint venture or strategic alliance has more of the means (*structural* and/or *cognitive power resources*) available to achieve their ends than their exchange partners, then *asymmetric nonzero-sum* and *zero-sum* outcomes can occur. If this does occur, then it is logical to argue that there has been an exercise of power in the horizontal business relationship in favour of one party and at the expense of the other.

As Figure 23 shows, in vertical business relationships there are no opportunities for harmonious exchange in this sense. The primary reason for this difference is because of the non-

252   Win-Win?

Figure 22: Contested and Harmonious Exchange in Horizontal Business Relationships

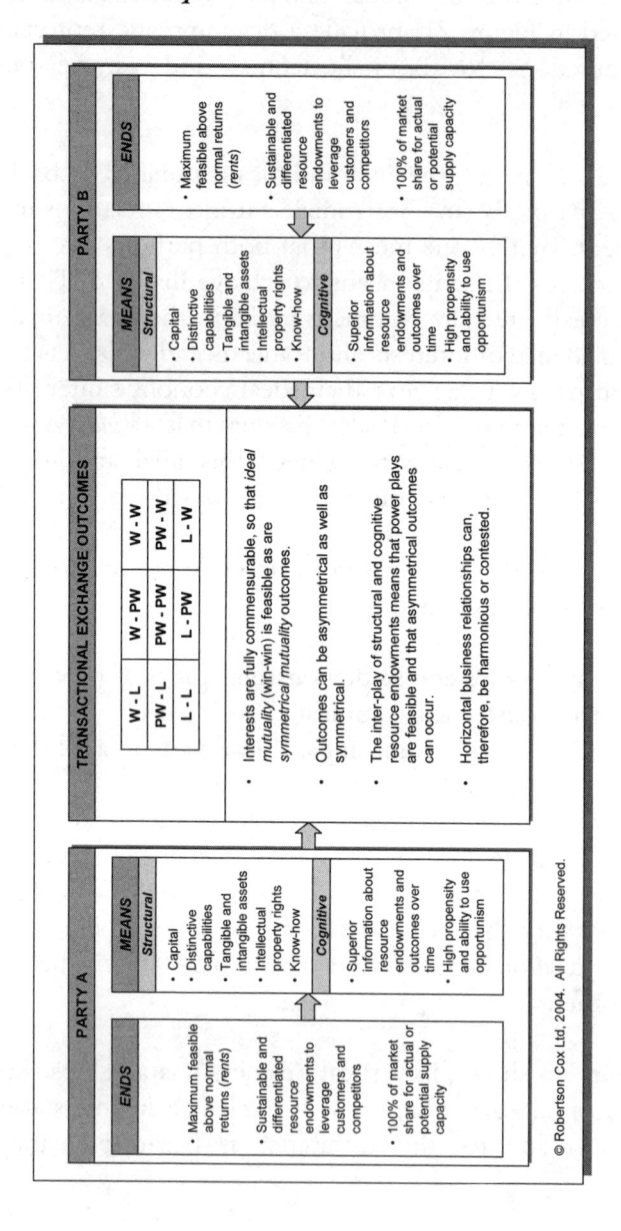

PARTY B

ENDS
- Maximum feasible above normal returns (*rents*)
- Sustainable and differentiated resource endowments to leverage customers and competitors
- 100% of market share for actual or potential supply capacity

MEANS

Structural
- Capital
- Distinctive capabilities
- Tangible and intangible assets
- Intellectual property rights
- Know-how

Cognitive
- Superior information about resource endowments and outcomes over time
- High propensity and ability to use opportunism

TRANSACTIONAL EXCHANGE OUTCOMES

W - L	W - PW	W - W
PW - L	PW - PW	PW - W
L - L	L - PW	L - W

- Interests are fully commensurable, so that *ideal mutuality* (win-win) is feasible as are *symmetrical mutuality* outcomes.
- Outcomes can be asymmetrical as well as symmetrical.
- The inter-play of structural and cognitive resource endowments means that power plays are feasible and that asymmetrical outcomes can occur.
- Horizontal business relationships can, therefore, be harmonious or contested.

PARTY A

MEANS

Structural
- Capital
- Distinctive capabilities
- Tangible and intangible assets
- Intellectual property rights
- Know-how

Cognitive
- Superior information about resource endowments and outcomes over time
- High propensity and ability to use opportunism

ENDS
- Maximum feasible above normal returns (*rents*)
- Sustainable and differentiated resource endowments to leverage customers and competitors
- 100% of market share for actual or potential supply capacity

© Robertson Cox Ltd, 2004. All Rights Reserved.

Figure 23: Contested Exchange in Vertical Business Relationships

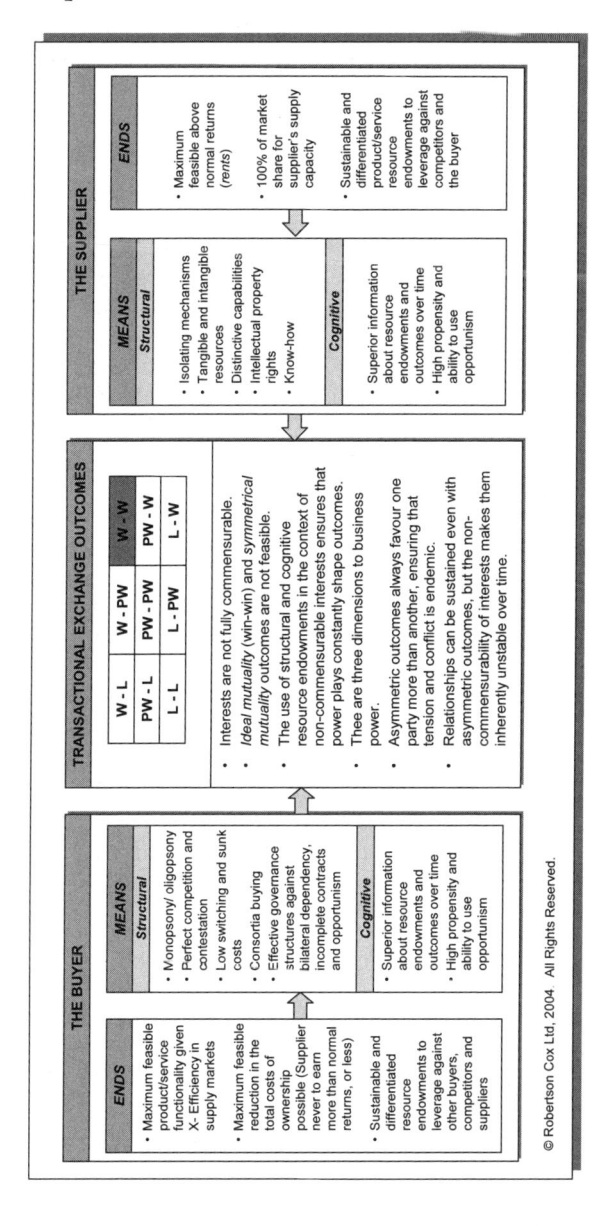

THE BUYER

ENDS	MEANS
• Maximum feasible product/service functionality given X- Efficiency in supply markets • Maximum feasible reduction in the total costs of ownership possible (Supplier never to earn more than normal returns, or less) • Sustainable and differentiated resource endowments to leverage against other buyers, competitors and suppliers	**Structural** • Monopsony/ oligopsony • Perfect competition and contestation • Low switching and sunk costs • Consortia buying • Effective governance structures against bilateral dependency, incomplete contracts and opportunism **Cognitive** • Superior information about resource endowments and outcomes over time • High propensity and ability to use opportunism

TRANSACTIONAL EXCHANGE OUTCOMES

W - L	W - PW	W - W
PW - L	PW - PW	PW - W
L - L	L - PW	L - W

• Interests are not fully commensurable.
• *Ideal mutuality* (win-win) and *symmetrical mutuality* outcomes are not feasible.
• The use of structural and cognitive resource endowments in the context of non-commensurable interests ensures that power plays constantly shape outcomes.
• Thee are three dimensions to business power.
• Asymmetric outcomes always favour one party more than another, ensuring that tension and conflict is endemic.
• Relationships can be sustained even with asymmetric outcomes, but the non-commensurability of interests makes them inherently unstable over time.

THE SUPPLIER

MEANS	ENDS
Structural • Isolating mechanisms • Tangible and intangible resources • Distinctive capabilities • Intellectual property rights • Know-how **Cognitive** • Superior information about resource endowments and outcomes over time • High propensity and ability to use opportunism	• Maximum feasible above normal returns (*rents*) • 100% of market share for supplier's supply capacity • Sustainable and differentiated product/service resource endowments to leverage against competitors and the buyer

© Robertson Cox Ltd, 2004 All Rights Reserved.

commensurability of the ends that buyers and suppliers pursue, and the tension between the operational means that are available to either party in the exchange to achieve their ideal interests (ends). Since the ideal goals of the buyer can only be achieved at the expense of the supplier *asymmetric nonzero-sum* and *zero-sum* outcomes involving 'contested exchange' are the only feasible outcomes in vertical business relationships.

This means that not only are *ideal mutuality* (a win-win in which both parties achieve their ideal goals) and *symmetrical mutuality* (both parties achieve the same non-ideal outcome) not feasible in buyer and supplier exchange, but also that all outcomes involve asymmetry. This also means that power plays, based on the use of *structural* and/or *cognitive power resources*, are predictable in vertical business exchange. This is because if one party can achieve their ideal it can only be at the expense of the objective interests of the other party and, if they have not achieved their ideal, there are always preferable outcomes for both parties, either with their current or an alternative exchange partner. This means that power plays are always an issue in buyer and supplier exchange.

The operationalisation of power developed here relies heavily on the assumption that, ultimately, it is when there is an objective non-commensurability of interests that exercises of power occur in business relationships. What this indicates is that conflict and tension are at the heart of most, but not all, business relationships and that, as a consequence, relationship outcomes that delight or equally satisfy all participants may not always be possible.

This is because a win-win is only feasible in horizontal forms of exchange, and even here it is not the only feasible outcome. Asymmetric outcomes favouring one party can also occur, because there is scope for the use of *structural* and *cognitive power resources* in horizontal and in vertical business relationships. Furthermore, *nonzero-sum* outcomes based on *mutuality* do not always eradicate conflict and tension in business relationships.

On the contrary, the analysis here shows that *mutuality* rarely involves symmetry of outcomes. Often it means only that a more or less temporary *nonzero-sum* accommodation has been arrived at, which may favour one party more than another. In these asymmetrical circumstances *mutuality* should be seen as a postponement of hostilities rather than its resolution—and particularly so in vertical business relationships where commercial interests are always non-commensurable, and exercises of power by one party over another are inevitable.

What all of this means is that business relationships cannot be managed effectively if those participating in them do not understand the objective conflicts of interest that inevitably arise, or the *structural* and *cognitive power resources* that allow one party to achieve more from the exchange than another. This implies that effective business relationship management is not likely to be achieved if managers are told that all they have to do for success is to trust others and be transparent in their dealings.

On the contrary, the analysis here shows that effective business relationship management requires three things. First, it requires an objective understanding of value in exchange from the perspective of both parties to the exchange. Second, it requires an understanding of the extent to which it is possible for one party to use a variety of operational means (structural and cognitive) to achieve their objective interests, or as close as they can come to them.

The third requirement is an understanding that business relationships have not failed if a win-win is not achieved. This is because it is not only *ideal* and *symmetrical mutuality* outcomes that sustain business relationships. The analysis here shows that a wide range of asymmetric outcomes can also sustain business relationships. The challenge in business relationships is not, therefore, necessarily to search for a win-win so much as to find the relationship outcome that the other party is willing to accept, which allows the maximum sustainable operational and commercial return, given the current power resources that both parties can mobilise.

Interestingly enough, this power circumstance may have an objective reality but, paradoxically, the subjective perception of this reality is also part of the reality of business exchange. This is true because managers often subjectively misconceive the objective levers that are available to them and fail to appropriate the level of commercial and/or operational value from relationships that they should, given their currently available power resources. Given this, it is clear that some managers understand the rules of the game of power and leverage better than others, and, as a result, they are able to achieve relationship outcomes that provide them with more value than they ought to, because the other side does not understand the rules of the game (Cox et al., 2004a, 2004b). Helping managers to improve their understanding of this problem and how to effectively create and mobilise their power resources is, however, the challenge for a future volume (Cox, forthcoming).

7.5 *The Implications for Future Academic Research and Managerial Action*

One of the major criticisms laid at the door of the proponents of the power perspective is that they have not always provided a robust and rigorous methodology through which the concept can be utilised in business thinking. Hopefully the objectively derived definitions of an exercise of power in horizontal and vertical business relationships provided here will assist in the development of a more thorough analysis of the circumstances within which parties to business relationships are, or are not, able to achieve their primarily commercial, but also operational, goals.

Perhaps most importantly of all, however, the discussion here has attempted to deal with one of the major epistemological criticisms raised against the power concept. This is the problem of falsification and the counter-factual (Popper, 1959; Ryan, 1970). In the discussion presented here it has been essential to provide an objective definition of the operational and, most importantly of all, the commercial goals of the parties in different types of business relationship. Only by doing so is it possible to avoid tautology and explain when, objectively speaking, an exercise of power has occurred. This, as we saw, is when asymmetric relationship outcomes occur and one side appropriates more of what they ideally value (in relation to their objectively defined economic interests) such that the other party cannot fully achieve their ideally valued outcome.

Unfortunately, this is not sufficient. To meet a proper test of rigour and robustness theoretically it is also necessary to be able to demonstrate when an exercise of power has not occurred. Since it is possible to explain when an exercise of power has occurred (i.e. when asymmetrical outcomes based on either mutuality or win-lose occur), and when it has not occurred (i.e. when symmetrical mutuality outcomes occur), then this deductively derived operationalisation of the concept should also meet the test of falsification. The ability to explain when power has, and has not, been exercised through falsification is an essential element for the development of a robust and rigorous scientific theory of explanation.

Given this, it is to be hoped that the way of thinking developed here may provide an opportunity for researchers interested in business relationships to understand whether or not power has been exercised in all types of transactions. More importantly perhaps, it ought to provide an opportunity for the development of a more rigorous and robust understanding of the *structural* and *cognitive power resources* that allow parties on both sides of an exchange transaction to appropriate value for themselves, and thereby exercise power over others.

Another task, perhaps, is the need by academic writers to begin to understand the significant differences between vertical and horizontal business relationships in more detail. Many analyses of transactions do not focus sufficiently on the similarities and dissimilarities between horizontal forms of exchange and vertical transactions between buyers and suppliers. Related to this is the failure by most academic writers to focus rigorously on the subject of interests and the meaning of value in exchange or, in particular, on the problem of subjective and objective interests.

What is most apparent when reading the current business management and economics literature is that most writing simply does not address the fact that the interests of buyers and suppliers may not be the same, and that what they value or want from exchange may not be fully commensurable. These important tensions in business transactions are not fully dealt with in the existing literature. Furthermore, the problem of understanding the impact of subjective interests on the behaviour of managers, and how these may significantly vary in relation to objective economic interests, is also not properly explained.

In particular, it is necessary to show how this divergence between subjectively perceived interests and objectively rational economic interests provides power resources for those who understand the rules of the game of transactional exchange better than others (Cox et al., 2004a; Cox, forthcoming). This is similar to the problem of the *power of initiation* and the *power of constraint* in political studies.

The *power of initiation* refers to the ability of human actors to pursue their own subjectively defined goals. The *power of constraint* refers to the objective economic reality in which human actors have to operate, which eventually forces them to modify their actions in the light of the objective consequences that flow from their subjective perceptions of reality (Cox, 1984). In economic and business management studies it is essential that this problem is more fully understood than it is today. This is because, working closely with major public and private sector organisations demonstrates that one of the major problems for all organisations is the fact that most managers either do not understand the principles of commercial exchange and, therefore, make serious errors when they work with exchange partners, and/or they are able to replace the objective goals of the organisation with their own subjectively defined personal goals.

It can be hypothesised from this that, when organisations allow managers to initiate policies based on subjective myopia and false consciousness, it is likely that the commercial and operational performance of organisations will be sub-optimal. This is an important research hypothesis that needs to be rigorously tested in the future.

What is also particularly surprising is the fact that the concept of power and the problem of false consciousness are so rarely remarked upon by leading writers within the business management and economics disciplines. This is despite the extensive literature that exists on power as a concept and the problems of bounded rationality, information asymmetry and opportunism. It is as if some of the major writers in the business management and economics disciplines have their own form of cognitive dissonance, and do not want to recognise that managers in the real world of business exhibit extremely high levels of false consciousness, or that power plays are a normal fact of business life—something that managers in the real world of business experience no difficulty in accepting.

Thus, while the current academic literature on business management and economics provides extremely interesting insights into the resources that may assist firms to develop sustainable competitive advantages and ways of making acceptable returns, how to think about the boundary of the firm decision, and how to economise on the costs of internal and external transactions, this does not currently provide managers with praxis. Praxis means the ability to take theory and use it in practically relevant ways. The primary reason for this malaise is, arguably, because the existing literature tends to be one-dimensional in its approach to the study of transactions and does not deal with the issue of subjective and objective interests effectively.

By one-dimensional one means that the strategising literature tends to focus on the firm as supplier and as competitor; while the governance literature tends to focus on the firm as a buyer seeking to economise on the costs of transactions. What managers need, however, is a way of linking these one-dimensional approaches to dyadic exchange so that a theoretical and practical fusion can be achieved.

This was a task that Michael Porter embarked upon, but which was never fully completed. This is because, while he outlined many of the structural resource endowments available to the firm, he did not link together the transactional outcomes, or dyadic power resource configurations, that occur when the resource endowments of buyers and suppliers interact. The primary reason for this was because he was concerned with how the firm achieves competitive advantage rather than with explaining the nature of transactional exchange. Because of this, Porter failed to fully articulate all of the *structural power resources* (especially those based on incomplete contracts) and *cognitive power resources* (especially those based on opportunism) that are available for buyers and sellers to utilise as they seek to appropriate value for themselves from exchange transactions (Porter, 1980).

The task of building on the work of the many writers who have written about the concept of power to develop a science of business transactions is now much more feasible because the resource-based literature and the governance and transaction costs economising perspective have provided a much more rigorous and robust understanding of the *structural* and *cognitive power resources* that are in play on both sides of the dyad of transactional exchange. All that remains now is for the work of linking these two aspects of transactions together to begin, so that the art and science of exchange transactions in business and economics, as well as in the social science of human behaviour, can be developed.

This art and science of business transactions will, however, necessitate a robust and rigorous delineation of objective and subjective interests. It will also require an understanding of the commensurability of these interests, and the scope for exchange partners to achieve *ideal mutuality*, as well as all of the other symmetrical and asymmetrical outcomes that fall short of a true win-win. If *ideal* or other forms of *symmetrical mutuality* are not feasible then the scope for exchange partners to use *structural* and *cognitive power resources* to leverage their objective and subjective ends in all forms of transactions will also need to be delineated.

This project is enormous because it will necessitate analysis not only of private sector business-to-business (B2B) exchange (the primary subject matter of this short volume), but also all of the other forms of public and private transaction. This includes, alongside B2B transactions, those transactions involving: business to consumer (B2C); business to public sector (B2P); business to quasi-government sector (B2Q); public sector to public sector (P2P); public sector to consumer (P2C); public sector to quasi-government sector (P2Q); quasi-government to quasi-government (Q2Q); consumer to quasi-government (C2Q); and consumer to consumer (C2C).

It is an interesting research question to speculate on whether or not the interests of participants in these different types of transaction vary and, as a result, whether or not the scope for *ideal mutuality* and the power resources available for exchange partners to leverage asymmetric outcomes, vary across different transactions (and in different cultures, epochs and physical

Interests, Power and Mutuality 263

locations) as well. This is a major research agenda for the future.

When this has been achieved it will then be possible to provide individuals and business and public sector managers with what they have always wanted—a simple recipe book of which levers to pull to augment their power in order to improve their ability to appropriate value when they are involved in particular transactions. When the cookbook is finished the twin problems of subjective interests and false consciousness will, however, remain. Some managers will still fail to recognise what their objective economic interests are, and will replace these with their own subjective preferences. This means that opportunities will always remain for those who objectively understand the rules of the game of exchange to appropriate a disproportionate share of value from transactions.

This is because, while there may be structural aspects to power, there are also cognitive aspects that provide opportunities for those who do not suffer from bounded rationality and false consciousness to achieve superior results than they should, even though they lack all of the *structural power resource* that they desire. This is another way of saying that many managers in the real world of business simply do not understand the difference between subjective and objective interests and/or transactional power resources. As a result of this commercial and operational myopia, or false consciousness, managers make significant commercial errors. These errors provide significant opportunities for those who do have a better understanding of the rules of the game to appropriate a disproportionate share value from those who do not.

This fact of life is unlikely to change even if a recipe book for transactional exchange is created. The primary reason is because human beings simply lack the time, resources and inclinations to eradicate their own bounded rationality and false consciousness. This is also why so much of the practice of business in the real world is subject to error and short-sightedness. Furthermore, even if this bounded rationality and false consciousness could be eradicated, the contested nature of most, if not all, exchange relationships will remain. This is because, whatever individuals believe subjectively, structural resource endowments and non-commensurable interests exist, and this ensures that power plays will continue to occur when non-commensurable interests arise.

This means that, although harmonious exchange can occur, "contested exchange" will persist even in a world of unbounded rationality. This may be a paradox for some, but not for those who understand objective interests in business relationships. While individuals pursue their subjectively defined interests, and may believe what they wish about the causes of success and failure in business exchange, in a world of absolute and relative scarcity, where harmonious exchange is of limited transactional utility, it is the possession and mobilisation of *structural* and *cognitive power resources* that ultimately determines who gets what, how and when.

References:

Achrol, R. S., Reve, T. and Stern, L. W. (1983), 'The environment of marketing channel dyads: a framework for comparative analysis', *Journal of Marketing*, 47.

Aghion, P. and Tirole, J. (1997), 'Formal and real authority in organizations', *Journal of Political Economy*, CV.

Akerlof, G. A. (1970), 'The market for lemons: qualitative uncertainty and the market mechanism', *Quarterly Journal of Economics*, 84.

Anand, P. and Stern, L. W. (1985), 'A socio-psychological explanation for why marketing channel members relinquish control', *Journal of Marketing Research*, 22.

Aoki, M., Gustafsson, B. and Williamson, O. E. (eds.) (1990), *The Firm as a Nexus of Treaties*, Sage, London.

Arndt, J. (1983), 'The political economy paradigm: a foundation for theory building in marketing', *Journal of Marketing*, 47.

Bacharach, S. and Lawler, E. (1981), *Power and Politics in Organizations*, Jossey-Bass, San Fransisco.

Bain, J. S. (1956), *Barriers to New Competition*, Harvard University Press, Cambridge, MA.

Balbus, I. (1971), 'The concept of interest in pluralist and marxist analysis', *Politics and Society*, 1.

Baran, P. and Sweezy, P. (1966), *Monopoly Capital*, Penguin, Harmonsdworth, Middlesex.

Barney, J. B. (1991), 'Firm resources and sustained competitive advantage', *Journal of Management*, 17.

Benson, J. K. (1975), 'The inter-organizational network as a political economy', *Administrative Science Quarterly*, 20.

Blau, P. M. (1964), *Exchange and Power in Social Life*, Wiley, New York.

Bowles, S. and Gintis, H. (1988), 'Contested exchange: political economy and modern economic theory', *American Economic Review*, 78 (2).

Bowles, S. and Gintis, H. (1993), 'The revenge of Homo economicus: contested exchange and the revival of political economy', *Journal of Economic Perspectives*, Winter.

Bowles, S. and Gintis, H. (1999), 'Power in competitive exchange' in Bowles, S., Franzini, M. and Pagano, U. (eds.), *The Politics and Economics of Power*, Routledge, London.

Brady, R. A. (1943), *Business as a System of Power*, Columbia University Press, New York.

Brown, J. R., Lusch, R. F. and Nicholson, C. Y. (1995), 'Power and relationship commitment: their impact on marketing channel member performance', *Journal of Retailing*, 71 (4).

Buchanan, L. (1992), 'Vertical trade relationships: the role of dependence and symmetry in attaining organizational goals', *Journal of Marketing Research*, 29.

Campbell, N. C. G. and Cunningham, M. T. (1983), 'Customer analysis for strategy development in industrial markets', *Strategic Management Journal*, 4.

Cannon, J. P. and Perreault, W. D. (1999), 'Buyer and seller relationships in business markets', *Journal of Marketing Research*, 36.

Carlisle, J.A. and Parker, R. C. (1989), *Beyond Negotiation: Redeeming Customer-Supplier Relationships*, John Wiley, Chichester.

Chamberlain, E. H. (1933), *The Theory of Monopolistic Competition*, Harvard University Press, Cambridge, MA.

Christopher, M. and Towill, D. R. (2002), 'Developing market specific supply chain strategies', *International Journal of Logistics Management*, 13 (1).

Coase, R. (1937), 'The nature of the firm', *Economica*, 4.

Commons, J. R. (1924), *The Legal Foundations of Capitalism*, Macmillan, London.

Commons, J. R. (1934), *Institutional Economics: Its Place in Political Economy* (Volume 1), Macmillan, London.

Connolly, W. E. (1972), 'On interests in politics', *Politics and Society*, 2.

Contractor, F. J. and Lorange, P. (1988), 'Why should firms cooperate? The strategy and economic basis for cooperative ventures', in Contractor, F. J. and Lorange, P. (eds.), *Cooperative Strategies in International Business: Joint Ventures and Technology Partnerships in Firms*, Lexington Books, New York.

Cook, K. S. (1977), 'Exchange and power in networks of interorganizational relations', *Sociological Quarterly*, 18.

Cook, K. S. and Emerson, R. M. (1978), 'Power, equity and commitment in exchange networks', *American Sociological Review*, 43.

Cook, K. S., Emerson, R. M., Gilmore, M.R. and Yamagishi, T. (1983), 'The distribution of power in exchange networks: theory and experimental results', *American Journal of Sociology*, 89.

Cowley, P. R. (1985), 'Modelling the effect of buyer and seller power on the margins of commodity plastics', *Strategic Management Journal*, 3.

Cowley, P. R. (1986), 'Business margins and buyer/seller power', *The Review of Economics and Statistics*, 68.

Cox, A. (1984), *Adversary Politics and Land: The Conflict over Land and Property in Post-War Britain*, Cambridge University Press, Cambridge.

Cox, A. (1997a), *Business Success: A Way of Thinking about Strategy, Critical Supply Chain Assets and Operational Best Practice*, Earlsgate Press, Stratford-upon-Avon.

Cox, A. (1997b), 'On power, appropriateness and procurement competence', *Supply Management*, October.

Cox, A. (1999a), 'Improving procurement and supply competence: on the appropriate use of reactive and proactive tools and techniques in the public and private sectors' in Lamming, R. and Cox, A. (eds), *Strategic Procurement Management: Concepts and Cases*, Earlsgate Press, Stratford-upon-Avon.

Cox, A. (1999b), 'Power, value and supply chain management', *Supply Chain Management: An International Journal*, 4 (4).

Cox, A. (2001), 'The power perspective in procurement and supply management', *Journal of Supply Chain Management*, 27 (2).

Cox, A. (2004a), "Strategic outsourcing: avoiding the loss of critical assets and the problems of adverse selection and moral hazard", in *Business Briefing: Global Purchasing and Supply Chain Strategies*, Business Briefings Ltd, London.

Cox, A. (2004b), 'The art of the possible: relationship management in power regimes and supply chains', *Supply Chain Management: An International Journal*, 9 (5).

Cox, A. (2004c), 'Business relationship alignment: on the commensurability of value capture and mutuality in buyer and supplier exchange', *Supply Chain Management: An International Journal*, 9 (5).

Cox, A. (forthcoming), *The Rules of The Game: How to Capture Value in Business*, Earlsgate Press, Stratford-upon-Avon.

Cox, A., Chicksand, D. and Palmer, M. (2004), *Business Relationship Optimisation in UK Red Meat Supply Chains*, Report for the Red Meat Industry Forum, Milton Keynes, July.

Cox, A., Furlong, P. and Page, E. (1985), *Power in Capitalist Societies: Theory, Explanation and Cases*, St Martin's Press, New York.

Cox, A., Ireland, P., Lonsdale, C., Sanderson, J. and Watson, G. (2002), *Supply Chains, Markets and Power: Mapping Buyer and Supplier Power Regimes*, Routledge, London.

Cox, A., Ireland, P., Lonsdale, C., Sanderson, J. and Watson, G. (2003), *Supply Chain Management: A Guide to Best Practice*, Financial Times/Prentice Hall, London.

Cox, A., Lonsdale, C., Sanderson, J. and Watson, G. (2004a), *Business Relationships for Competitive Advantage: Managing Alignment and Misalignment in Buyer and Supplier Transactions*, Palgrave Macmillan, Basingstoke.

Cox, A., Lonsdale, C., Sanderson, J. and Watson, G. (2004b), 'Managing appropriately in power regimes: relationship and performance management in 12 supply chain cases', *Supply Chain Management: An International Journal*, 9 (5).

Cox, A., Sanderson, J. and Watson, G. (2000), *Power Regimes: Mapping the DNA of Business and Supply Chain Relationships*, Earlsgate Press, Stratford-upon-Avon.

Cox, A. and Townsend, M. (1998), *Strategic Procurement for Construction*, Thomas Telford, London.

Das, T. K. (1990), *The Time Dimension: An Interdisciplinary Guide*, Praeger, New York.

Das, T. K. (2004), 'Time-span and risk of partner opportunism in strategic alliances', *Journal of Managerial Psychology*, 19 (8).

Das, T. K. and Rahman, N. (2002), 'Opportunism dynamics in strategic alliances' in Contractor, F. J. and Lorange, P. (eds.), *Cooperative Strategies and Alliances*, Pergamon, London.

Das, T. K. and Teng, B. S. (2002), 'A social exchange theory of strategic alliances' in Contractor, F. J. and Lorange, P. (eds.), *Cooperative Strategies and Alliances*, Pergamon, London.

David, R. J. and Han, S. (2004), 'A systematic assessment of the empirical support for transaction cost economics', *Strategic Management Journal*, 25 (1).

Dosi, G. (1995), 'Hierarchies, markets and power: some foundational issues on the nature of contemporary economic organizations', *Industrial and Corporate Change*, 4 (1).

Dwyer, F. R. and Sejo, O. (1987), 'Output sector munificence effects in the internal political economy of marketing channels', *Journal of Marketing Research*, 24.

Dwyer, F. R. and Summers, J. O. (1986), 'Perceptions of interfirm power and its use within a franchise channel of distribution', *Journal of Marketing Research*, 23.

El-Ansary, A. and Stern, L. W. (1972), 'Power and measurement in the distribution channel', *Journal of Marketing Research*, 9.

Emerson, R. M. (1962), 'Power-dependence relations', *American Sociological Review*, 27.

Etgar, M. (1976), 'Channel domination and countervailing power in distributive channels', *Journal of Marketing*, 44 (3).

Finkelstein, S. (1992), 'Power in top management teams: dimensions, measurement and validation', *Academy of Management Journal*, 35.

Fisher, M. (1997), 'What is the right supply chain for your product?', *Harvard Business Review*, 75 (2).

Ford, D. and McDowell, R. (1999), 'Managing business relationships by analysing the effects and value of different actions', *Industrial Marketing Management*, 28 (5).

Ford, D. (ed.) (1998), *Managing Business Relationships*, John Wiley, Chichester.

Ford D. (ed.) (2002), *Understanding Business Markets and Purchasing: An Interaction Approach,* International Thompson, London.

Foss, N. J. (2003), 'The strategic management and transaction cost nexus: past debates, central questions, and future research possibilities', *Strategic Organisation*, 1.

Foss, K. and Foss, N. J. (2000), 'Competence and governance perspectives: how much do they differ? And how does it matter?' in Foss, N. J. and Mahnke, V. (eds.), *Competence, Governance and Entrepreneurship*, Oxford University Press, Oxford.

Foss, K. and Foss, N. J. (2001), 'Assets, attributes and ownership', *International Journal of the Economics of Business*, 8.

Frazier, G. L. (1983), 'Inter-organizational exchange behaviour in marketing channels: a broadened perspective', *Journal of Marketing*, 47.

Frazier, G. L. and Anita, K. (1995), 'Exchange relationships and inter-firm power in channels of distribution', *Journal of the Academy of Marketing Sciences*, 23.

Frazier, G. L. and Rody, R. C. (1991), 'The use of influence strategies in inter-firm relationships in industrial product channels', *Journal of Marketing*, 55.

French, J. R. and Raven, B. (1959), 'The bases of social power', in Cartwright, D. (ed.), *Studies in Social Power*, University of Michigan Press, Ann Arbor.

Gabel, H. L. (1983), 'The role of buyer power in oligopoly models: an empirical study', *Journal of Economics and Business*, 35.

Galbraith, C. S. and Stiles, C. H. (1983), 'Firm profitability and relative firm power', *Strategic Management Journal*, 4.

Gallie, W. B. (1955-6), 'Essentially contested concepts', *Proceedings of the Aristotelian Society*, 56.

Gaski, J. F. (1986), 'Interrelations among a channel entity's power sources: impact of the exercise, referent and legitimate power sources', *Journal of Marketing Research*, 23 (1).

Goldman, A. I. (1972), 'Towards a theory of social power', *Philosophical Studies*, 23 (4).

Granovetter, M. (1985), 'Economic action and social structure: the problem of embeddedness', *American Journal of Sociology*, 91 (3).

Grant, R. (1991), 'The resource-based theory of competitive advantage: implications for strategy formulation', *California Management Review*, 33.

Grossman, S. and Hart, O. (1983), 'An analysis of the principal-agent problem', *Journal of Financial Economics*, 20.

Grossman, S. and Hart, O. (1986), 'The costs and benefits of ownership: a theory of vertical and lateral integration', *Journal of Political Economy*, 94 (4).

Gummesson, E. (2002), *Total Relationship Marketing*, Butterworth Heinemann, Oxford.

Gundlach, G. T. and Cadotte, E. R. (1994), 'Exchange interdependence and inter-firm reaction: research in a simulated channel setting', *Journal of Marketing Research*, 31.

Hadeler, B. J. and Evans, J. R. (1994), 'Supply strategy: capturing the value', *Industrial Management*, 36 (4).

Håkansson, H. and Gadde, L. E. (1997), 'Supplier relations', in Ford, D. (ed.) *Understanding Business Markets: Interactions, Relationships and Networks*, Dryden Press, London.

Harsanyi, J. C. (1962), 'Measurement of social power in *n*-person reciprocal power situations', *Behavioural Science*, 7.

Hart, O. (1989), 'An economist's perspective on the theory of the firm', *Columbia Law Review*, 89 (7).

Hart, O. (1995), *Firms, Contracts and Financial Structure*, Clarendon Press, Oxford.

Hart, O. and Moore, J. (1990), 'Property rights and the nature of the firm', *Journal of Political Economy*, 98 (6).

Heidi, J. and John, G. (1988), 'The role of dependence balancing in safeguarding transaction-specific assets in conventional channels', *Journal of Marketing*, 52.

Hines, P., Lamming, R., Jones, D., Cousins, P. and Rich, N. (2000), *Value Stream Management: Strategy and Excellence in the Supply Chain*, Financial Times/Prentice Hall, London.

Homans, G. (1958), 'Social behavior as exchange', *The American Journal of Sociology*, 65 (6).

Hunt, K. A., Mentzer, J. T. and Danes, J. E. (1987), 'The effects of power sources on compliance in a channel of distribution: a causal model', *Journal of Business Research*, 15 (5).

Jacobs, J. (1974), 'Dependency and vulnerability: an exchange approach to the control of organizations', *Administrative Science Quarterly*, 19 (1).

Kim, H., Hoskisson, R. E. and Wan, W. P. (2004), 'Power dependence, diversification and performance in keiretsu member firms', *Strategic Management Journal*, 25.

Knight, F. H. (2002), *Risk, Uncertainty and Profit*, Beard Books, Washington.

Kumar, N., Sheer, L. K. and Steenkamp, J. E. M. (1995), 'The effects of perceived interdependence on dealer attitudes', *Journal of Marketing Research*, 32.

Lamming, R. C. (1993), *Beyond Partnership: Strategies for Innovation and Lean Supply*, Prentice Hall, London.

Lamming, R. C., Caldwell, N. D., Harrison, D. A. and Phillips, W. (2001), 'Transparency in supplier relationships: concept and practice', *Journal of Supply Chain Management*, 37 (4).

Lee, H. L. (2002), 'Aligning supply chain strategies with product uncertainties', *California Management Review*, 44 (3).

Lippman, S. A. and Rumelt, R. P. (2003a), 'A bargaining perspective on resource advantage', *Strategic Management Journal*, 24 (11).

Lippman, S. A. and Rumelt, R. P. (2003b), 'The payments perspective: micro-foundations of resource analysis', *Strategic Management Journal*, 24, Special Issue.

Lukes, S. (1977), *Power: A Radical View*, Macmillan, Harmondsworth, Middlesex.

Lustgarten, S. H. (1975), 'The impact of buyer concentration in manufacturing industries', *The Review of Economics and Statistics*, 57.

Macbeth, D. and Ferguson, N. (1994), *Partnership Sourcing*, Pitman, London.

Macneil, I. R. (1974), 'The many futures of contacts', *Southern California Law Review*, 47 (May).

Macneil, I. R. (1983), 'Values in contract: internal and external', *Northwestern University Law Review*, 78 (2).

Maloni, M. and Benton, W. C. (2000), 'Power influences in the supply chain', *Journal of Business Logistics*, 21 (1).

March, J. G. (1966), 'The power of power', in Easton, D. (ed.), *Varieties of Political Theory*, Prentice Hall, Englewood Cliffs, NJ.

March, J. G. (1988), *Decisions and Organizations*, Basil Blackwell, Oxford.

Marx, K. (1967), *Capital*, Vol. 1, International Publishers, New York.

Maslow, A. H. (1943), 'A theory of human motivation', *Psychological Review*, 50.

McDonald, F. (1999), 'The importance of power in partnership relationships', *Journal of General Management*, 25 (1).

McMillan, J. (1992), *Games, Strategies and Managers*, Oxford University Press, Oxford.

Milgrom, P. and Roberts, J. (1992), *Economics, Organization and Management*, Prentice Hall, Englewood Cliffs, NJ.

Mintzberg, H. (1983), *Power In and Around Organizations*, Prentice Hall, Englewood Cliffs, NJ.

Molho, I. (1997), *The Economics of Information: Lying and Cheating in Markets and Organisations*, Blackwell, Oxford.

Nagel, J. (1968), 'Some questions about the concept of power', *Behavioural Science*, 13 (2).

Olson, M. (2000), *Power and Prosperity*, Basic Books, New York.

Oxley, J. E. (1999), 'Institutional environment and the mechanisms of governance: the impact of intellectual property protection on the structure of inter-firm alliances', *Journal of Economic Behaviour and Organization*, 38.

Penrose, E. T. (1959), *The Theory of the Growth of the Firm*, Oxford University Press, Oxford.

Peteraf, M. A. (1993), 'The cornerstones of competitive advantage: a resource-based view', *Strategic Management Journal*, 14 (3).

Pfeffer, J. (1981), *Power in Organizations*, Pitman, Marshfield, MA.

Pfeffer, J. and Salancik, G. R. (1978), *The External Control of Organizations: A Resource Dependency Perspective*, Harper & Row, New York.

Popper, K. (1959), *The Logic of Scientific Enquiry*, Hutchinson, London.

Porter, M. E. (1980), *Competitive Strategy: Techniques for Analysing Industries and Competitors*, Free Press, New York.

Provan, K. G. and Gassenheimer, J. B. (1994), 'Supplier commitment in relational contract exchange with buyers: a study of inter-organizational dependence and exercised power', *Journal of Management Studies*, 31.

Rajan, R. G. and Zingales, L. (1998), 'Power in a theory of the firm', *The Quarterly Journal of Economics*, May.

Ramsay, J. (1994), 'Purchasing power', *European Journal of Purchasing and Supply Management*, 1 (3).

Ramsay, J. (1996a), 'Power measurement', *European Journal of Purchasing and Supply Management*, 2 (2/3).

Ramsay, J. (1996b), 'The case against purchasing partnerships', *International Journal of Purchasing and Materials Management*, Fall.

Ramsay, J. (2004), 'Supplier value: an undiscovered dimension of value in business-to-business trade', *Proceedings of the 13th IPSERA Conference*, Catania, Italy.

Roberts, J. (2004), *The Modern Firm: Organizational Design for Performance and Growth*, Oxford University Press, Oxford.

Robertson, D. H. (1928), *The Control of Industry*, Nisbet & Co., London.

Robinson, J. (1933), *The Economics of Imperfect Competition*, Macmillan, London.

Rumelt, R. P. (1987), 'Theory, strategy and entrepreneurship', in Teece, D. (ed.), *The Competitive Challenge: Strategies for Industrial Innovation and Renewal*, Harper & Row, New York.

Ryan, A. (1970), *The Philosophy of the Social Sciences*, Macmillan, London.

Salancik. G. R. and Pfeffer, J. (1977), 'Who gets power and how do they hold on to it: a strategic-contingency model of power', *Organizational Dynamics*, 6.

Sanderson, J. (2004), 'Opportunity and constraint in business-to-business relationships: insights from strategic choice and zones of manoeuvre', *Supply Chain Management: An International Journal*, 9 (5).

Schul, P. L., Pride, W. L. and Little, T. L. (1983), 'The impact of channel leadership behavior in intra-channel conflicts', *Journal of Marketing*, 47.

Scott, C. and Westbrook, R. (1991), 'New strategic tools for supply chain management', *International Journal of Physical Distribution and Logistics Management*, 21 (10).

Shapiro, B. P., Kasturi Rangan, V., Moriarty, R. T. and Ross, E. B. (1987), 'Manage customers for profits (not just sales)', *Harvard Business Review*, September-October.

Simon, H. A. (1955), 'A behavioural model of rational choice', *Quarterly Journal of Economics*, 69.

Smith, A. (1776), *The Wealth of Nations*, Penguin, 1985 edition, Harmondsworth, Middlesex.

Stern, L. W. and Reve, T. (1980), 'Distribution channels as political economies: a framework for comparative analysis', *Journal of Marketing*, 44 (3).

Stiglitz, J. E. (1987), 'The causes and consequences of the dependence of quality on price', *Journal of Economic Literature*, XXV (March).

Stolt, J. F. and Emerson, R. M. (1977), 'Structural inequality, position and power in network structures' in Hamblin, R. and Kunkel, J. (eds), *Behavioral Theory in Sociology*, Transaction, New Brunswick, NJ.

Thorelli, H. (1986), 'Networks: between hierarchies and markets', *Strategic Management Journal*, 7.

Turnbull, P. W. and Zolkiewski, J. M. (1995), 'Customer portfolios: sales, costs and profitability', *Manchester School of Management*, UMIST, UK.

Walsmsley, G. L. and Zald, M. N. (1973), *The Political Economy of Public Organizations*, Lexington Books, Lexington, MA.

Wathne, K. H. and Heide, J. B. (2000) 'Opportunism in inter-firm relationships: forms, outcomes and solutions', *Journal of Marketing*, 64 (4).

Watson, G. and Sanderson, J. (1997), 'Collective goods versus private interests: lean enterprise and the free rider problem' in Cox, A. and Hines, P. (eds.), *Advanced Supply Management: The Best Practice Debate*, Earlsgate Press, Stratford-upon-Avon.

Wernerfelt, B. (1984), 'A resource-based theory of the firm', *Strategic Management Journal*, 5 (2).

Wilkinson, I. (1981), Power, conflict and satisfaction in distribution channels', *International Journal of Physical Distribution and Materials Management*, 11 (7).

Wilkinson, I. F. and Young, L. C. (2002), 'Business dancing: the nature and role of inter-firm relations in business strategy', in Ford, D. (2002) (ed.), *Understanding Business Markets and Purchasing*, Thomson Learning, London.

Williamson, O. E. (1975), *Markets and Hierarchies: Analysis and Antitrust Implications*, Free Press, New York.

Williamson, O. E. (1985), *The Economic Institutions of Capitalism*, Free Press, New York.

Williamson, O. E. (1991), 'Strategizing, economising and economic organization', *Strategic Management Journal*, 12.

Williamson, O. E. (1993), 'Opportunism and its critics', *Managerial and Decision Economics*, 14 (2).

Williamson, O. E. (1995), 'Hierarchies, Markets and Power in the Economy', *Industrial and Corporate Change*, 4 (1).

Williamson, O. E. (1996), *The Mechanisms of Governance*, Free Press, New York.

Williamson, O. E. (1999), 'Strategy research: governance and competence perspectives', *Strategic Management Journal*, 20 (12).

Williamson, O. E. (2000) *Empirical Microeconomics: Another Perspective*, unpublished paper, University of California, Berkeley, CA.

Womack, J., Jones, D. and Roos, D. (1990), *The Machine That Changed the World*, Rawson Associates, New York.

Womack, J. and Jones, D. (1996), *Lean Thinking: Banish Waste and Create Wealth in Your Organisation*, Simon Schuster, New York.

Yamagishi, T., Gillmore, M. R. and Cook, K. S. (1988), 'Network Connections and the Distribution of Power in Exchange Networks', *American Journal of Sociology*, 93 (4).

Zajac, E. J. and Olsen, C. P. (1993), 'From transaction cost to transactional value analysis: implications for the study of inter-organizational strategies', *Journal of Management Studies*, 30 (1).

Zald, M. N. (1970), 'Political economy: a framework for comparative analysis' in Zald, M. N. (ed.), *Power in Organizations*, Vanderbilt University Press, Nashville, TN.

Index:

A

above-normal returns, 48, 53-54, 68, 89, 102, 104, 110, 117, 139, 178-179, 202, 230, 243
absolute scarcity, 204, 264
Achrol, R. S., 200
Aghion, P., 201
Akerlof, G. A., 29,176
Anand, P., 200
Anita, K., 200
alliance, 116
alliancing, 8-9, 40
Aoki, M., 31
Arndt, J., 200
arm's-length relationships, 20-22, 24-25, 35, 41-42
asset specificity, 231-233, 247
asymmetric exchange, 235
asymmetric information, 249
asymmetric mutuality, 126, 142, 144, 152-153, 206, 225, 244
asymmetric nonzero-sum outcomes, 244, 251, 254
asymmetric outcomes, 12,15, 25, 27, 57-61, 69, 71, 73, 95, 101-102, 105, 112-113, 121-122, 124-126, 130, 133, 135, 137-138, 151-153, 204, 226, 228, 231-233, 236, 238-240, 244, 246, 250-251, 254, 256-258, 262
authority, of the state, 214

B

Bacharach, S., 200
Bain, J. S., 200
Balbus, I., 194
Baran, P., 200
Barney, J. B., 202
barriers to trade, 217
benchmarking, 174
Benson, J. K., 200
Benton, W. C., 201
best practice, 197
bilateral dependency, 21, 231, 233, 237, 247
Blau, P. M., 78

281

282 Win-Win?

BMW, 10
bottom line performance, 181, 223
boundary of the firm decisions, 212-213, 219-221, 260
bounded rationality, 32, 36, 38, 42, 150, 176, 206-207, 235, 237, 239, 242, 248, 260, 263-264
Bowles, S., 30, 40-41, 77-78, 121,200, 201, 209, 245, 248
Brady, R. A., 200
brand, 100
break even, 53, 99, 110, 116, 119-121, 139, 140-143, 151-152, 156, 167, 190-191
British Aerospace, 10
Brown, J. R., 200
Buchanan, L., 200
business relationship alignment, 162, 189
Business Schools, 171
business to business (B2B) exchange, 262
business to consumer (B2C) exchange, 262
business to public sector (B2P) exchange, 262
business to quasi-government sector (B2Q) exchange, 262
buyer and supplier exchange, 15, 41, 73-107, 118-120, 127, 142-143, 150, 161, 189, 191, 206
buyer dominance, 99, 244
buyer dominant collaboration, 97
buyer dominant relationships, 40
buying consortia, 230

C

Cadotte, E. R., 200
Campbell, N. C. G., 78, 200
Cannon, J.P., 21
capacity utilization, 115
capitalists, 217
car assemblers, 166
car industry, 166-167
Carlisle, J. A., 22
cash flow, 152
Chamberlain, E. H., 200
cheating, 239
Chicksand, D., 168
Christopher, M., 74
Coase, R., 200, 210
Coasean perspective, critique of, 198, 210-224
cognitive dissonance, 260
cognitive power resources, 16, 226, 228-229, 236-242, 244, 247-249, 254-255, 258, 261-264

Index   283

coincidence of interests, 251
Cold War, 219
collaboration, 7-10,
collaborative relationships, 7-11, 20-22, 24-25, 35, 39-43, 53-71, 168, 170
collaborative sourcing, 34-35, 39-43, 73-74, 81, 84-85, 94, 97, 100-104
comprehensive clause contracts, 246
commensurability of interests, 78-79, 84, 90, 93, 117, 121-122, 138-141, 161, 188-189, 192-193, 208, 225-226, 234, 236, 238, 240-241, 243, 250-255, 258-259, 262, 264
commercial cost, 82
commercial ends, 168, 170-171, 208
commercial exchange, 170, 237
commercial goals, 171
commercial incompetence, 172
commercial myopia, 168, 170, 174-175
commercial risks,168
commercial value, 166-179, 181, 188, 192
commercial value outcomes, 77-79, 82, 84-85, 106-107, 109-163
commodity exchange, 217, 259
Commons, J. R., 199, 204
competing claims, 248
competitive advantage, 212, 224, 260-261
competitive markers, 229
complete contracts, 246-247
conflicts of interest, 162, 204-205, 244, 247, 255
conflicts in relationships, 92, 138-139, 161-162, 197, 204, 206, 208, 236, 244, 254-255
Connolly, W. E., 194
construction industry, 167
consumer to consumer (C2C) exchange, 262
consumer to quasi-government (C2Q) exchange, 262
contestation, 87, 100, 110, 230
contested exchange, 40, 77-78, 121, 142, 153, 161, 198, 225, 243-256, 264
contested markets, 93, 99
contingent renewal, 249
Contractor, F. J. 38, 61, 66
contractual safeguards, 233-237
control of the means of production and exchange, 199, 210, 216
Cook, K. S., 78,,200, 209, 245
cost reductions, 122
counter-factual, problem of, 257
Cowley, P. R., 200
Cox, A., 14, 20, 40-41, 46, 77-79, 81, 89, 94, 98, 106, 121, 142, 145, 167, 168, 169,174, 183, 189, 194, 200, 201, 204, 210, 229, 237, 242, 244, 257, 259
credible commitment contracting, 208, 233, 235
critical assets, 210-211, 221-222
critical supply chain assets, 212

cultural norms and bonds, 98
Cunningham, M. T., 78, 200
customer responsiveness, 115
cycle time, 115

D

Das, T. K., 29, 39, 70, 80, 117, 122, 138, 241
David, R.J., 224
dedicated investments, 98
dependency, 80-81, 151-152, 157-158, 168, 239
dependent party, 59-61, 69
Direct Line, 169
differentiated products and/or services, 114
differentiation, 146, 221-223
direct selling methods, 168
distinctive capabilities, 230
dominance, 247
dominant buyer, 162
dominant party, 59-62, 69, 100, 232
dominant supplier, 102, 162
Dosi, G., 171
DTI, 168
duopoly, 100
Dwyer, F. R., 200
dyadic exchange, 74-75, 197, 230, 242, 261

E

economic rationality, 175, 187-188, 208, 236-237, 239, 259
El-Ansary, A., 200
Emerson, R. M., 78, 200, 209, 245
end customers, 167
endogenous enforcement, 249
enforcement, of competing claims, 248-249
entrepreneurs, 211, 214-218, 220-224, 237
entrepreneurship, 171, 214-218
epistemology, 201, 205, 257
Etgar, M., 200
Evans, J.R., 200
ex-ante relationships, 202, 245-247
ex-post relationships, 202, 245-247
ex-post structural power resources, 241, 248

exchange asymmetry, 234
exchange partners, 169, 225-226, 228-229, 231, 233, 235-236, 240-241, 251, 254, 259, 262
exchange theory, 209
exchange transactions, 21, 25, 113, 197, 199, 202-204, 207, 210, 214-215, 223, 225-256, 261
exchange trade-offs, 86, 127
exchange value, 82, 85, 88-89, 93, 199
exploitation of labour, 216
external contracts, 215
external processes, 166
externalities, 213

F

false consciousness, 12, 16, 29, 162, 165-195, 229, 237, 239-241, 260, 263-264
falsification, test of, 257-258
farming industry, 167-168
Ferguson, N., 74
Finkelstein, S., 200
firm, theory of, 211-224
first dimension of power, 240, 247, 249
Fisher, M., 74
fmcg industries, 167
food industry, 167
Ford, D., 74, 76
Foss, N.J., 202, 224
Frazier, G. I., 200
free riders, 116-117
French, J. R., 200
functionality, 82-90, 92-93, 97-100, 104, 110-112, 116-117, 119,122, 139, 142-143, 145-159, 179, 189, 231, 241, 244
fungibility of assets, 247
Furlong, P., 194, 200

G

Gabel, H. I., 200
Gadde, L.E., 200
Galbraith, C. S., 200
Gallie, W. B., 194,
Gaski, J. F., 200
Gassenheimer, J. B., 78, 200

Gintis, H., 30, 40-41, 121, 200, 201, 209, 245, 248
Goldman, A. I., 200
governance perspective, 209, 224-225, 242-243, 261
governance structures, 230, 233
Granovetter, M., 200
Grant, R., 202
Grossman, S., 212, 215
Gummesson, E., 23
Gundlach, G. T., 200

H

Hadeler, B. J., 200
Hakanssson, H., 200
Han, S., 224
harmonious exchange, 250-251, 264
Harsanyi, J. C., 200
Hart, O., 29, 212, 215
headcount, 223
Heide, J. B., 138
Heidi, J., 200
hierarchies of need, 46, 48
Hines, P., 74
hold-up, 41, 81, 102, 167-168, 247
Homans, G., 204, 225
homo economicus, 235
Honda, 10-11
horizontal business relationships, 14-15, 30, 35-39, 45-72, 79-80, 84-85, 109, 116, 121-138, 142-143, 150, 161, 166, 170, 176, 182, 187-188, 204, 206, 228, 230, 233, 241, 243-244, 246, 250-251, 257-258
hostages, 233
Hunt, K. A., 200

I

IBM, 168
ideal mutuality, 23, 26, 28, 39-42, 45-46, 53-54, 77-78, 94-95, 106, 111-112, 124-126, 135, 138, 141-143, 161, 165, 189-190, 206, 225-226, 228, 243, 244, 251, 254, 256, 262
ideal symmetrical mutuality, 125
ignorance, 242, 249
IMP school, 74-76
imperfect information, 237

imperfect markets, 229-230
improve profitability, 113
improvements in capacity utilization, 115
improvements in customer responsiveness, 115
improvements in process cycle times, 115
improvements in product and service quality, 115
improvements in supplier and supply chain management, 115
incompetence, 246
incomplete contracts, 41, 230, 236-237, 245-247, 261
industrial revolution, 220
industry standard practice, 169
inefficient contracting, 208
information asymmetry, 30, 33, 36, 38, 41-42, 89-90, 150, 176, 206-207, 235, 237, 239, 242, 248-249, 260
insourcing, 211-212, 219-220, 233
intangible assets, 230
intellectual property, 230
interactions approach, 74
interdependence power structures, 98-99
interests, 71, 162, 172, 177, 191, 197-264
intermediaries, 168
internal contracts, 215
internal processes, 166
internet economy, 219
isolating mechanisms, 54-56, 114, 230
IT industry, 168

J

Jacobs, J., 200
joint-stock limited liability companies, 213, 217-219
joint ventures, 8, 11, 15-16, 23, 34-38, 43, 45-46, 53-61, 110, 116-117, 121, 128-131, 133-135, 137, 182, 188, 230, 251
John, G., 200
Jones, D., 85
junk bond status, 166

K

Kim, H., 78, 201
Knight, F. H., 215
know how, 230
Kumar, N., 200

L

labour theory of value, 199-200
Lamming, R. C, 74, 76
Lawler, E., 200
lean production, 166-167
lean supply, 166-168
lean tools and techniques, 166-168
Lee, H. E., 74
legitimacy, of the state, 214
leverage, 13-14, 19, 162, 171-172, 202, 208, 210, 222-223, 226, 228-230, 236, 238, 242, 247, 249-250, 256, 262-263
limited liability, 210, 217-219
Lippman, S. A., 224
lock-in, 9-10, 19, 41, 81, 149
Lorange, P., 38, 61, 66
lose-lose, 15, 25, 27, 55, 57, 64, 66-67, 101-103, 112, 118, 120, 144, 147
lose-win, 94, 104, 118-120, 144, 169
loss leaders, 52-53, 102-105, 110-111, 119-121, 149-150, 152, 156, 241
low returns, 87, 162, 166-168, 181, 244
Lukes, S., 194, 240
Lustgarten, S. H., 200
lying, 239, 247

M

Macbeth, D., 74
Macneil, I. R., 20, 76
make/buy decision-making, 210, 219-220, 222-223
Maloni, M., 201
management academics, 171
market analysis, 246
market closure, 90, 110, 112, 116-122, 139, 188, 202-203, 230, 239, 245
market contestation, 230
market exchange, 233-234
market failure, 201-202
market inefficiency, 217
market power, 202-203
March, J. G., 200, 205, 209, 228
market tested sourcing, 34-37, 39-43, 73-74, 80-81, 84-85, 94-95, 97, 99-101, 103-104
Marx, K., 199-200, 210-211, 216
Maslow, A. H., 46
maximisation, 47-48, 88, 109-110, 122, 145, 152-153, 157-158, 185, 212, 221, 245
McDonald, F., 201

McDowell, R., 76
McMillan, J., 22
means of production and exchange, 218, 221
Milgrom, P., 29, 81,167
MOD, 168
Molho, I., 29,176
monopoly, 80, 202, 230
monopolists, 190
monopsony, 80, 230, 239
moral hazard, 41
Moore, J. 212
Mintzberg, H., 200
mutuality, 12, 16-17, 24, 28-29, 32, 42-43, 70-71, 73-76, 78, 94-99, 101, 105, 112, 124-127, 137, 142, 162, 165, 191, 195, 197-264
myopia, 229, 231, 233, 237, 240-241, 246, 259-260, 263

N

Nagel, J., 200
network relationships, 75
non-commensurability of interests 78-79, 84, 90-93, 117, 121-122, 138-141, 161, 188-189, 192-193, 208, 225-226, 234, 236, 238, 240-241, 243, 249-255, 258-259, 262, 264
nonzero-sum mutuality, 154
nonzero-sum outcomes, 20, 112, 138, 141-142, 144, 151, 155-157, 159, 161, 165, 206, 226, 244, 250, 255
nonzero-sum asymmetrical mutuality, 141, 244
nonzero-sum symmetrical mutuality, 141
normal returns, 48-49, 53, 68, 87, 97, 99, 102, 104, 110-111, 116, 119-121, 139, 142, 152, 156, 181, 190-191, 202-203
nous, 229, 237

O

obedience, to commands, 248-249
obfuscating, 239
objective interests, 14-16, 23, 29, 41, 45-53, 77, 99, 109-112, 121, 124, 128, 138, 161-163, 165-166, 177-179, 188-195, 203-204, 208, 225-226, 228-229, 231, 234-235, 238-240, 242, 254-255, 258-259, 260, 262-264
objective reality, 239
oligopoly, 100, 230
oligopsony, 230
Olsen, C. P., 75, 77

Olson, M., 201
one-dimensional thinking, 260-261
one-off games, 104-106
open book, 97
operational means, 168, 171, 208, 214, 226, 254-255
operational myopia, 175-176
operational value, 166-179
operational value outcomes, 77-79, 82, 84-85, 106-107, 109-163
opportunism, 29-30, 32-33, 35-36, 41-42, 80, 115, 128, 130, 149, 176, 188, 197, 201, 206-208, 230, 233, 235-236, 239, 242, 245-246, 248-249, 260-261
outsourcing, 211, 213, 219-220, 223
ownership of the means of production and exchange, 199, 210, 216, 250
Oxley, J. E. 224

P

Page, E., 194, 200
Palmer, M., 168,
Parker, R. C., 22
partial win outcomes, 23, 25-27, 42-43, 52-66, 68-71, 95-101, 104-106, 112, 116, 118-122, 126-127, 141-143, 145, 151-159, 169, 179, 181, 190, 193-194, 226, 228, 251
partnership sourcing, 7-8, 40
partnerships, 40
path-dependency, 171
Penrose, E. T., 202
perfect competition, 201
perfect markets, 203, 229
performance measurement, 246
performance management, 246
Perreault, W. D., 21
Peteraf, M.A., 202
Pfeffer, J., 78, 200, 209, 245
Physiocrats, 199
political economy perspective, 16, 198, 209
Popper, K., 257
Porter, M. E., 78, 200, 209, 229, 245, 261
positive-sum outcomes, 138, 155, 165, 206
post-contractual hold-up, 167-168, 237
post-contractual relationships, 202, 213, 246
power, 13-14, 19, 78-79, 138, 162, 197-264,
power and leverage perspective, 78-79, 225-264
power balance, 248
power in exchange, 199
power of constraint, 259
power of initiation, 259

Index 291

power plays, 254, 260, 264
power resources, 79, 176, 204, 222, 226, 228-229, 236-239, 242, 256, 259, 261-263
praxis, 260-261
pre-contractual relationships, 202, 213, 237
preferences, 146-161, 185-188, 191-195
price fixing, 246
principal-agent relationships, 215-216, 218-222, 232
profit maximisers, 47-48
profitability, 148, 181, 223
profits, 48-49, 149, 157, 168-169, 202, 210-213, 215, 217, 222
property rights, 212-213
Provan, K. G., 78, 200
public sector to consumer (P2C) exchange, 262
public sector to public sector (P2P) exchange, 262
public sector to quasi-government (P2Q) exchange, 262
putting out system, 218-219

Q

quality fixing, 246
quality standards, 231
Quesnay, 199

R

Rahman, N., 29, 122
Rajan, R. G., 200
Ramsay, J., 77, 78, 200
rank ordering of preferences, 146-161, 185-188, 191-195
Raven, B., 200
reciprocal collaboration, 40-41, 98
relational approach, 74-76
relational specific adaptations, 98
relative scarcity, 204, 242, 264
relative utility, 242
rents, 48-49, 55, 87-90, 93, 98, 110-111, 113, 116-117, 119-120, 130, 135, 139, 143, 148-150, 153, 156, 159, 167, 170, 178, 181, 188, 190-191, 193-194, 202-203, 230, 241, 243-245, 251
repeat games, 106
resource-based approach, 202-204, 224, 261
resource-dependency school, 209, 231-233, 239, 242
resource endowments, 210, 214, 228-234, 236, 238-239, 242, 261
returns, 89-91, 110-111, 114, 119-120, 122, 130, 148-159, 187, 192, 211-212, 244, 260

Reve, T., 200
revenue, 89-91, 110, 113-114, 117-120, 135, 139, 142-143, 148-159
risk aversion by managers, 173-175
risk taking, 174-175, 215-218, 220, 234
Roberts, J., 29, 81,167,
Robertson, D. H., 200
Robinson J. 200
Rody, R. C., 200
Rover, 10-11
rules of the game, 237, 256, 259, 263
Rumelt, R. P., 54, 114, 224, 230
Ryan, A., 257

S

Salancik, G. R. 78, 200, 209, 245
sanctions, use of, 247-249
Sanderson, J., 78, 117, 168, 201, 242, 244
satisficers, 47-48, 86
scarcity, 201
Schul, P. I., 200
Scott, C., 78, 200
second dimension of power, 240-241, 248
Sejo, O., 200
Shapiro, B. P., 77
shipbuilding industry, 167-168
Simon, H.A., 32,176
slavery, 232-234
Smith, A., 81-82, 93-94
social goals, 171
social sciences thinking, 199-201, 204-205, 209, 225, 250, 262
standardized demand, 167
Stern, L. W., 200
Stiglitz, J. E., 246
Stiles, C. H., 200
Stolt, J. F., 200
strategic alliances, 11, 15-16, 23, 34-35, 37-39, 43, 45-46, 54, 61-71, 110, 116-117, 121, 128, 130, 132-137, 182, 188, 231
strategising literature, 261
structural power resources, 226, 229-231, 233, 236-242, 244-245-248, 251, 254-255, 258, 261-264
subject conceptions, 172
subjective interests, 16, 45-53, 99, 148, 162-163, 165-166, 173-174, 177-179, 183, 188-195, 204, 209, 228-229, 231, 234-235, 258-259, 260, 262-264
subjective misconception, 180-188

subjective myopia, 16, 173, 237, 259-260
sub-optimal outcomes, 151, 260
Summers, J. O., 200
sunk costs, 230
supplicancy, 235-236
supplier dominance, 99, 245
supplier dominant relationships, 40, 98
supplier responsiveness, 115
supply chain management, 115
surplus value, 216
sustainability, 94-107, 138, 161-162, 165, 185-186, 202-203, 260
switching costs, 101, 230
Sweezy, P., 200
symmetrical mutuality, 125, 138, 141-142, 155, 161, 206, 225-226, 228, 243-244, 251, 254, 256, 258, 262
symmetrical outcomes, 12,15, 23, 25, 27, 56-61, 67-70, 73, 95-96, 101, 112-113, 121-122, 124-126, 130, 133, 135, 137-138, 141, 161, 204, 225-226, 228, 262

T

tangible assets, 230
tautological reasoning, 22, 49, 165, 205, 209, 257
Teng, B. S., 39
tensions in relationships, 92, 117-118, 138, 161-162, 177, 191, 197, 206, 236, 254-255, 259
third dimension of power, 241-242, 248
time-based strategic moves, 246
Tirole, J., 201
Thorelli, H., 200
total cost of ownership, 82-90, 92-93, 97-100, 104, 112, 114, 119-121, 139, 142-143, 145-159, 179, 190, 193, 231, 241, 244
Towill, D. R., 74
Townsend, M., 167
Toyota, 162
transaction cost economics, 16, 74-76, 210-225, 231, 261
transaction partners, 176
transactions, 198-207, 209, 225-256, 262
transactional exchange, 16, 78, 171-173, 175-176, 192, 197-264
transactional utility, 264
transparency, of information, 30, 33, 38-39, 89, 97, 162, 176, 206, 208, 255
trust, 162, 176, 206-208, 255
Turnbull, P. W., 77

U

unbundled pricing, 149
uncertainty, management of, 215-218, 220, 234
use value, 85-89, 93, 116, 142, 190, 193, 202

V

value, 19, 21-22, 24-27, 35, 45, 71, 73-107, 113-116, 122, 147, 151, 153, 159-160, 162-163, 167-170, 172, 177, 183, 185, 188-190, 192, 200, 205, 210-211, 213-214, 216-221, 223-224, 226, 229, 236, 238, 243, 247, 249, 256-258, 261, 263
value appropriation, 163, 199, 210-211, 213-214, 217-221, 223-224, 226, 228-229, 236, 243, 249, 256, 258, 261, 263
value creation, 216
value for money, 82-84, 89, 93, 100
value from supply, 90-93
value in exchange, 255
value in use, 82
value propositions, 82-84, 145
value trade-offs, 166
vendor managed inventory, 167
vertical business relationships, 14-15, 30, 35-36, 39-43, 71-107, 109, 117, 121-122, 128, 138-163, 166, 169-170, 176, 182, 187, 189, 193-194, 206, 228, 230, 241, 244, 250-251, 254, 257-258
vertical exchange, 155
vertical exchange transactions, 146
vertical integration, 211-212, 219-221, 233

W

Wal-Mart, 162
Walmsley, G I., 200
Walrasian economics, 225, 245
waste, removal of, 166
Wathne, K. H., 138
Watson, G., 78, 117, 201, 242, 244
wealth creation, 221
Wernerfelt, B., 202
Westbrook, R., 78, 200
withholding information, 239
Wilkinson, I., 76, 200

Williamson, O. E., 21, 29, 32-33, 41, 74, 81,176,200,205,208,209,210,224,228,233,236,245
willing supplicant, 156, 162
win-lose, 8, 10-11, 15, 20, 23, 25-27, 50-51, 54-55, 58-60, 63-65, 68, 78, 94, 103-104, 106, 118-120, 126, 144, 153, 226, 258
win-win, 7-9, 11-16, 19-30, 32-33, 39-40, 42-43, 46-107, 118, 120, 124, 127, 133, 135, 137-138, 141, 143-144, 165, 171, 177-179, 182-185, 187-189, 195, 206, 226, 254, 256
Womack, J., 85

X

x-efficiency, 86-88, 98-99, 101, 110, 117, 119-121, 139, 142, 153, 156

Y

Yamagishi, T., 200
Young, L.C., 76

Z

Zald, M. N., 200
Zajac, E. J., 75, 77
zero-sum outcomes, 73, 112-113, 126-127, 141-142, 144-145, 148, 151, 155, 225-226, 244, 250-251, 254
zero-zero outcomes, 112, 147
Zingales, L., 200
Zolkiewski, J.M., 77